DECONSTRUCTING THE WELFARE STATE

T0141242

Who are NHS middle managers? What do they do, and why and how do they do it?

This book explores the daily realities of working life for middle managers in the UK's National Health Service during a time of radical change and disruption to the entire edifice of publicly-funded healthcare. It is an empirical critique of the movement towards a healthcare model based around Health Maintenance Organization (HMO)-type providers such as Kaiser Permanente and United Health. Although this model is well known internationally, many believe it to be financially and ethically questionable and often far from 'best practice' when it comes to patient care.

Drawing on immersive ethnographic research based on four case studies – an acute hospital trust, an ambulance trust, a mental health trust, and a primary care trust – this book provides an in-depth critical appraisal of the everyday experiences of a range of managers working in the NHS. It describes exactly what NHS managers do and explains how their roles are changing and the types of challenges they face. The analysis explains how many NHS junior and middle managers are themselves clinicians to some extent, having hybrid roles as, simultaneously, nurse and manager, midwife and manager, or paramedic and manager. While commonly working in 'back office' functions, NHS middle managers are also just as likely to be working very close to or actually on the front lines of patient care. Despite the problems they regularly face from organizational restructuring, cost control, and demands for accountability, the authors demonstrate that NHS managers – in their various guises – play critical, yet undervalued, institutional roles.

Depicting the darker sides of organizational change, this text is a sociological exploration of the daily struggle for work dignity of a complex, widely denigrated, and largely misunderstood group of public servants trying to do their best under extremely trying circumstances. It is essential reading for academics, students, and practitioners interested in health management and policy, organizational change, public sector management, and the NHS more broadly.

Paula Hyde is Professor of Organizations and Society at Manchester Business School, UK. Her research interests lie in the sociology of work and critical explorations of how care is organized.

Edward Granter is Lecturer in Organization and Society at Manchester Business School, UK. His research focuses mainly on the sociology of work and organizations, and Frankfurt School Critical Theory.

John Hassard is Professor of Organizational Analysis at Manchester Business School, UK. His main research interests lie in organization theory, management history, and corporate change.

Leo McCann is Professor of Organization Studies at Manchester Business School, UK. His research focuses on the impact of neo-liberal restructuring on economies, organizations, and workers.

This book represents an impassioned indictment of the misapplication of business principles to healthcare in the NHS. It offers a dystopian peek into the lived experience of dedicated health professionals struggling to maintain their professional integrity and a national institution in the face of a disturbing tension between business imperatives and ethics of care.

Roy Suddaby, Winspear Chair of Management,
Peter B. Gustavson School of Business, University of Victoria, Canada
and Research Professor, Newcastle University Business School, UK

This fine book deconstructs the English welfare state (notably the NHS) in two ways: it critically explores what current health policy is doing to the NHS; and it tracks the NHS's possible morphing into a new commercialized entity. It draws on extensive case study work to explore the experience of middle managers in such change, placing empirical work in a theoretical and political economic context. This important contribution informs a major area of policy, political and also public concern.

Ewan Ferlie, Professor, Department of Management, King's College London, UK

This book offers a brilliant analysis of the work of healthcare managers in an age of major public sector reform. Lucid and thought-provoking, it provides much needed insight into the ethical and philosophical issues facing our public services today. Most of all, it offers a deep sociological appreciation of the movement towards 'marketization' and the threats this poses to publically-funded healthcare.

Mary Jo Hatch, Professor Emerita, University of Virginia, USA

Shattering the myth that NHS middle managers are costly pen-pushers, this book emphasizes their critical contributions. With financial pressures and constant change, however, they are faced with 'managing the impossible'. But is this deliberate policy? The authors suggest that the mix of complex governance systems, funding restrictions, and unrealistic targets ensure that the NHS is always seen to be failing, thus reinforcing the case for privatization – which is already happening. This is essential reading for anyone concerned about how the NHS is managed, locally and nationally.

David A. Buchanan, Emeritus Professor of Organizational Behaviour,
Cranfield School of Management, UK

This book is a treasure in two important senses. Firstly it showcases first rate scholarly empirical research that seeks to explore what middle managers do in a number of important health care contexts. Junior and middle management roles are often overlooked by organizations and indeed by academics and policy makers. It is refreshing to see a spotlight being placed on these critical roles. Secondly it offers a thoughtful and impactful analysis of the changes seen in health care as part of the welfare state. The stealth revolution is highlighted where the scope of its availability is being questioned.

Sue Dopson, Rhodes Trust Professor of Organizational Behaviour,
Saïd Business School, UK

DECONSTRUCTING THE WELFARE STATE

Managing healthcare in the Age of Reform

Paula Hyde, Edward Granter, John Hassard and Leo McCann

Routledge
Taylor & Francis Group

LONDON AND NEW YORK

First published 2016
by Routledge
2 Park Square, Milton Park, Abingdon, Oxon OX14 4RN

and by Routledge
711 Third Avenue, New York, NY 10017

Routledge is an imprint of the Taylor & Francis Group, an informa business

© 2016 P. Hyde, E. Granter, J. Hassard and L. McCann

British Library Cataloguing-in-Publication Data
A catalogue record for this book is available from the British Library

Library of Congress Cataloging in Publication Data
A catalog record for this book has been requested

ISBN: 978-1-138-78719-3 (hbk)
ISBN: 978-1-138-78720-9 (pbk)
ISBN: 978-1-315-76674-4 (ebk)

Typeset in Bembo
by Saxon Graphics Ltd, Derby

For Johnny, Jill, Roisin and Kate

CONTENTS

ACKNOWLEDGEMENTS

We would like to thank the hundreds of NHS managers and professional and support staff who volunteered to be interviewed about their work and/or observed doing their jobs in the course of this study. Without their help and co-operation, this research would not have been possible. We would also like to thank the National Institute for Health Research, Service Delivery and Organisation (NIHR SDO) programme for funding three years of research. The research was entitled Roles and Behaviours of Middle and Junior Managers: Managing New Organizational Forms of Healthcare (NIHR SDO 08/1808/241). Without this funding, we would not have been able to complete the fieldwork on which this book is largely based. We should add that the views and opinions expressed in the book are those of the authors and do not necessarily reflect those of the NIHR SDO programme or the Department of Health.

ABOUT THE COVER

In choosing an image for the paperback cover, we searched through many before settling on this scene from the Marx Brothers' film *A Day at the Races* (Metro-Goldwyn-Mayer, 1937). The early scenes of this well-known film concern comedic and often bizarre relationships between clinicians, administrators, private investors and patients at a medical facility. Specifically, they revolve around the antagonistic dealings between the clinical head of healthcare (Dr Hugo Z. Hackenbush – played by Groucho Marx), the head of healthcare administration (Mr Whitmore – Leonard Ceeley), a banker who is attempting to gain control of the facility (J. D. Morgan – Douglas Dumbrille) and the richest and most important patient (Mrs Upjohn – Margaret Dumont). We chose this image because it appeared somewhat emblematic (to us at least) of many of the themes emerging from our research: the habitual and structural enmity assumed between clinicians and healthcare managers; the incipient *shoeshine capitalism* of medical functions under modern healthcare models; healthcare practices being fragmented and pushed and pulled in different directions under neo-liberalism; and the emergent chaos on the ground as changes to socialized healthcare are rolled out against an increasingly laissez-faire economic backcloth. *A Day at the Races* was the ninth film by the Marx Brothers and like their preceding MGM feature, *A Night at the Opera*, a major hit. In 2000, the American Film Institute ranked it one of funniest movies of the last 100 years.

PREFACE

The 'highest law'

Walworth Road in south London is not a place one would readily associate with ancient Roman political philosophy. Yet, implausible as it may seem, a sharp-eyed observer might locate a statement by Cicero etched in stone above a doorway facing this traffic-clogged, unprepossessing street. The building is Walworth Road Clinic, and the text proclaims the value, centrality and nobility of citizenry and public service. A passenger sat on the top deck of one of the many buses crawling through the traffic would be at the perfect elevation to read it:

THE HEALTH OF THE PEOPLE IS THE HIGHEST LAW

We cannot know for sure what the designers and funders of this building had in mind, but one can imagine the carving of this statement to represent an appeal to socialist and progressive thought around the universal state provision of healthcare. An elaborate statue in Greco-Roman style on the clinic's roof is redolent of classicism, spiritualism and mysticism, featuring a serpent coiled around the rod of Asclepius – an ancient yet familiar symbol of healing. The usage of Cicero adds rhetorical weight to the organizational mission of the clinic as a provider of free medical services to the people of the London borough of Southwark. Opened in 1937 and predating the establishment of the National Health Service, the clinic is now one of many thousands of municipal, charity, or church-based healthcare facilities around Britain that were brought under the aegis of the state-run NHS from 1948 onwards.

Although long outmoded as a care facility, today this clinic technically remains a community services care provider under the administration of Guy's and St Thomas' NHS Foundation Trust. According to a rather poorly maintained website, care services currently offered from this location are an odd combination of Abdominal Aortic Aneurysm Screening, At Home Service, Foot Care, and

Reproductive and Sexual Health.[1] Community services are now part of something called SLIC – Southwark and Lambeth Integrated Care – an organization that involves the new Clinical Commissioning Groups that were controversially legislated into existence by the Conservative–Liberal Democrat coalition government of 2010–15. The acronym SLIC is apposite – the organization has its own IP address, separate branding, and a much glossier and more businesslike website. SLIC, like so much of the NHS, now looks to be right on the margins of public provision and ready to be contracted out to a commercial operation.

Such is the extent of NHS inpatient, outpatient and community service provision that most readers who have spent any time in Britain will have at least some practical knowledge of services provided by the NHS. Unlike our previous workplace studies, this in-depth ethnographic study of the NHS took us into familiar settings – the types of places with which we all had considerable personal experience. In fact, during the three-year period of the study and as part of our lives outside work, we all had occasion to spend time at NHS specialist departments; on the one hand, receiving care as inpatients or outpatients and, on the other, as visitors to various friends and relatives. The study took us beyond the public spaces we knew and understood in acute hospitals, mental health facilities, community services and ambulances and into the buildings, vehicles and back offices where much unseen work takes place.

This book is an examination of the daily experiences and practices of working life in a changing NHS seen through the eyes of occupational groups that are typically undervalued and poorly understood, namely junior and middle managers. *Deconstructing the Welfare State* demonstrates the vital roles of junior and middle managers in the daily functioning of healthcare organizations, even when they are typically derided as wasteful and distracting to the real work of caring for patients. It documents our experiences in four NHS organizations: an acute trust, an ambulance trust, a mental health trust and a primary care trust. It derives from the extensive time we spent observing the work of middle and junior managers as it took place and from our conversations and interviews with NHS staff and managers at all levels. The managers for each of these services were facing financial challenges, mandated structural changes and increases in demand for services. By the end of the study, the acute hospital encompassed many services provided by private companies under an NHS banner; the ambulance service was losing contracts for patient transport to private providers and struggling with performance targets whilst facing yet another structural reconfiguration; and the mental health trust had won so many primary care community service contracts that mental health service provision was overshadowed by more extensive non-mental-health community services. Finally, the primary care service was legislated out of existence to be replaced by several local and regional commissioning services with many of the services it previously provided being advertised for open tender to 'any qualified provider'.

We borrow Wendy Brown's (2015) term 'stealth revolution' to describe the effects of such neo-liberalism on the welfare state in the UK. Despite official government claims to the contrary, our analysis of the daily managerial climate of four NHS trusts demonstrates that the NHS *is* being privatized, its scope of availability *is* being narrowed, and its very future as a *free at the point of need* health service on the basis of social solidarity *is* fundamentally threatened. The 'health of the people' is no longer the 'highest law' – it is more of a side issue, relegated in favour of laws of commerce: increased shareholder value and business decisions based on profitability. As a result, we see how the NHS becomes a brand or *Kitemark* under which healthcare is increasingly delivered by private providers according to the logic of the market where turning a profit comes before assessment of need as a means of deciding where and how to deliver care.

Note

1   www.guysandstthomas.nhs.uk/our-services/community/southwark/walworth-road-clinic.aspx

1

DECONSTRUCTING THE WELFARE STATE

Undoing 'one of the greatest achievements in history'?

The National Health Service was established on 5 July, 1948. It formed the cornerstone of the welfare provisions devised and enacted by the UK's post-war Labour government under Prime Minister Clement Attlee and was conceived following the experiences of the First and Second World Wars and their aftermath. The welfare state represented a radical attempt at changing the social, economic and class structures of Britain. It was a technocratic, state-led solution to the challenges of providing education and reducing poverty, unemployment, homelessness and ill health; a programme not uncommon in other post-war countries (McCann, 2014). One of the motivating principles was the fact that government ownership, administration, rationing and investment had worked successfully in wartime, which supported the belief that the same could be achieved in peacetime. Aneurin Bevan, Minister for Health at the time and often referred to as the architect of the NHS, founded the service on the collective principle that 'no society can legitimately call itself civilized if a person is denied medical aid because of lack of means' (1952: 100). As a result, the nationalized health service was built on the principle of care to be given free of charge at the point of need. The NHS has been the most popular and enduring element of Britain's post-war settlement (Pierson, 1994: 132; Taylor, 2013).

State welfare provision has never received universal support and the nationalization of healthcare was not without its critics. Most notable perhaps was the initial resistance from the British Medical Association and Bevan's frustrated observation that he had pacified doctors by 'stuffing their mouths with gold' as he was forced to accept continued private practice of NHS consultants. Since then, clinicians of all kinds have typically given strong support to the NHS's single payer (tax-funded) principles, which (usually) allowed clinical professionals to focus all their attention on clinical needs without being distracted or constrained by considerations of financial cost (Harrison, 1999). As a result of the improvements in the health of the UK population, the NHS has been described by a former British Medical Association council chairman as 'one of the greatest achievements in history'.[1]

This book was intended to follow on from our *Managing in the Modern Corporation* (Hassard *et al.*, 2009) in its in-depth coverage of the intensification of managerial work following organizational downsizing. That study featured themes of stress, exhaustion, demoralization and resentment about top management strategy. Certainly, all of these themes remain very much present in this current text. However, in researching NHS organizations, it was impossible to avoid a much bigger and more clearly political and moral story; that of the disturbing tension between business imperatives and ethics of care and, in many cases, a rapid sense of loss of control among many working for the NHS – hence *Deconstructing ...* . This made everyday working life in the NHS effectively a political space into which employees, including junior and middle managers, projected their moral and political values about the meaning and importance of their work. Yet, despite the efforts of governments and consultants to encourage the NHS to be more businesslike (Davies and Gubb, 2009), it remains a public service, not a profit-driven enterprise. Patient care remains the number one priority for NHS trusts, both in official pronouncements and in a great deal of practice.

Deconstructing the Welfare State therefore offers a critical examination of working life in a changing NHS as seen through the eyes of junior and middle managers. As this book demonstrates, those working for the NHS are beset on all sides by pressures for marketization, policy reforms and system-wide restructuring, resource shortages, and increasing demand for services. This chapter describes the broader sociopolitical environment in which our managers found themselves, and as such, it serves as an introduction to the various themes of the book. It opens by sketching out the background to the NHS in order to demonstrate that organizational and policy change in this field is highly politicized and deeply infused with ideological and moral rhetoric. The chapter then moves on to describe the current condition of the NHS, drawing attention to the profound challenges it is facing in terms of growing patient demand, shrinking resources, and the rise of external competition. These challenges are then explained in more detail with reference to a resurgent neo-liberal attack on the idea of free public healthcare and the autonomy of clinical professions. This has a dual form, as manifested in: i) policy drives to open up public services to *free market* competition; and ii) an intensification of attempts to control public servants and attenuate professional discretion, often using various forms of performance indicators. Broadly speaking, these trends are labelled as New Public Management (Hood, 1991), a pervasive and powerful form of *managerialism* (Klikauer, 2013). The chapter concludes with an explanation of why we have chosen to draw a distinction between management and managerialism. We do this not least because, as seen in Chapter 2, the deconstruction of the NHS is played out through middle managers in particular as an imposed form of managerialism; yet many managers believe strongly in the foundational ethos of the NHS as a public service for patient care rather than as a business or commercial enterprise. Chapter 2, in keeping with our interest in middle managers, details how the deconstruction of the NHS has been achieved incrementally over recent decades. It examines how these policy changes were effected through and by NHS managers.

Throughout our study, we drew together macro, meso and micro levels of analysis (Mills, 1959). Chapter 3 details the distinctive Critical-Action perspective we used to examine how organizational structures and processes were influenced by overt and covert ideological factors and forces. In Chapters 4 to 7, we see how these interactions played out in the lives and work of junior and middle NHS managers in four types of NHS organization: an acute trust (Chapter 4), an ambulance trust (Chapter 5), a mental health trust (Chapter 6) and a primary care trust (Chapter 7). Each of these empirical chapters portrays the significant effects of this changing environment on a distinct type of NHS organization. The final section (Chapter 8) draws the conclusion from our findings that something more than a simple NHS reorganization is underway. There is a new ideology to consider – of care provision linked to business income rather than patient need. We see how this thinking pervades the mindset of politicians, senior managers and business consultants. We argue that this deconstruction of public welfare ought to be subjected to critical scrutiny if we are to genuinely consider what marketization does to care. The reforms are all the more insidious for being largely conducted through stealth, without proper oversight, and without adequate public accountability, approval, or even debate (Leys and Player, 2011; Tallis, 2013). This is what we mean by *Deconstructing the Welfare State* – the NHS is our subject of enquiry amid much larger social, political, economic and organizational debates about the shrinkage of public service provision and the effacement of democracy by a neo-liberal 'stealth revolution' (Brown, 2015).

The NHS: politically untouchable?

It is widely argued that changes to public welfare provision are difficult for governments to enact because they potentially create constituencies who lose out through cutbacks and reform (Pierson, 1994). This is nowhere more apparent than with the NHS. In 2014, a US think tank rated the NHS overall as the best value health system in the world (Campbell and Watt, 2014). In 2000, the World Health Organization ranked the UK in eighteenth place (out of 184 national systems) for 'overall health system performance', with France coming first and the US, thirty-seventh (World Health Organization, 2000). The NHS is currently Europe's largest employer (with around 1.38 million staff in 2014) and is one of the world's largest and most famous public service institutions, designed to provide universal healthcare on the basis of patient need, not on their ability to pay. Over and above its national importance as an employer, it is also popular with patients. Recent reported levels of patient satisfaction with the NHS are high. British Social Attitudes surveys from 1983 to 2000 show a trend line of between 40 per cent and 50 per cent of patients self-reportedly either 'very satisfied' or 'satisfied', but this has been climbing rapidly since the 2000s to a high point of 70 per cent in 2010.[2] A Care

Quality Commission survey of NHS patient care in England reports in 2014 that 84 per cent of around 56,300 respondents rated their treatment at between seven and ten out of ten (NHS Confederation, 2015). It has proved to be a mostly effective and very popular institution – one whose existence is widely supported by the British public, by patients and by clinical professionals.

Its much-loved status is quasi-mystical, and it is often described as being politically untouchable; so much so that small-state Conservative politicians are often forced to promise that it will be 'safe in their hands' (Pierson, 1994: 133). The late Tony Benn, once a symbol of the Old Left in British politics, when interviewed by the US left-wing documentary film-maker Michael Moore for *Sicko* – a film about the failings of the largely private American healthcare system – described the existence of the NHS as follows:

BENN: [I]t's as non-controversial as votes for women; nobody could come along and say 'why should women have the vote?' now because people wouldn't have it; and they wouldn't have in Britain – they wouldn't accept the deterioration or destruction of the National Health Service.
MOORE: If Tony Blair would have said 'I'm going to dismantle the national healthcare' ...
BENN: [interrupting] There'd have been a revolution.[3]

Perhaps Benn was right. If a government had *announced* such plans then widespread opposition would indeed be likely. It's perhaps best, therefore, not to announce them. Despite discouraging polling data on the British public's opinion of how well the Conservative Party would handle the NHS, the Conservatives won an overall majority in the UK general election of 2015. In the first Prime Minister's Questions session of the new Parliament, in June 2015, David Cameron again committed to a publicly funded NHS, claiming his government would raise an extra £8 billion in funding that it had not committed to prior to the election. Once more we see public claims about a much-loved NHS that is *safe in Conservative hands*. But, as we see in more detail below, there is every reason to be sceptical about these claims.

Recent years have seen a radical reshaping of the NHS in ways not always open to public scrutiny. This is why we adopt the phrase 'stealth revolution' (Brown, 2015) to describe the changes to the NHS. Political rhetoric continues to uphold the sanctity of the NHS while legislation quietly opens the doors wide to 'any qualified' provider. We see in Chapter 2 how public and professional criticism of reforms only seems to have emboldened neo-liberal policymakers.

Taking a pulse: assessing the current health of the NHS

The NHS in England treats about one million patients every 36 hours, almost all free of charge (NHS Choices, n.d.), and it is facing continued increased demand for services at a time of severe financial pressure. Austerity measures designed to tackle government budget deficits in the wake of the financial crises of 2007–8 have placed practically all organizations and staff in the NHS under added pressure. The NHS as a whole was ordered to achieve £20 billion in cost savings out of a total budget of £100 billion by 2015 (Taylor, 2013: 82). This is alongside the growth of anticipated funding shortfalls estimated at between £20 billion and £40 billion due to a growing and ageing population (Appleby *et al.*, 2009: 2). Budget cutbacks are combined with pressures related to performance improvement and accountability to taxpayers and patients. With standards of NHS care officially under intense scrutiny (if not always in practice), the NHS is assailed by challenges and criticisms from: government that wishes to reform the NHS in the direction of greater marketization and better value for money for taxpayers; from patient support groups such as Cure the NHS who regard the everyday working culture of the NHS as callous and uncaring; and from corporate interests that believe they can offer high-quality healthcare services at lower cost than traditional public providers such as NHS hospitals, mental health trusts, community services and ambulance services. Many trusts are in chronic financial distress (amounting to nearly a billion pounds in deficit in financial year 2014–15: Walshe and Smith, 2015). As the Chartered Institute of Public Finance and Accountancy (CIPFA) projected a £2.1 billion deficit for 2015–16 – two and a half times the previous year's record – many previously financially sound foundation trusts have been brought into difficulty (CIPFA, 2015) and the financial position of the NHS 'is indeed dire' (Walshe and Smith, 2015).

Many parts of the NHS are at the cutting edge of patient care and medical research. But other areas are woefully underfunded and understaffed, repeatedly offering insufficient or patchy patient care. Staff shortages are endemic, with the Royal Colleges that represent the various medical professions and para-professions clamouring in desperation for workable staffing levels. Patients in many areas of the country face long waits for GP appointments, and Accident and Emergency (A&E) units are often overcrowded and 'on a cliff edge' (McCann *et al.*, 2015a: 777). Ambulance trusts have had to deal with a 25 per cent rise in the volume of emergency calls over five years (AACE, 2014: 17) and have turned to privately run ambulance companies and charities to plug gaps. Non-emergency patient transport services now compete directly with commercial transportation companies for regional care contracts. Mental health care provision has been very problematic, especially as regards out of hours services, with widespread unavailability and variation in care services (CQC, 2015). Scandals around substandard care and basic patient safety failures have enveloped several NHS Trusts, none more so than the notorious failings at Mid Staffordshire NHS Trust. The subsequent investigation (HCC, 2009) and public inquiry (Francis, 2013) cast long shadows over the NHS; the Stafford failings symbolically depict the NHS as an organization in some difficulty.

Heavy workloads, rationing and severe pressure have long characterized working life in the NHS. When these conditions have combined with austerity measures and business-driven changes then crisis tendencies have become magnified. For how much longer can it struggle on when facing budget cuts and increasingly open competition for care contracts? News – typically bad – of cutbacks, reorganizations and patient treatment failures are often headline-making. The NHS as a whole has been through many rounds of restructuring and reform since at least the early 1980s. None of this is new. But with the passage of the Health and Social Care Act of 2012, the policy agenda for radical reorganization rapidly gained momentum. Not a word of this coming legislation appeared in either the Conservative's or the Liberal Democrats' pre-2010 election manifestoes (Tallis, 2013). What we had instead was political leaders' explicit promises of no more 'top-down' or 'pointless reorganisations' of the NHS (Eaton, 2013). The Health and Social Care Act abolished the broad meso-level administrative structures that existed in the form of the strategic health authorities and primary care trusts and instead provided for widespread outsourcing of government-run health provision and commissioning; with its controversial competition clause, it mandated the opening of care contracts to 'any qualified provider'. The Act solidified into law (at least in England) the principles that were already long underway – NHS organizations were increasingly recast as independent care commissioners and providers competing with other non-NHS organizations (for-profit healthcare corporations, insurance companies, charities, even transport conglomerates) for business in a healthcare market (Leys and Player, 2011; Pollock, 2005; Tallis, 2013).

Unlike other public service organizations, such as the police or the armed forces, the chain of command from central government to NHS trusts has been severed by the Health and Social Care Act – the Secretary of State for Health is no longer directly responsible for healthcare commissioning and delivery. Indeed, how can a minister be directly responsible for the healthcare system of England when commissioning and provision are now effectively market based and executed by competing independent business units? Rather than the health of the people being the highest law, the laws of capitalism – as in the US model of *managed care* – will in all likelihood govern health provision. The US healthcare system is consistently ranked poorly by international standards where it is

> evolving into a three-tier system, with the best professional care that money could buy for the affluent; managed care, HMOs, preferred partner and other health insurance plans for the middle class and working class; and … public hospital emergency rooms and clinics for the working poor.
>
> *(Pious, 2008: 211–12)*

This is the model the NHS is in danger of emulating.

A note of caution is needed here. Observers have predicted the collapse, decay and privatization of the NHS for decades, although not always in that order. The NHS seems, like its staff, to be always on the edge – overworked, underfunded, reorganized to no determinable gain, and under intolerable pressure. Blog-based literature by NHS clinicians or news media and TV programmes regularly draw on metaphors of 'extreme' and 'on the edge' (Granter *et al.*, 2015; Lyng, 2004) working environments, as witnessed in television programmes such as *24 Hours in A&E* or *An Hour to Save Your Life*. The NHS and its staff are often portrayed as much loved but troubled; as battle-hardened survivors. NHS workers often describe 'the system' as 'at the point of collapse' (e.g. see Reynolds, 2006: 275), yet somehow it has struggled on and the Department of Health and senior politicians continue to deny the existence of any plans for privatization.

Shock therapy? The neo-liberal policy environment of cutbacks, flexibility and enterprise

Viewed from a long-term historical perspective, we are arguably coming full circle. The post-war welfare state was part of a larger trend in which a technocratic government would act as monopolistic provider of health and welfare services as entitlements to citizens. This position has been progressively challenged since the 1970s with fiscal conservatives across the developed world increasingly arguing that the entitlements of the post-war settlement are unaffordable, encourage welfare dependency, and act as a barrier to the growth of a more dynamic, innovative private sector (Pierson, 1994). Welfare reforms (typically involving the attenuation of public spending, privatization and the introduction of competition into former public monopolies) were promoted not just by the 'restrained government' advocates of the neo-liberal New Right but also by the Third Way reformists of Clinton's New Democrats or Blair's New Labour (Brown, 2015; Clarke *et al.*, 2000; Jordan, 2010; Steger and Roy, 2010). Although annual spending on the NHS did rise significantly during 1997–2009,[4] the Blair government simultaneously pursued an aggressive project of managerialism in an attempt to control the behaviour of clinical professionals. They aimed to raise standards, reduce waiting times and restrain the cost of treatments (Noordegraaf, 2007) largely through the use of batteries of performance indicators and rankings (Dent, 2008). Marketizing reforms were also introduced such as the establishment of foundation trusts and the promotion of patient choice (see Clark *et al.*, 2002 and Chapter 2).

Before the Second World War and the subsequent emergence of welfare states, healthcare and social services were largely provided on a market basis with some charitable provision, meaning that those without the means to pay would often face destitution. French sociologists Luc Boltanski and Eve Chiapello famously wrote of three eras or 'spirits' of capitalism: the first being the pre-war era of largely unregulated markets with extremely basic and patchy welfare safety nets; the second, the post-war settlement of Keynesian demand management, technocratic government and universalistic welfare systems; and the third, the neo-liberal era of restrained government and the break-up of the post-war settlement (which almost returns us to the first spirit). They argue that each era's 'spirit' mobilized ideological and moral arguments in order to justify and reproduce itself (Boltanski and Chiapello, 2005). Often these arguments would have their roots in criticism of the prior era. In the post-war era of managerial capitalism (Chandler, 1977) – or the second spirit of capitalism (Boltanski and Chiapello, 2005) – many of the behaviours and structures established by the privileged white-collar managerial and professional ranks were implicit and opaque (Freidson, 1986). Combined with the protection afforded by government monopoly provision of public services, professionals could close ranks, cover up bad practice, fob off complaints and hush up potential whistle-blowers. But the professional system also worked on and inspired public trust; legally protected job titles, professional and academic qualifications, and trappings such as uniforms and badges conveyed messages to the public that their holders are trustworthy, honest, financially disinterested experts who are uniquely qualified to serve the public (du Gay, 2006).

The currents of the Conservative Party's neo-liberal philosophy and policy agenda of low taxes, curtailed government borrowing and spending, and wide scope for business and enterprise runs against the traditions of a publicly owned and operated NHS free at the point of need and paid for out of taxes and government borrowing. There is nothing *conservative* about these changes – to the contrary, the neo-liberal project promises to radically reshape the relationships of people to government (Brown, 2015; Klein, 2007; Peck, 2010; Steger and Roy, 2010). Rather than access to healthcare (or any other public service) being something a citizen can expect of the state, health services are increasingly delivered on a *patient as customer* basis with markets and private insurance, rather than welfare and universal tax-funded provision, at their core.

Today's neo-liberal attack on tax and spend welfare is couched in the justificatory rhetoric of removing professionals' artificially granted powers and the stifling red tape and bureaucracy associated with it. The turn away from government and back to markets connects with widely proliferated and popular themes about liberation, flexibility and agility. A market for healthcare means more choice for the patient/customer and not having to submit to professional or governmental authority or to sit for months on waiting lists. Cash, not government means-testing or social solidarity, gives the entitlement. In brief, the UK moved from commercial provision of services available to those who can pay to a nationalized and centralized model available to all on the basis of universal provision paid for by taxation before returning towards a more marketized and fragmented system involving a multitude of providers and questions about which treatments might remain free at the point of need.

The absence of personal wealth under marketized systems means little, slow or no access to services (Sandel, 2013). It implies 'rationing by income' – an idea out of kilter with most European welfare systems but tolerated (even championed) in the US (Royce, 1997: 156–7). Yet the socialistic notions of progressive taxation and solidarity – that most working-age adults *pay in* and individuals only *take out* when unfortunate enough to need medical attention – are, if not openly attacked, becoming ever more attenuated and unlikely as policy options. Deconstructing the welfare state through lowering taxes, turning NHS trusts into businesses and rationing healthcare has not been uncontroversial (Pierson, 1994); but resistance has been muted and ineffective (Tallis, 2013). There has been a failure of progressive political parties to offer any real defence of post-war settlement ideals of solidarity and entitlements. David Graeber in *The Utopia of Rules* describes a 'pathetic rearguard action' (2015: 6) against the destruction of welfare states by labour/ moderate left parties, largely because such political parties long ago left behind their founding values of social solidarity. Prime Minister Tony Blair and his pro-market New Labour government presented neo-liberalism not as the destruction of welfare but as 'essential to the modernization and improvement' of public services. He would claim that 'we are at our best when at our boldest' (*The Guardian*, 2002). Being 'bold' effectively meant embracing markets and the private sector and making sure that when government spending on public services was increased, the workers and occupations were bound ever more tightly in bureaucratic performance management targets and metrics. Professions were not to be trusted; sometimes they were regarded with 'open contempt' (Tallis, 2013: 6). A Blair speech implied that traditionalist public sector trade unionists were 'wreckers' (Sparrow and Womack, 2002), and he once told the British Venture Capital Association that he bore 'scars on [his] back' from just the first two years of trying to reform public sector organizations and professions (Assinder, 1999).

New Labour's health reforms have been dramatically accelerated by the Conservative–Liberal Democrat coalition government elected in 2010. The Health and Social Care Act 2012 is the most dramatic change thus far – one that lays the ground for shrinking the *free at the point of need* service in England and replacing it with what is approaching a US-style 'Managed Care' system. This is all the stranger given the desperate struggles and controversies in the US since 2008 around the establishment of a federally backed healthcare insurance scheme (so-called Obamacare). Just when the US is perhaps finally starting to embrace elements of a state-governed entitlement to medical care and insurance, the NHS – one of the world's best-ranked systems – is moving in the opposite direction towards commercial commissioning of care, increased rationing of treatments based on market principles, and the control of clinical practice according to cost considerations rather than prioritizing patients by need (for an overview of the dynamics of managed care, see Enthoven, 1993; Fairfield *et al.*, 1997; Royce, 1997; Scott *et al.*, 2000).

Managers and managerialism: the New Public Management

The same neo-liberal and managerialist trends are afoot in other public sector professions – policing and probation services, social work, schools (Exworthy and Halford, 1999) and even the armed forces (Godfrey *et al.*, 2013). Higher education, for example, has been the target of reforms such as the White Paper of June 2011 that similarly champions more choice and competition, and claims to put 'students at the heart of the system' (BIS, 2011). All of these changes aim to reinvent citizens as customers who will vote with their wallets in selecting whichever services they do or do not value and, hence, utilize the lever of the 'efficient market' to break up what Eliot Freidson famously described as the 'professional dominance' model (Freidson, 1986: 210) of public services (see also Le Grand, 2003). Facing the onslaught of managerialism and neo-liberalism, professions are struggling to survive under their traditionally remote 'second spirit of capitalism' guise and have had to reinvent themselves partially as managers, executives, leaders or customer-facing entrepreneurs in order to adapt to the New Public Management (Noordegraaf, 2007).

The structures and justifications of the second spirit of capitalism have been assailed by a whirlwind of fragmenting forces in which the organizing actors of the prior regime struggle to remain relevant; regulators, professions, unions and even management all get reformed or erased. NHS trusts are reinvented as more businesslike, more responsive, more flexible, more entrepreneurial while, in reality, they are struggling to meet their fundamental duties to patients. New Public Management implicitly attacks professional privilege and professionals' claims to expertise and exceptional status outside of market discipline, making it hard for doctors to defend themselves using habitual arguments of clinical autonomy – i.e. Hippocratic models of care. Many other occupations in the NHS (such as occupational therapists or paramedics) have never enjoyed such professional power, and these arguments are not really available for them. General managers also have little in the way of professional power or clinical credentials to fall back on and are thus especially exposed to the logics and discourses of market competition and targets-led control. These changes are difficult to resist, partly because they consistently privilege economic metrics over social or moral arguments (Brown, 2015).

These neo-liberal pressures derive from two distinct but deeply entwined areas. The first is the rise of markets and competitive pressure. The second is the managerialism of audits with performance metrics that have put professionals on the back foot, always having to justify themselves according to targets and measures that are derived and enforced externally. Managerialism thus provides the organizational or front-line operating procedures of neo-liberal marketization (Brown, 2015; Kliakauer, 2013; Styhre, 2014). The justificatory rhetoric of the 'third spirit of capitalism' is an odd mixture of markets, leadership and liberation from control, yet managerialism reimposes the rules of monitoring, auditing, control and inspection as opposed to relationships built on professional trust. Even as the neo-liberal discourse of leadership and liberation rhetorically attacks the management traditions of bureaucracy, control, and management by numbers, the 'utopia of rules' (Graeber, 2015) or 'rituals of verification' (Power, 2000) are re-enforced by managerialism.

These changes are labelled New Public Management (Hood, 1991), a pervasive and powerful form of managerialism (Klikauer, 2013). In some ways, our argument may seem confusing as surely the advance of New Public Management and the managerialist attack on professions might be expected to *strengthen* the hands of the middle managers we will focus in upon. However, we argue that this type of managerialism is attractive only to commercial interests, senior executives and reformist policymakers; managers at junior and middle level are under threat from these reforms and are typically resentful of them. In many ways, managerialism specifically targets middle managers as being in need of reform or removal. They are pressed upon to become more effective, more efficient, more entrepreneurial.

Thus management (an occupational group and practice) is distinct from managerialism (an ideology and policy agenda).

In recent years, overly bureaucratic management has been cited as a problem for the NHS; and it has not been uncommon for doctors, in particular, to criticize an influx of managers and the unwelcome intrusion of commercial interests over their practice. A notable example is the satirical paper in the otherwise serious *Journal of the Royal Society of Medicine* that attacks managerialism, the cult-like attraction for business consultants, and their questionable and meaningless 'research'. Here is a flavour:

> We identified several over-lapping reasons for reorganizations, including money, revenge, money, elections, money, newly appointed leaders, money, unemployment, money, power-hunger, money, simple greed, money, boredom, and no reason at all.
>
> [...]
>
> *Data collection*
>
> We used a large trash bin on wheels.
>
> *(Oxman et al., 2005: 564)*

Such anger is reflective of a deep frustration, unease and helplessness about how professional dominance over decisions made about care has been eroded and replaced by finance-driven administration and engaged in ceaseless 'redisorganization' (2005: 566; see also Smith *et al.*, 2001). But doctors bemoan the direction of change and attack managerialism, they also acknowledge that many managers (usually at mid-level and below) uphold the traditional ethos of the NHS and also resent the ways in which NHS trusts are being turned into businesses as budgets are cut and workloads broadened. An open letter to the *Health Services Journal* in December 2014 – signed by various senior healthcare leaders and several chairs of the Royal Colleges – appealed for 'a change in attitudes towards NHS managers', arguing that 'managers make an essential contribution', 'work long hours' and are 'as dedicated to the service as any other group of staff' (HSJ, 2014). Such arguments are supported by the findings presented in this book.

The antipathy, therefore, between professionals and managers is much less clear-cut than it might appear, each side having to find ways to accommodate and collaborate with various agendas (Exworthy and Halford, 1999: 121). Moreover, many managers in the NHS are also clinicians of various types and exposed, therefore, to the tensions between the 'second spirit of capitalism' – the traditional model of professional dominance and universal healthcare – and the 'third spirit' – business-driven neo-liberalism. We argue that while managerialism is indeed a major threat to the existence of the NHS, this threat is not one emerging from the managers themselves, especially not mid-level and junior managers. Instead, it is important to appreciate a degree of separation between managers (as an occupational group) on one side and managerialism (the discourses and ideologies of business, leadership, commercialism and financialization) on the other.

Notes

1   Dr John Marks, quoted in BBC News (1998).
2   For an overview, see The King's Fund (2015).
3   *Sicko* (2007), dir. Michael Moore: 1:02:32–1:02:50.
4   From £61 billion in 1997 to £122 billion in 2009 (in real terms and at 2013 prices) (Nuffield Trust, n.d.).

2

DECONSTRUCTING THE NHS

The changing roles of junior and middle managers

This book is broadly about the NHS and the managers who work in it. Building on extensive prior research and writing on managerial work and organizational change (Granter *et al.*, 2015; Hassard *et al.*, 2009; Hyde *et al.*, 2012; McCann *et al.*, 2008), it explores work and change in the NHS through the eyes of junior and middle managers who are charged with the myriad tasks of trying to keep it running. As we detail in Chapter 1, the book is partly an organizational and political story – one that brings NHS managers into confrontation with organizational and policy transformations that are reshaping their roles and their means of organizing care. But it is just as much a human story, a discussion and illumination of the drama and conflict involved as NHS staff – very often clinicians turned managers – engage with the day-to-day challenges, severe pressure, bureaucratic absurdities, and small losses and victories of healthcare work. There are indeed large and growing literatures on organizational change, on public sector management and on middle managers. This chapter restricts itself to a brief overview of some of the basic contours of these debates so that the reader can gain an understanding of where this study locates itself before detailing how managers have been co-opted into the incremental deconstruction of the NHS over several decades.

Central questions

Fundamentally, the central questions of the book are: who are NHS middle managers; what do they do; and why and how do they do it? As such, it plans to follow in a long line of acclaimed studies into the realities of managerial work in other contexts (such as Kanter, 1977; Mintzberg, 1973; Osterman, 2009; Tengblad, 2006; Watson, 1977, 1996). These questions are answered by the use of immersive ethnographic research, involving the authors spending days and weeks observing managers at work and conducting in-depth life history interviews with them. Participants included nurse managers in the acute trust, emergency control managers and paramedic clinical team leaders in the ambulance trust, clinical and functional managers in the mental health trust and those managing care commissioning and care provision in the primary care trust. These NHS organizations allowed extended access, which enabled us to study managers at close range over three years.

Early studies of managerial work often took a somewhat structural and descriptive approach, exemplified by Henry Mintzberg's pioneering observational study of managers' time usage (1971, 1973). Work in a similar vein includes that of Rosemary Stewart who also wrote in depth on the NHS (1989, 2003; see also Dopson and Stewart, 1990). Elsewhere, a valuable and highly discursive overview of the earliest research on managerial work is provided by Hales (1986). This literature provides much detail on the complex, varied, intense, messy and demanding nature of managerial work; it has a tendency to be highly managerialist and seemingly apolitical, though it frequently seems to privilege the perspectives and goals of executive and senior managers (Klikauer, 2013). Studying the mechanics of managerial work solely in terms of organizational effectiveness or leadership assumes that the only purpose and value to be derived from exploring management is to learn lessons for encouraging higher performance; that is, to learn about how to encourage *better* management, provide more management development, identify training needs, etc. Far less attention is given to the contradictions and tensions of managerial work, especially when it comes to the profound challenges faced when managing overstretched resources (Perlow, 1999). In general, the technical tone of this type of literature excludes human elements such as the reality of life or death decisions, workplace dignity and morality, conflicts about occupational or professional identity and the struggle for recognition. Such issues are especially important in healthcare management where much of the work can be emotionally laden and on which human lives may depend (Bolton, 2000; Boyle and Healy, 2003; Theodosius, 2008).

For these reasons, we are more attuned to qualitative literature on managerial work and organizational change based on in-depth interviews and ethnographic observation. Such studies include Allcorn *et al.* (1996), Barley and Kunda (2004), Fraser (2001), Heckscher (1996), Jackall (1988), Kanter (1977), Kunda (1992), Smith (1990) and Watson (1977, 1996). Our portrayal of NHS management reflects not only what managers told us their lives were like, but also our personal, first-hand experience of team meetings, training events and daily work in offices, wards or ambulance stations. This allowed us to see and interpret for ourselves the world of managerial work in various areas of the NHS (Tope *et al.*, 2005; Watson, 2011). To some extent, we pre-empt the chapters to follow in detailing the broad scope of NHS managerial roles linked to incremental NHS reform; but given the complexity of the political and social environment NHS managers have faced in recent decades, we feel an early account is necessary.

An easy target: restructuring NHS middle managers

A common-sense view of middle managers regards them as time-servers and pen-pushers who represent levels of wasteful and *faceless* bureaucracy in large organizations.

This is especially true with the rise of discourses about leadership, which often disparage management (McCann, 2016). However, in-depth sociological research into middle managers takes a different view, suggesting that they are neglected, often unsung characters who are attuned to the 'reality on the ground' and are essential in keeping organizations running (Hassard *et al.*, 2009; Huy, 2001; Osterman, 2009). Middle managers are often overstretched, especially after restructuring exercises in which organizational levels are reduced and spans of control broadened. They are constantly faced with the difficulty of juggling competing demands, often without adequate resources. Much of their work involves almost a kind of 'street-level bureaucracy' (Lipsky, 1980), which is traditionally seen as the preserve of front-line workers – muddling through, making the best of the resources they have, and often using informal means to work through problems and serve patients as best they can (McCann *et al.*, 2015a). This is why we essentially regard middle managers as *workers*. Such a categorization applies more so in the NHS where many managers are simultaneously managers and clinicians. Their work is challenging – balancing the competing demands of patient care and business efficiency.

In our previous book (Hassard *et al.*, 2009; see also McCann *et al.*, 2008: 365), we argued that corporate executive management levels were becoming increasingly detached from the mid-level management ranks. This situation was causing considerable resentment among middle management who tended to regard executive leaders to be remote, removed from the realities on the ground and vicious in the increasing demands they made on middle management. These issues re-emerge in even starker form in the NHS. At the time of writing, the annual salaries of junior and middle managers are much lower than those of corporate middle managers who, in some roles, earn as much as £70,000 plus £30,000 in bonuses. The most junior supervisory or administrative-type positions can start at NHS Agenda for Change[1] Band 5 (£21,692–£28,180) with most middle management jobs in Bands 6 or 7 (£26,041–£40,964), only getting up to Bands 8a–8d (£39,632–£81,618) or 9 (£77,850–£98,453) for the most senior management roles such as chief financial manager, Estates manager (Higher Level Operations) or head of Human Resources (HR). They are contractually meant to work a 35-hour week, although there is considerable evidence to show they work well beyond this in order to keep up with work demands. NHS mid-level managers tend not to face quite as long working hours as many of those 'extreme job' holders in the private sector who work 60+ hours per week (Hewlett and Luce, 2006), although top managers and upper-level mid-managers in the NHS are heading in that direction, if not already there (Buchanan *et al.*, 2013).

The previous chapter implied a question: if financially distressed NHS trusts can't afford to cut back on nurses because of patient safety risks, where can they make cost savings? One idea is to downsize management and administration. Junior and middle managers in the NHS have come under sustained criticism for being emblematic of public sector waste or an uncaring faceless bureaucracy, and they have become palpable targets for redundancies and cost savings (e.g. see Smith, 2011). Middle management, administration, auditing, paperwork and bureaucracy are unpopular in many walks of life; often regarded as dull, wasteful, frustrating and unnecessary (Graeber, 2015; Hassard *et al.*, 2009; Osterman, 2009). So why not cut them back? Managerial positions in the NHS can be especially vulnerable for they receive sharp criticism not only from politicians, patient groups and sections of the media, but also from NHS clinicians. Management can be a low-status occupation in the NHS, and high-status clinical professionals can be difficult characters to manage because of their traditional claims to clinical autonomy (de Bruijn, 2011; Harrison, 1999; Mintzberg, 1998). Middle managers in particular appear to be one of the undisputed and less contentious targets for UK government reforms.

Cutting back on management costs is one obvious tactic that many organizations deploy under the pressure of demands for cost savings. However, an emerging literature dating back to the 1990s attests to the difficulties and unanticipated consequences of corporate downsizing (Cascio, 1993). Cutting costs in a rush and without consultation destroys morale and operational effectiveness (Cameron *et al.*, 1991). Morale often suffers considerably as a result of alienating and disruptive organization change (Allcorn *et al.*, 1996). Delayering – intended to strip out unnecessary rungs on the bureaucratic ladder to improve flexibility and communication – in fact increases the distance between managers by creating spans of control that become too large to manage successfully (Hassard *et al.*, 2009; McCann *et al.*, 2008). After delayering, it is typical for surviving mid-level managers to face markedly increased workloads, and this is without additional support as they rarely get to even see the next manager above them whose workload is even larger (Fraser, 2001; Hassard *et al.*, 2009). When the managerial structure is flattened, middle managers also face career motivation problems as their next move is typically sideways rather than upwards (Lindorff, 2009). A powerful study of downsizing in a US hospital, for example, paints a vivid and disturbing picture of a workplace in severe distress. Part of the study involved middle managers completing word-association tasks with results such as:

Job – *Frustrating*. Morale – *Low*. Efficiency – *Pathetic*.

and

Job – *Oh, God*. Morale – *Low*. Efficiency – *Poor*.
(*Allcorn* et al.*, 1996: 153, 159*)

Organizational change initiatives have been widely championed in the NHS, such as Lean Systems, Balanced Scorecard, Six Sigma, flatter hierarchies, Total Quality Management, leadership programmes and the replacement of groups of managers with digital Management Information Systems. Senior leaders talk of pushing 'the operational stuff' downward to line management and try to sell such changes by claiming this amounts to a devolving of authority and discretion, making mid-level managerial jobs more involving and valuable. But these changes also typically mean widening the span of control, and managers regularly experience 'devolved authority' as the 'dumping' of yet more work duties onto their already overburdened shoulders. Classical management theorists such as V. A. Graicunas or Lyndall Urwick believed that any more than five or six direct reports was too many for any manager to realistically cope with. Such views appear Luddite today and are readily dismissed by contemporary management consultancies who champion the role of lean, agile, digitally enhanced practices that can dispense with bureaucracy. In reality, IT-enabled devolution of authority to the line tends to impose huge extra workload pressures on middle managers, who are increasingly scarce due to prior rounds of downsizing and delayering (Hassard *et al.*, 2009).

In fact, according to official figures, the total number of middle managers in the NHS is not especially large. The NHS Confederation (2015) reports that in 2014 the NHS employed 150,273 doctors, 377,191 qualified nurses, 155,960 qualified scientific, therapeutic and technical staff, and 37,078 managers – just 2.67 per cent of the 1.388 million NHS staff. It is unclear whether those counted as managers are people who are managers by profession rather than hybrid clinician-managers. When researching NHS trusts, it is often hard to identify staff in NHS organizations as 'middle managers' (Hyde *et al.*, 2012). This is because many staff who carry out managerial work and bear managerial responsibilities are themselves clinicians; medical directors, nurse or midwife managers, clinical team leaders, paramedic area managers, for example. It has long been recognized that NHS middle managers have hybrid manager/clinician identities (e.g. see Bolton, 2003; Currie, 1997; Currie and Procter, 2005). This can be a major source of personal conflict – the partially marketized nature of the NHS intensifies the ways in which professional clinical judgement can clash with market/business logic (McCann *et al.*, 2015a). Patient care has to be seen to take priority, but budgets also need to be balanced. Crises can be ever-present as newspaper headlines about complaints and failures in patient care are just around the next corner and regular audits and inspections require increasing volumes of data.

'Liberating the NHS': assessing the impact of policy changes on middle managers

Amid the furore over the Health and Social Care Act of 2012, it is easy to forget that the NHS has been the subject of regular policy reform and change. Although it expanded rapidly in the first 30 years, the NHS experienced only one major reorganization aimed at improving co-ordination across the system. But coinciding with the economic turmoil of the 1970s/1980s, welfare and public services increasingly came under scrutiny as they conflicted with the emergent neo-liberal ideology. Governments began to embrace the notion that public services needed the discipline of commercial-style general management in order to control, monitor, audit and, in many ways, restrict the discretion of public service professionals. Since then, NHS reorganizations have become both more regular and more ambitious until – following the financial crisis and economic contraction of 2008/9 – reforms paved the way for the wholesale private provision of public services, reflecting political preferences for market economics in the public sector. This trajectory towards private provision of NHS services has been well documented elsewhere, particularly given its rapid acceleration in recent years. Recent accounts of the transformation programme range from Allyson Pollock's searing critique *NHS Plc* (2005) to contrasting accounts detailing those who 'lose out' – *NHS SOS: How the NHS was Betrayed* (Davis and Tallis, 2013) – and those who 'win out' – *The Plot against the NHS* (Leys and Player, 2011). These books document the transition of the NHS from national ideal to brand for sale.

More recently, managers and management have been central to NHS reforms, being named at various times as either the cause of or the cure for inefficiencies. Middle managers were introduced in the 1980s to make the NHS more efficient and then removed by the coalition government in the 2010s for the same reason. As we chart the journey of the NHS from a publicly provided service towards one that is commercially provided, we see how management and managerialism have played central roles in the narratives surrounding successive reforms.

Nigel Lawson, Chancellor of the Exchequer for much of Margaret Thatcher's time as premier, famously wrote that 'the NHS was the closest thing the English have to a religion' and, seemingly frustrated, added 'with those who practice in it regarding themselves as a priesthood' (1992: 613). Lawson recognized that free public healthcare, enacted through the NHS, was an important and positive component of identity for UK citizens. Nevertheless, successive governments came to see retrenchment of the welfare state as a necessary good with the NHS remaining the subject of attention for an increasingly aggressive and pervasive neo-liberal political agenda. As is well known, the first White Paper of the incoming coalition government (Department of Health, 2010) was subtitled *Liberating the NHS*. In true 'third spirit of capitalism' style (Boltanksi and Chiapello, 2005), the claims to liberation seem to rest on emancipating healthcare from the dead hand of state bureaucracy and professional closure. It promised a 45 per cent cut in management costs. Eventually passed into law as the aforementioned Health and Social Care Act 2012, this liberation has brought the NHS almost full circle towards a pre-1948 system of healthcare. Changes to commissioning arrangements provided a major point of entry for private providers, and the controversial Section 75 regulations covering procurement, patient choice and competition meant that most services had to be put out to tender to 'any qualified provider'.

Although front-line services may, for a time, remain relatively unchanged during these transitions – regardless of who is the provider – government reforms certainly affect managers, who are cast in a variety of roles as they are required to perform distinct and competing functions from public administrator to business manager to entrepreneur. Ultimately, front-line healthcare and the services that patients receive will be affected as changes in service provider and managerial roles demand different decisions to be made about how to allocate scarce resources to either improve the nation's health or meet financial targets. In the remainder of this chapter, we chart the journey of the NHS from inception to (neo)liberation and detail the consequent effects on managerial work in the NHS. We see managers cast into five roles, which pervaded to a greater or lesser degree in each type of NHS organization we studied (see Chapters 4–7).

Deconstructing the NHS: from public institution to efficient business

We have seen how ideas about management have undergone significant shifts in recent years (see also Hassard *et al.*, 2009 and McCann, 2016). We now consider how government reforms in relation to the management of the NHS have reflected these changes and how those changes affect the working lives of NHS managers. As noted, the backdrop to these changes was an aggressive neo-liberal agenda – a 'stealth revolution' (Brown, 2015) – alongside turbulent economic circumstances. Various governments came to realize the enormity of the task of transforming the NHS for market competition, and we argue that the transition took place in many stages and through a series of major reforms that cast NHS managers into a variety of roles before portraying them as the source of the problem.

This section provides a brief overview of government policy as it has prepared the NHS for commercialization and how this has affected NHS managers over the life of the NHS to date (for fuller accounts of NHS policy reforms, see Davis and Tallis, 2013; Harrison and McDonald, 2008; Lister, 2008). These changes can be broadly grouped into five stages of NHS deconstruction that cast managers into the roles of administrator, bureaucrat, business person, leader and, finally, reluctant entrepreneur.

1 Steady state, 1948 to 1982: the manager as public administrator

The NHS was founded in 1948 on the three principles of: universal coverage, being free at the point of delivery, and being provided on the basis of need rather than ability to pay (Klein, 2010). It operated as a professional bureaucracy with clinicians exerting considerable influence and autonomy. Hospitals were managed by an administrator, a chief nurse and a medical consultant. No *one* person had overall responsibility. The shape of the emergent NHS reflected the political challenges of its establishment; the British Medical Association, which was a fierce opponent, negotiated substantial concessions for its members. General practitioners remained self-employed subcontractors, and consultants were appointed at regional level, thus protecting them from local managerial control. They had professional sovereignty in clinical practice and could use NHS facilities for their private practice. Governing boards and committees had substantial medical representation (Harrison and McDonald, 2008).

Until the publication of the Griffiths Report (in 1983), management in the NHS operated on a consensus basis, which saw agreement between members of the medical profession and hospital administrators. Medical professionals held the dominant position, and research during the 1970s suggested that consultants tended to have more influence than management teams (Harrison, 1982: 387). Throughout the 1950s and 1960s, these arrangements for NHS management came into question, but it took a scandal about mistreatment of long-stay patients at Ely Hospital to lead to the creation of the Health Advisory Service (first known as the Hospital Advisory Service), which undertook hospital inspections.[2] The first major reorganization of the NHS took place in 1974, bringing together GPs and community and hospital services into single local NHS organizations. Decision-making continued to follow a triumvirate consensus-management arrangement, which was extended to several levels of the local organization. Throughout this period, GPs and consultants shaped service development. The net result was that management plans, decisions and capital expenditure reflected their priorities. Managers, as *administrators*, were inward-looking and reactive, solving problems and gathering resources to satisfy their medical staff (Harrison and McDonald, 2008). Elements of this triumvirate, largely consensus-driven management was still in evidence among managers, consultants and lead nurses in the acute trust we studied (see Chapter 4).

2 First comes managerialism, 1983 to 1988: the manager as bureaucrat

The Griffiths Report institutionalized management in the NHS, and the role of manager was to control clinical activity, budgets and performance. The 1980s saw a new Conservative government that was under continued economic and financial pressure. Attempts to manage perceived declining NHS performance included two changes, both from 1983. The first saw the introduction of annual top-down reviews against a rudimentary set of performance indicators. These reviews allowed the performance of local health authorities to be compared. Although these reviews were said to have had little immediate effect (Harrison and McDonald, 2008), they did institutionalize the idea of performance against quantitative targets. Second, the *NHS Management Inquiry* by Roy Griffiths (Department of Health, 1983), Chairman of Sainsbury's PLC, attempted to abolish 'consensus management' in favour of 'general management' and provided the structural arrangement for a *rational* management system. This shift in relationships involved a move away from the high levels of trust involved in consensus management towards the low trust of rational management (Hunter, 1984). Griffiths' recommendations generated a long-standing rift between clinicians and managers. The report suggested the appointment of general managers, the introduction of management budgets, value for money reforms, and management training and education. General managers from inside and outside the NHS were appointed to hospitals and health authorities by the end of 1985. Management budgets were introduced alongside greater financial controls. Savings arising from those reforms were to be returned to improving services for patients, and the NHS Training Authority was established in order to extend management instruction, especially for doctors, who were to become more closely involved in financial matters and budgeting. Managers had fixed-term contracts and so arguably, as *bureaucrats*, became more responsive to government demands.

The Griffiths Report spurred the development of a field of literature in the social sciences/organization studies around *NHS management* as a subject in itself.

Researchers such as Cousins (1988) and Anthony and Reed (1990) focused on the report's effects on the management of healthcare in the NHS. Cousins argued, for example, that 'the introduction of market rationality has obscured the purposes of state welfare work' (1988: 211). Central to Cousins' claims about the threats posed to NHS management by market rationality was the imposition of cost reduction targets. Thus three themes – market rationality, policy pressures from the centre, and targets in various forms – entered the discourse on healthcare management around that time. Despite the introduction of more formal management structures, informal methods of management have remained important. Utilizing interview techniques, Anthony and Reed elicited responses from nurse managers that, in hindsight, could be seen to typify later findings. Nurse managers were *reluctant* middle managers in that they did not perceive themselves as managers at all. Instead, they found themselves torn between patient care and organizational concerns for resource management and the like (Anthony and Reed, 1990: 22). Anthony and Reed provided a taxonomy of management roles and behaviours. In terms of roles, they listed: crisis management, administrative chores, task-based or craft-based management (including co-ordination) and corporate management. In addition, they detailed the following behaviours: (the application of) personal skills, personal networks of relationships, personal obligation, acquired wisdom and skill, formal authority and constitutional authority (1990: 28).

3 Then the market, 1989 to 1996: the manager as business person

The period 1989–96 saw the first attempts to prepare the NHS for market competition. The 1989 White Paper *Working for Patients* passed into law as the NHS and Community Care Act in 1990. It introduced an (internal) quasi-market for healthcare by encouraging services to split along 'purchaser' (health authority and some GPs) and 'provider' (acute, mental health, ambulance and community services) lines. Purchasers were given budgets to buy healthcare from providers. Providers became NHS trusts (independent organizations with their own management teams), and trusts would then compete with each other to provide services to the purchasers. Between 1991 and 1995, all providers became NHS trusts. GPs could hold budgets (GP fundholding) to purchase care for their patients from the NHS or private providers. Some GP fundholders were able to accelerate care for their patients, leading to accusations of a two-tier health system emerging. As well as attempting to increase managerial control of services, these changes were also designed to introduce competition and a business culture. The management role was thus oriented towards *business* matters.

The Patient's Charter (Department of Health, 1991) saw the patient as consumer with expected standards of service. This was followed by *The Health of the Nation* (Department of Health, 1992), which set the scene for further development of targets as a means of performance management. Although NHS quasi-market institutions were originally abandoned by the New Labour government of 1997, these early experiences paved the way for market-oriented changes in the coming years.

Research at the time found that enmities between clinicians and managers triggered by the Griffiths reforms continued to the extent that 'general managers have been singularly unsuccessful in involving clinicians in managing their services' (Dopson, 1994: 27). Further, 'many empirical studies have highlighted the reluctance of doctors to be involved in management as a key issue in health-care management' (1994: 28).

Dopson contrasted the 'thought styles' of NHS doctors and managers (1994: 28) and found that the former focused on evidence and short-term operational goals while the latter, more on organizational interests. She went on to highlight the role of clinical director, which emerged, structurally, as the archetypal doctor-manager role. Basing her findings on interviews with consultant doctors, Dopson suggested that they had a largely negative attitude towards both management and managers. A similar conclusion was reached by Fitzgerald (1994). In her analysis, consultants taking on senior management roles were motivated primarily by a desire to maintain their professional power within the organization – to 'considerably strengthen the sphere of influence of the medical profession' (1994: 42). Perhaps unsurprisingly, Dopson and Stewart (1990) found that middle management was more stressful under the move to marketization and that middle managers in the public sector were more resistant to change than their private sector counterparts.

As the 1990s progressed, interest in NHS nurse manager (as well as NHS middle manager) roles began to develop. It was argued that clinical nurse managers now performed a *pivotal* organizational role (Oroviogoicoechea, 1996: 1273). In terms of definition, Oroviogoicoechea placed clinical nurse managers firmly in the role of *first-line* managers; that is, in what we might term a junior management role. Six 'role functions' of the nurse manager were suggested: 'management of clinical nursing practice and patient care; management of human, fiscal and other resources; development of personnel; compliance with regulatory and professional standards; strategic planning; [and] fostering of interdisciplinary, collaborative relationships' (1996: 1275–6). The role of first-line nurse manager was increasingly associated with managerial rather than clinical functions, reflecting associated 'role confusion and conflict' (Duffield, 1991: 1248). In this, Duffield was largely in concert with Anthony and Reed (1990; see above). Duffield noted the uncertainty experienced by first-line nurse managers over whether or not they should still have been providing direct patient care (1991: 1249).

4 New business units and the foundation trust, 1997 to 2009: the manager as leader

Along with New Labour came a centralization of NHS management and an emergent culture of *leaderism*; the new NHS manager was someone capable of leading many changes and, counter-intuitively, of being directed by the national agenda (Bresnen et al., 2015). Labour came to power having promised to 'save the NHS', and this period saw unprecedented change involving the formation, dissolution and rearrangement of structures and responsibilities of NHS authorities and trusts. *The New NHS: Modern, Dependable* (Department of Health, 1997) saw the abolition of the internal market and dismantling of GP fundholding. This was an era of centralized management of the NHS as one organization. It involved target setting, intended to reduce waiting times and improve access to services. It also saw the introduction of a star rating system for NHS organizations. Organizations were rated by the newly established Commission for Health Improvement (CHI). Although national targets were subsequently abandoned, along with the star rating system, priorities continued to be indicated through the *Operating Framework for the NHS*, published annually. The National Institute for Clinical Excellence (NICE) was created to make decisions on the adoption of treatments. These two institutions (CHI and NICE) took over areas previously controlled by the medical profession. Decisions about suitable treatments were now being made by NICE, and clinical governance was being carried out by CHI (subsequently named the Health Care Commission and then the Care Quality Commission). The (ten-year) *NHS Plan* (Department of Health, 2000a) described the NHS and National Service Frameworks, which for the first time set standards for specialist services such as mental health and cardiac care.

Decades of underspending on healthcare meant that England had notably poor health outcomes compared to other developed nations. In 2000, Tony Blair promised to increase health spending to European levels. This meant a rise from 6.6 per cent (1999/2000) to 9 per cent (2005/6) of GDP, and real terms increases in spending of 7.1 per cent were projected (Wanless, 2002); by 2007/8, spending reached £113 billion. Much of the increased spending went on pay and price inflation (Harrison and McDonald, 2008). However, this period of major investment followed a period of spending cuts, and substantial improvements were made to infrastructure and equipment. Clinical activity also increased.

A code of conduct for NHS managers was introduced in 2003, codifying ethical managerial conduct. This guidance included: putting the care and safety of patients first; the need for honesty and integrity; and being responsible for their work and the work of those they manage. Breaking this code could lead to dismissal and being barred from working for the NHS. There is, however, little evidence of it ever being used in this way.

Although the targets and associated penalties were initially successful in reducing waiting times, increasingly disturbing behaviours linked to intense centralized control preceded a radical change in direction towards decentralization and the readoption of market-based reforms. These included the promotion of patient choice and competition between providers as well as allowing for organizations based on not-for-profit structures – NHS foundation trusts.

The first wave of foundation trusts came into being in 2004. At the same time, the previous system of block contracts to service providers was replaced by a new funding system called Payment by Results. This system was aimed at reducing waiting times by targeting payments towards specific treatments and thus providing a powerful incentive for trusts to direct activity towards areas of greatest need. This move towards payments per treatment proved difficult to introduce in mental health services (see Chapter 6). The Darzi Review (Department of Health, 2008) laid out the second ten-year plan for the NHS although it was rapidly displaced by the unfolding financial crisis. The review laid out plans to increase patient choice, to improve public health provision and to extend the role of doctors as managerial leaders. This era encapsulated ideas of the manager as *leader* – leading change and complying with rapid-fire structural and policy changes.

For some time before this (e.g. see Hood, 1991), academic authors had begun to relate developments in the management of healthcare to what had become known as New Public Management or NPM. Hunter (1996: 801) listed the chief dimensions of NPM:

> Hands-on professional management in the public sector
>
> Standard setting, performance measurement and target setting, especially for professional services
>
> Emphasis on output controls linked to resource allocation
>
> The disaggregation or 'unbundling' of previously monolithic units in the public sector into provider/producer functions, and the introduction of contracting standards
>
> Stress on private sector management style and greater flexibility coupled with a move away from formal, inflexible public service ethic
>
> Discipline and parsimony in resource use: cost cutting, doing more with less, controlling labour union demands.

Currie and Brown (2003) adopted an explicitly narratological approach in their account of group and individual identities of senior and middle managers in an NHS hospital. While narratives of senior managers were held by the authors to perform as legitimating discourses, individuals had their own stories to tell, and they did so as part of a process of identity construction (2003: 563). They noted that while the 'sectoral transference' of managers, and management styles, from the private sector initially had an empowering effect on NHS middle managers (2003: 568, 569), this ran up against another dynamic that typified corporate change in the last 20 years: delayering. Thus middle managers found themselves in a vulnerable position. Once again, we were reminded of the key tenets of New Public Management (see the sixth point in Hunter's schematic, above), with senior managers encouraging the use of 'business plans' by middle managers as a way of controlling ever-scarcer resources (2003: 571). As Currie and Brown highlighted, the construction of robust business plans by individual managers could not fully mitigate against the risk of job losses as part of organizational restructuring.

Preston and Loan-Clarke found that NHS managers knew they were viewed negatively by the media, by the general public and even by their own families (2000: 104). They found that the managers' jobs were difficult and stressful (a theme across much of the NHS management literature) and yet the difficulty of the work was largely unacknowledged. Managers felt that they received pressure from all sides (2000: 106) as they worked to organize the functioning of a highly complex organization. Merali (2003) found NHS managers to be committed to the core values of improving people's health and being socially useful to the extent that these values were expressed by the managers themselves. However, like Preston and Loan-Clarke, managers interviewed by Merali believed that they were negatively viewed by clinicians, politicians, the media and the public at large.

Nurse managers became a focus of attention in many studies of NHS management. Willmott (1998) examined the transition from senior nurse to newer ward manager roles. This change in role was implemented as part of the continued and increasing emphasis on quality and effectiveness of patient care, which had come to characterize NHS policy. Willmott noted various potential criticisms of this restructuring; for example, the moving of expert clinical staff away from front-line patient care could be seen to be at odds with precisely that – patient care at the bedside. Further, the move away from more direct clinical work could undermine ward managers' credibility with junior staff. Willmott also noted that the integration of clinical professionals into management structures could be difficult (1998: 420). Despite these potential difficulties, many (61 per cent) of Willmott's respondents were positive about their new role as charge nurse/ward manager.

Some responses were less positive. Some ward managers complained about growing distance between themselves and their nursing staff. Others felt distanced from patients and wondered if their extensive experience of caring for patients was being put to best use in their new, more office-based role (1998: 423). Increased levels of stress were noted by 81 per cent of Willmott's interviewees. This finding was supported by Adams *et al.* (2000) who found that nurse managers had an increasing workload – the increasing number of students to supervise being one example. A key finding in the piece by Adams *et al.* was that when attempting to *juggle* the myriad demands on their time, ward managers retained a sense of prioritizing patient care above all else, often stepping in and returning to a hands-on role when necessary. According to Adams *et al.* and indeed across the literature, shortage of staff and resources due to financial constraints was a central reason for increased work intensity and longer working hours. In the cost-conscious environment of the NHS, nurse managers often preferred to do patient-facing work themselves in order to save money on additional staffing costs (2000: 547).

Elsewhere, Cooke was quite scathing about the whole project of New Public Management, which could be seen as a means of extracting more work for less money whilst at the same time maintaining *de facto* hierarchies under the guise of flexibility and decentralization (2006: 224). The contradictions of NPM were summarized as follows: '[i]ncrease political control but free managers to manage; [s]ave money but raise standards; [m]otivate and empower staff but intensify work and downsize; [r]educe bureaucracy but increase audit, measurement and juridification; [d]ecentralize responsibility but centralize control' (2006: 224–5).

Nurse managers were often being referred to as 'hybrid managers' (Dopson and Fitzgerald, 2006; Savage and Scott, 2004). The role of modern matron (introduced in 2002) was described by Savage and Scott (2004: 419, citing Hewison, 2004) as embodying this hybridity: 'a new type of management in which non-medical health care professionals engage in aspects of general (or "generic") management, combining this with their clinical management responsibilities'.

By this point in the historical development of NHS middle management, nurses and other clinicians in the NHS were increasingly expected to demonstrate qualities of *leadership* as well as management. Leadership was a less tangible expectation of managers that included: improving the quality of patient care; influencing improvements in population health; promoting the NHS as being well led, managed and accountable; and developing strategies to motivate and develop NHS staff (Bresnen *et al.*, 2015).

Martin and Learmonth (2012) noted the upward discursive trajectory of concepts of leadership in the NHS. Their perspective on leadership was more critical than that found in much of the literature. For these authors, leadership was 'generally seen as a nefarious political project, one concerned with facilitating subtle forms of control: leaders seducing their followers into accepting what may not be in their interests' (2012: 282). Discourses of leadership were intended to influence healthcare workers' sense of self. By having NHS managers, for example, buy in to the leadership discourse, policymakers and senior managers were able to co-opt them into ongoing reforms that may not have been in their best interests. Martin and Learmonth, however, asserted that although policy and trust management discourse presented an image of ownership and leadership at local levels, ultimately, real power continued to lie with the centre. Such power was enforced through inspection regimes, performance targets and resource allocation. Discourses of devolved leadership could serve to obviate this contradiction in the consciousness of workforce and patients alike in suggesting that seemingly liberatory management discourses could be ideological vehicles for more effective domination of the workforce.

The Healthcare Commission (HCC; latterly known as the Care Quality Commission, CQC) in March 2009 published *Investigation into Mid Staffordshire NHS Foundation Trust*. This report was highly critical of the use of performance targets in NHS management. Hood (2006) noted the risks associated with targets in the NHS in particular. While authors tended to acknowledge that target setting had been successful in some cases – reducing waiting times in A&E, for example – many have been critical of the inflexibility of centrally set targets (Bevan and Hood, 2006). This somewhat ambivalent approach recognized that while target-based governance regimes were problematic, the absence of an effective hierarchy in the NHS made their use unavoidable (Bevan and Hood, 2006). Managers as leaders were expected to implement policy by convincing clinicians of the necessity for change.

5 Open door to 'any qualified provider', 2010 to the present: the manager as reluctant entrepreneur

The first White Paper of the Conservative–Liberal Democratic coalition government in 2010 brought health policy almost full circle by proposing the removal of management layers to improve efficiency. They advocated what were said to be the most significant changes to the NHS since it began (Whitehead *et al.*, 2010). The White Paper *Equity and Excellence: Liberating the NHS* (Department of Health, 2010) proposed to reduce management costs by 45 per cent over four years and to delayer the NHS by abolishing 151 primary care trusts and 10 strategic health authorities. However, these layers were to be replaced by two new layers: 300–500 GP consortia overseen by the national NHS Commissioning Board (for more detail, see Chapter 7). Critics have argued that decentralizing budgets to local GP consortia complicates cost containment in a pluralistic system (Leys and Player, 2011). The Health and Social Care Act 2012 took the changes even further by lessening the emphasis on GPs as commissioners and providing for private sector commissioning. The *liberation* came to refer to the liberation of provider services to make public or private provision in a competitive consumer market. Thus managers of provider services had to become increasingly *entrepreneurial* in a multi-commissioning, competition-driven health service. As we see later, entrepreneurial activities were undertaken somewhat reluctantly in order to ensure organizational survival year by year.

More recently, scholars of healthcare management began looking at the use of *Lean* management techniques in healthcare settings. Waring and Bishop (2010) argued that Lean techniques might not be directly translatable from industrial to healthcare settings. Further, some of the apparent performance improvements achieved by Lean techniques appeared to result from work intensification and heightened (peer) supervision. In a similar manner to Cooke's (2006) take on empowerment and Martin and Learmonth's (2012) analysis of discourses of leadership, Waring and Bishop considered the rhetorical status of Lean. Lean thinking could be seen to synthesize, rhetorically at least, the direct functional priorities of management (efficiency) and clinicians (patient care). This synthesis was achieved by creating a supposed logical trajectory from the first set of priorities to the second: improve efficiency and, thus, improve patient care.

Each stage of what we term the 'deconstruction of the NHS' describes three overarching themes: institutional reform; the changing balance of power; and attempts at performance management. These policy themes have been driven by an underlying belief in the power of both rational management and markets to increase efficiency. This review provides an historical backdrop against which our empirical work exploring the realities of managerial work can be assessed. Moreover, in the empirical chapters that come later, it is clear that the effects of these changes are still in evidence today; albeit to a greater or lesser extent depending on the type of NHS organization, the degree of change it has faced and the context of the local political landscape.

Notes

1 Agenda for Change was the name for a new pay spine for all NHS staff except doctors and senior managers. Introduced in December 2004, it involved a major change to pay for nurses, allied health professionals and other non-clinical staff. All affected NHS jobs were subject to job evaluation and grading under the new scheme.

2 NHS inspectorates undergo regular name changes and reorganization. At the time of writing, the inspectorate for health and social care organizations is the Care Quality Commission.

3

EXPLORING NHS WORK

A Critical-Action perspective

This chapter outlines the theories and methods we have drawn upon – and also developed – in carrying out research into the management of modern UK healthcare. Basically, it explains our efforts to develop a research perspective appropriate for directing our empirical investigations into managerial work (see Chapters 4–7). We do this in four phases. First, we explain our initial analysis of the various theoretical, methodological and philosophical options available to us in the process of developing a research perspective. Second, we discuss the main research issues that have influenced the development of this perspective, which is basically a hybrid approach to sociological analysis. Third, we unpack our research perspective – Critical-Action Theory – to show how it can contribute to management and organization studies generally. And fourth, we describe the process by which we have applied our Critical-Action perspective to studies of managerial work in four health service sectors. In realizing this research, our objective has been to address one generic question: what are the effects of the New Public Management ethos on management roles and behaviour in UK healthcare? Ultimately, readers will appreciate how our empirical investigations suggest one generic answer: that managerial work in UK healthcare is changing because the business-oriented ethos of the New Public Management has seen an associated shift in emphasis from public service to managerialism. This chapter describes, therefore, the philosophical, theoretical and methodological journey we have taken from initially framing our research question to arriving at this answer through empirical analysis.

Explaining theoretical and methodological options

The first phase of the research process was consideration of the research options available to us, their appropriateness to the project aims, and how as a team we felt these married with our own professional skills. In our initial meetings, one of the first tasks set was to define and locate an appropriate research paradigm for our theoretical and methodological enquiries. Although the members of the research team had skill sets relevant to one generic research field – management and organization studies (MOS) – they individually came from various social science backgrounds; namely, psychology, social psychology and sociology. The first objective, therefore, was to develop a common theoretical and methodological outlook – one that would see the team 'singing from the same (research) hymn sheet'.

To accomplish this, it was suggested that we go *back to basics* and consider epistemological issues relevant to our project. It was hoped that a philosophically oriented approach would provide us with a unified perspective on the methodological options available to contemporary research in MOS and our study in particular. To arrive at this position, the team initially conducted a theoretical and methodological reading programme – one that offered a broad sweep of intellectual terrain in MOS. One contribution that immediately came to mind was work associated with the well-known model of research paradigms provided by Burrell and Morgan (1979; see also Morgan, 1980, 1986). This model offered not only the advantage of familiarizing us with a range of research literatures and styles in MOS, but also – in addressing the various philosophical principles which underpinned them – tools to consider how different methodological positions could potentially be adapted in novel ways to meet the needs of our specific project, or what was basically a contingency orientation.

Put briefly, the Burrell and Morgan model classifies MOS theories and methods within a matrix based on the intersection of two sociological axes: subjective–objective and regulation–radical change (basically a reworking of the traditional dualisms of agency–structure and consensus–conflict, respectively). The resulting two-by-two matrix produces four major research paradigms: *functionalist* (objective-regulation); *interpretive* (subjective-regulation); *radical humanist* (subjective-radical); and *radical structuralist* (objective-radical). These four paradigms are founded upon mutually exclusive views of the social and organizational world; each stands on its own terms and generates its own distinctive analyses. Taken together, the paradigms offer a map for negotiating the various subject areas of MOS – one which offers a convenient means of identifying similarities and differences between the works of researchers, and in particular, the underlying frames of reference they variously adopt.

We noted from the start, however, that despite the Burrell and Morgan model being one of the most cited in the history of MOS (with almost 9,000 Google Scholar citations), it was produced three decades prior to our study. As such, the question remained of how applicable it was for contemporary theoretical and methodological developments in MOS. We thus set ourselves the subsequent task of reviewing and accounting for generic developments in theoretical and methodological thinking in the interim period. These discussions (including significant input from Julie Wolfram Cox, Monash University; see Hassard and Wolfram Cox, 2013) suggested that in addition to the main social science orders discussed by Burrell and Morgan – structure and agency (or as we redefined them, structural and anti-structural positions) – recent decades had also seen a so-called 'third order' of sociological analysis come to the fore in the form of post-structuralism and more broadly postmodernism. Thus to appreciate the range of methodological options available for contemporary MOS enquiries, we directed ourselves subsequently to mapping the terrain of MOS research *post* Burrell and Morgan.

Tables 3.1 and 3.2 summarize these early discussions about the development of MOS in the post–Burrell and Morgan period and the domains of research that currently present themselves. Our analysis adopted the framework originally developed by Burrell and Morgan in arguing that theories of management and organization inherently reflect a 'philosophy of science' and a 'theory of society' (Burrell and Morgan, 1979: 1). For the former, we proposed an argument that research in MOS adopting a broadly post-structural or postmodern approach can be characterized as ontologically *relativist*, epistemologically *relationist*, and methodologically *reflexive*; it is also work that, in decentring human agency, is arguably *deconstructionist* in its orientation to human nature. Although other terms from social theory and philosophy can be substituted to characterize such third-order analysis, we have argued that these are particularly expedient for researchers' purposes.

When we expanded this analysis to consider Burrell and Morgan's second dimension – 'the nature of society' – we found our three core MOS paradigms expanded into six research domains. Table 3.2 lists these domains together with examples of the theories, theorists and research that comprise them. This analysis was realized by delineating the underlying political and ideological assumptions of scholarly communities within our three paradigm orders. However, to make sense of such assumptions for contemporary MOS analysis, instead of deploying Burrell and Morgan's original terminology of the sociology of regulation and sociology of radical change, we felt it more appropriate to talk of differences between 'normative' (Habermas, 1986; Jacobs and Hanrahan, 2005; Peters, 2005) and 'critical' (Alvesson and Willmott, 1992, 2003; Grey and Willmott, 2005; Parker, 2002a) accounts, especially given the now established use of the latter term as an identifier for ideologically Leftist analysis across several MOS traditions (Fournier and Grey, 2000; see also Alvesson and Deetz, 2000; Corbett *et al.*, 2011; Deetz, 1996).

TABLE 3.1 Metatheories for MOS paradigms

	Structural paradigm	*Anti-structural paradigm*	*Post-structural paradigm*
Ontology	Realist	Nominalist	Relativist
Epistemology	Positivist	Constructionist	Relationist
Human nature	Determinist	Voluntarist	Deconstructionist
Methodology	Deductive	Interpretive	Reflexive

TABLE 3.2 Typology of MOS research domains: examples of theories, theorists and research

Paradigm	Research domain	Organizational theories (OT) (e.g.)	Influential theorists and writers (e.g.)	Research and analysis in OT (e.g.)
Structural	**Normative structural**	Contingency theory Institutional theory Population ecology	Alfred Chandler Philip Selznick Eugene Odum	Donaldson (2001) Greenwood et al. (2008) Aldrich (2008)
Structural	**Critical structural**	Labour process theory Radical Weberianism Socialist feminism	Harry Braverman Max Weber Shulie Firestone	McCann et al. (2008) Mouzelis (1975) Walby (1986)
Anti-structural	**Normative anti-structural**	Ethnomethodology Phenomenology Social constructionism	Harold Garfinkel Edmund Husserl Alfred Schutz	Llewellyn and Hindmarsh (2010) Holt and Sandberg (2011) Hosking and McNamee (2006)
Anti-structural	**Critical anti-structural**	Anti-organization theory Critical discourse Critical theory	Herbert Marcuse Norman Fairclough Jürgen Habermas	Anthony (1977) Phillips et al. (2008) Burrell (1994)
Post-structural	**Normative post-structural**	Actor-network theory Archaeo-genealogy Process theory	Bruno Latour Michel Foucault Henri Bergson	Hardy et al. (2001) Hodgson (2000) Tsoukas and Chia (2002)
Post-structural	**Critical post-structural**	Autonomism Post-structural feminism Post-colonialism	Antonio Negri Julia Kristeva Gayatri Spivak	Harney (2007) Thomas and Davies (2005) Jones (2005)

Based on ideological characteristics, therefore, we have argued that our three paradigms reflect the following analytical domains: *normative structural*; *critical structural*; *normative anti-structural*; *critical anti-structural*; *normative post-structural*; and *critical post-structural*. In MOS, the first four domains have been accounted for regularly in terms of their theoretical positions and research contributions (see Bottomore, 1975; Burrell and Morgan, 1979; Hassard, 1993; Hearn and Parkin, 1983; Jennings *et al.*, 2005; Lewis and Grimes, 1999). Indeed they basically reflect the four original Burrell and Morgan paradigms in terms of their metatheoretical and methodological philosophies (i.e. normative structural *qua* functionalist; critical structural *qua* radical structuralist; normative anti-structural *qua* interpretive; critical anti-structural *qua* radical humanist). Within these domains, we found not only research traditions that were accounted for in the original Burrell and Morgan model (e.g. anti-organization theory; ethnomethodology; labour process theory) but also many others that have emerged since (e.g. critical discourse analysis; institutional theory; population ecology; process theory). In one important case, however, Social Action Theory (see below), we disagreed with its original (functionalist) location in Burrell and Morgan and repositioned it within an anti-structural research domain.

This initial exercise allowed us, therefore, to become familiar with the range of methodological and research opportunities available within MOS and, on this basis, to begin to look for goodness of fit with the specific aims of our project. Our model formed the generic basis from which methodological options could be narrowed down. It formed a springboard to developing our own theorizing and a unified research position. This line of analysis was considered particularly useful in that it allowed us to reflect not only on methodological appropriateness (through the comparison of various subjectivist and objectivist and, thus, qualitative versus quantitative strategies and methods) but also on the nature of political interpretation. Reflective, sociologically, of traditional consensus versus conflict perspectives, this was felt important in light of the concept of *ideology* being one that, from our early literature searches and discussions on the management of healthcare, loomed increasingly large.

Finally, as MOS has benefitted previously from developments linking pluralistic theorizing with research methodology, we felt that, as a by-product of our analysis, one of the potential benefits for future research may be through promoting a methodology for *paradigm triangulation*. By identifying the metatheoretical assumptions underpinning core analytical orders in MOS, scholars may utilize such assumptions to produce a new form of paradigm-based research enquiry. Similar in strategy to approaches such as paradigm interplay (Schultz and Hatch, 1996) and meta-triangulation (Lewis and Grimes, 1999) and based on a philosophy of highlighting areas of analytical overlap as well as sites of contradiction (Okhuysen and Bonardi, 2011), this method would draw upon a range of paradigms and domains to explain, in a more inclusive fashion, contemporary organizational phenomena such as new professional identities, hybrid organizational forms, and social networks. In so doing, this approach would seek to formalize methodologically, and thus advance, the call by Bechara and Van de Ven (2011) for researchers to triangulate their philosophies of science in order to understand complex organizational and managerial problems.

Towards a hybrid research position

Given the backcloth provided by our methodological review, the next stage in the research process saw us attempt to determine an analytical orientation appropriate to the political context of analysis (see Chapter 1). This would see our various theoretical and methodological interests considered vis-à-vis specification of a formal research position.

On the one hand, for our theory of social science, the aims set out in our study specified examination of the realities, roles and behaviours of healthcare managers in various NHS organizations. In terms of sociological investigation, the research direction suggested by these aims was an interpretive approach founded upon a constructionist epistemology. On the other hand, for our theory of society, the election of a new UK government and its launch soon thereafter of a White Paper directed at *Liberating the NHS* appeared to reflect, contextually, a heightened political and ideological climate for healthcare and its management – one which, in Burrell and Morgan's terms, was characterized more by *change, conflict, disintegration* and *coercion* than *stability, integration, co-ordination* and *consensus*. That is, a context reflecting, sociologically, a *radical change* more than a *regulation* position.

The research orientation which seemed appropriate to our project needs, therefore, appeared one that would marry a methodology characteristic of interpretivism (or, in our terms, *normative anti-structuralism*) and a theoretical position directed at understanding the influence of political and ideological forces, with such analysis, in MOS, potentially reflecting a *critical anti-structural* approach. In short, our discussions drew us to explore the possibilities for developing a hybrid approach to research – one representing a blurring or synthesis of two established sociological traditions: Action Theory and Critical Theory.

In our research, the influence of Action Theory (strictly speaking Social Action Theory) stems from an attempt some decades ago to develop an alternative analysis of organizations in work by David Silverman (who in turn was drawing upon Action Theory as developed variously by Max Weber, Alfred Schutz, Wilhelm Dilthey and Peter Berger). In Silverman's work on the 'action frame of reference' (see 1970, pp. 126–7 for a summary), for example, he argued that sociology should be concerned with *understanding* rather than observing behaviour (as under positivism) and that this distinction was crucial in that it is meanings that define social reality rather than social reality being self-evident through observation. As meanings were predisposed to deteriorate, they required regular reaffirmation in everyday actions. Social reality did not just occur 'out there', but instead had to be made constantly to *re*-occur intersubjectively. The inference was that through social interaction, people could adjust and even change meanings.

Explanations of social action, therefore, needed to take account of the meanings that those participating in everyday events attached to such actions. For Silverman, social researchers should build their theories upon foundations that view social reality as being socially constructed, sustained and changed. In the study of organizations, he argued that the social actor should be at the centre of the analytical stage, for it is crucial that researchers understand subjective and intersubjective meanings if they are to understand the significance of organizational actions. Silverman therefore offers a view of the social world that emphasizes the processual nature of human affairs – a world where organizational actors interpret the situation in which they find themselves and act in ways that are meaningful to them. For Silverman, special interpretive or qualitative methods are required to research this social world in order to yield explanations that are 'adequate at the level of meaning'.

The other main influence on our methodological position has been Critical Theory. Our early theoretical discussions turned on issues of knowledge, language and ideology in healthcare politics at both national and local levels. As such, we directed our early attentions at ideas associated with, for example, Antonio Gramsci and the concept of *ideological hegemony*, Herbert Marcuse and *technological rationality*, and especially Jürgen Habermas and *communicative distortion* – in other words, social theorists whose work is associated centrally with understanding relationships between ideology, language and society. On examining their work, we started to consider whether such theorizing could be married with our suggested methodological stance – stemming from Action Theory – of constructionism and interactionism. In line with writing on Critical Management Studies (Alvesson and Willmott, 2003; Fournier and Grey, 2000), our discussions suggested increasingly that critical social scientists accept it is necessary to appreciate the lived experience of people in context – a view which, as suggested by our reading, Critical Theory also shared with ideas and methodologies of some interpretive theories. What made scholarship in Critical Theory different from our interpretive methodology, however, was that it interprets social action and the symbols of society in order to understand the ways in which social groups are *ideologically* dominated. For Critical Theory, knowledge is power – it asks questions about the ways in which competing interests clash and the manner in which conflicts are resolved in favour of particular groups.

A major focus of Critical Theory therefore is *communication*, which is addressed through two kinds of problems. On the one hand, the *politics of textuality* concerns the various ways that media produce encoded messages and audiences decode those messages as well as the power and domination apparent in these processes. Research on this theme might examine, for example, the ways certain kinds of media content are produced and how such depictions are understood by audiences so as to perpetuate or oppose the power of dominant institutions, such as government. On the other, the *problematic of culture* examines the relations among media, other institutions and the ideology of culture. Researchers are interested in how the dominant ideology of a culture subverts other ideologies via social institutions. Crucially, like interpretive analysis, both emphasize the ways social forces are produced and reproduced in the daily activities of individuals, groups and institutions. The task such analysts address is revealing how such ideological forces operate in society, their method being directed at exposing the underlying tension between opposing forces. The argument is that only by becoming intimately aware of such forces – for example, in an ideological power struggle – can we genuinely question the nature of political motives.

For several decades, Jürgen Habermas has been the most influential scholar working in this tradition. From the 1970s, Habermas, along with Herbert Marcuse, helped shape the New Left in Germany and, later, the US. Habermas argues that society must be understood as a combination of three main interests – work, interaction and power. By work, he means the efforts to create necessary material resources, or what he calls the 'technical interest'. By interaction, he means the use of language (and symbols) for communication, or what he calls the 'practical interest'. And by power, he means the tendency for ideologies to dominate in society, or what he refers to as the process of 'distorted communication'. For Habermas, social life cannot be performed from the view of only one interest: work, interaction or power. No particular activity is wholly contained by one of these, but includes some arrangement of them all. Thus all three are essential for a comprehensive appreciation of society. Only by becoming aware of the interplay of such forces can groups themselves become empowered to transform society.

Central to our concerns has been Habermas' (1964) early and influential work on the concept of the *public sphere* where he takes as a point of departure work by the Chicago School and notions of the ideological and *consciousness-shaping* function of media. Habermas' argument here is that the public sphere is realized in every conversation where individuals assemble to form a public body. This sphere mediates between society and state where conversation is critical to the construction of that entity we call *the public*. Like the Chicago School, Habermas argues that the creation of opinion takes place at the community and peer group level; in other words, the formation of a rational public depends upon the information available, together with the situations available, for discussing the significance and meaning of information. Such explanations suggest that the representations of social reality we receive depend upon organized effort for their production and dissemination. In studying the political context of management and organization, therefore, the emphasis we take from Habermas is on the *means and experience* of communication in work, institutions and society.

In sum, the suggestion is that communication practices are an outcome of the tension between political creativity in framing messages and the social reception of them. It is the job of the critical theorist to identify ideology in such as way that alternative explanations of such ideologies can be heard. Here an ideology can be defined as a set of ideas that structures a group's notion of reality, a system of representations or a code of meanings governing how individuals and groups see the world (Hall, 1997).

The Critical-Action Theory perspective

Our discussions on research positioning, therefore, suggested the adoption of what Clifford Geertz (1983) once referred to as a 'blurred genre' – one in which social researchers access concepts from across disciplines and utilize various frames of reference in their work. In our research, the suggestion is that we blur the domains of Action Theory and Critical Theory with the goal of providing what we might call a 'Critical-Action Theory' perspective for MOS, specifically in relation to understanding everyday events of healthcare management.

We have noted how interpretive research has emphasized the importance of symbolic action and social interaction. Here, findings represent researchers' interpretations of informants' interpretations of their experiences; that is, through words, symbols and actions. We have also suggested that the emphasis placed by the interpretive researcher on human agency and localized experience may appeal potentially to critical management scholars, who seek an alternative to the *over-determinism* characteristic of mainstream structural and functional research. However, despite the potential theoretical and methodological rewards from such a synthesis, there appear to have been relatively few attempts to reap them. Those works that come to mind are mainly contributions from sociology before the so-called 'defeat of the Left' (Anderson, 2000) in Marxist scholarship, or the *death of the subject* under postmodernism.

In MOS, perhaps the most notable examples of such a synthesis or blurring of Action Theory and Critical Theory appeared in the mid 1970s; in particular, Huw Beynon's (1973) study of car workers' experiences of 'factory class consciousness' in *Working for Ford*, Stewart Clegg's (1975) analysis of power relations on a building site in *Power, Rule and Domination* and Paul Willis' (1977) study of how 'working class kids get working class jobs' in *Learning to Labour*. Despite the higher sociological profile of *Working for Ford* and *Learning to Labour*, Clegg's work represents perhaps the most explicit *statement* of a synthesis of the kind we have in mind. Clegg's thesis on how organizational power relations can only be understood as part of a wider 'form of life' resonates strongly with the hermeneutic critique of our focal social theorist, Habermas, as well as other critical theorists interested in the role of language and ideology in the construction (and *communicative distortion*) of social life. In Clegg's work, however, the accent is placed more strongly on *critique* – and focally Marxist critique – than *action*, whereas our approach seeks to achieve a more equitable balance between ethnographic enquiry and ideological criticism, hence our conscious use of a hyphenated phrase: Critical-Action Theory.

Apart from the defeat of the Left and death of the subject, another reason for a lack of popularity in sociological investigations may be a view that our preferred research position of Critical-Action actually appears oxymoronic. A view often expressed in Critical Management Studies is that interpretive research in MOS, commonly realized through ethnographic field studies, tends to be rather atheoretical. Alternatively, critical scholars are frequently deemed to be too ideological in their theoretical orientation and thus excessively sociologically biased in their research evaluations. For some sociologists, therefore, the blurring of research domains on the lines we suggest may represent an uneasy alliance – one that raises serious questions about the compatibility of theory-driven social agendas and interpretive field research.

We argue, however, that to accept this assertion is to neglect the many advantages of adopting a Critical-Action approach for MOS research. Although not laying out a programmatic research strategy, or systematic theory or statement, for Critical-Action, Willis' *Learning to Labour* acts almost as a poster child for such an endeavour, notably through his description of how ethnography can provide an active or praxis-oriented methodological vehicle for making advances in critical theorizing. As Willis (1977: 3–4) suggests:

> The ethnographic account, without always knowing how, can allow a degree of the activity, creativity and human agency within the object of study to come through into the analysis and the reader's experience. This is vital to my purposes where I view the cultural, not simply as a set of transferred internal structures (as in the usual notions of socialization) nor as the passive result of the action of dominant ideology downwards (as in certain kinds of Marxism), but at least in part as the product of collective human praxis.

Ethnographic research thus allowed Willis to situate his working-class adolescent informants as more than mere victims of false consciousness. Instead, he portrays them as rational actors who clearly perceive the structural constraints on their social class. However, through their opposition to dominant culture, they come to adopt the very attitudes that predestine them to a life of factory labour.

In line with interpretive ethnography, the methodology of Critical-Action adopts a similar qualitative methodological approach. This is one directed at understanding cultural phenomena that, in turn, reflect the system of meanings guiding the actions of a social group – in our case, healthcare managers. Critical-Action also shares with interpretivist ethnography the belief that research subjects' perceptions of social reality are themselves theoretical constructs. While subjects' constructs are more 'experience-near' (Geertz, 1983) than the researcher's, they remain, nevertheless, reconstructions of social reality.

However, Critical-Action diverges from traditional interpretive enquiry in maintaining that the subject's reconstructions are frequently infused with meanings that sustain subjugation. We argue that subjects' cognisant representations serve to maintain social phenomena as much as to explain them. In Critical-Action research, therefore, the emphasis is not so much on ordaining the subjects of study as seeking to reveal their political essence in relation to issues of work, management and organization. Such a perspective is not restricted merely to documenting the everyday actions of subjects but is also directed at deconstructing wider ideological forces related to such interpretive enquiries.

Concepts typically deployed to construct theory and explanation in MOS – such as *empowerment*, *leadership* and *motivation* – are thus not necessarily treated as neutral descriptors of work, management and organization but are potentially viewed as signifiers of wider, frequently ideological, processes that are produced and reproduced in the social setting under investigation. In other words, under

Critical-Action Theory, management concepts are ideological when they promote the production and reproduction of particular social and economic relations. In studies of healthcare management, for example, a Critical-Action account would not treat concepts such as *choice*, *lean* and *quality* as unproblematic but potentially as ideological forces whose accepted definition and maintenance can operate to the benefit of wider political interests and, notably, ones associated with a neo-liberal agenda.

In fieldwork, therefore, a Critical-Action study would entail more than accounting for macro-level forces that influence the local domain under investigation. Instead, such a perspective would suggest that such external factors are a fundamental part of the internal composition of that domain and should be recognized as such even at the most micro level of interaction. A Critical-Action approach suggests that the social production of meaning in work organizations is intrinsically linked to economic and political concerns and that the ideological character of organization is habituated in the infusion of such economic and political interests in everyday knowledge, elements of which may make reference to MOS knowledge itself.

Finally, in some respects, Critical-Action Theory resonates with what Fairclough (2003) has described as the macro- and meso-level concerns of Critical Discourse Analysis, notably through concern with language, social context, and issues of political ideology and how power relations are reproduced. Critical-Action Theory, however, through its primary recourse to ethnographic rather than close textual investigation, offers a more anthropologically oriented analysis – one which places the social subject, rather than just language forms, at the centre of the sociological stage. This reflects origins in ethnographic and interpretive sociology rather than in critical linguistics. Further, at the micro level of analysis, Critical-Action Theory is far removed from the focus on syntax, metaphoric structure and other elements of linguistics characteristic of Critical Discourse Analysis. Above all, under Critical-Action Theory, the human subject is *thrown into the world alive and kicking* rather than being, under genres of postmodernism, for example, philosophically *dead*.

Researching healthcare managers

In this general introduction to the forms of research perspective we considered in seeking to frame our research enquiries, the aim has been to introduce the theoretical and methodological assumptions that came to underpin our examination of managerial work in four healthcare settings: an acute trust (Chapter 4), an ambulance trust (Chapter 5), a mental health trust (Chapter 6), and a primary care trust (Chapter 7). In the chapters that follow, we explain these investigations into the realities, roles and behaviour of healthcare managers in greater detail, notably in terms of how such managers deal with the demands of a neo-liberal economic agenda and specifically with the policies and practices associated with the New Public Management.

For each case organization, our research has been framed by the theory and practice of our preferred Critical-Action Theory perspective – a hybrid approach developed from synthesizing Action Theory and Critical Theory. In terms of fieldwork, this has seen the development of an ethnographic approach to investigation founded on two research techniques: interviewing and observation. Our interviews have been based mainly on a semi-structured instrument directed at addressing issues related to the core aims of the project. In addition, we conducted a number of interviews that were largely unstructured; this being the case, for example, with those conducted near the end of the research with managers recently demoted or made redundant. The interview process generally saw managers interviewed at their place of work, commonly in their offices, or else in a private room if a manager worked in a shared office or open-plan setting. Exceptions were for our recently redundant managers plus interviews with academics who are experts in a certain field of healthcare management research, all of which were held at Manchester Business School. The duration of interviews was generally between 60 and 90 minutes, although interviews could last for over two hours in some exceptional cases. The process of interviewing commonly saw one or two members of the team meet with a single interviewee and record the discussion on a digital recorder. These recordings were later transcribed by an external agency. Some interviewees, however, were reluctant to have their views digitally recorded, and so, on these occasions, the interviewer(s) took detailed notes by hand. In total, 80 recorded and 39 unrecorded interviews were conducted during the period of field investigations.

In addition to semi-structured and unstructured interviews, our fieldwork involved periods of direct observation, specifically non-participant observation. This research concerned, in the main, observations of managers at work, team meetings, board meetings and training sessions. Data were recorded mainly by handwritten notes, made either at the time of observation or in the hours immediately afterwards. These notes represented the direct description of events plus reflections and comments on particular issues and incidents. During the fieldwork, the team conducted 63 periods of non-participant observation; a 'period' lasted anything from a one-hour meeting to a half day training session to a day spent *shadowing* a manager for 6 to 12 hours at a time. While conducting observational research had been envisaged at all four case sites, we must note that due to the proposed abolition of one form of NHS organization (primary care trusts), access negotiations resulted in this only being feasible at three – the acute hospital, the ambulance service, and the mental health service. In the case of the primary care organization (the last organization to be researched), it was felt by our access gatekeepers that observation of managers and meetings would be too sensitive – notably so given that the Human Resources Department was one of the functions to be studied. As such, an agreement was reached that access would be permitted to the organization on the basis that we restricted our analysis, almost exclusively, to interview-based research.

Therefore, in the chapters that follow, we describe our research in terms of four case study accounts. As noted, these accounts reflect our preferred theoretical and methodological perspective of Critical-Action research. In addition, they also reflect elements of the approach to qualitative case research and theory building suggested by Eisenhardt (1989) in that to provide a logical explanatory structure for each case account, we present our data in relation to managerial context, roles, and behaviour. This structure is adopted so as to discuss our main research themes at three levels of analysis: macro, meso and micro. Thus our analysis of managerial context deals with *macro* issues of ideology, policy and governance; roles with *meso* issues of responsibilities, domains and practices; and behaviour with *micro* issues of attitudes, experiences and perceptions. Although such categories offer a basic guide for analysing relevant issues of policy, practice and perception, as this research is based on qualitative analysis of ethnographic data, we do not suggest that these levels of analysis are hermetic or watertight. Rather, they frequently reflect overlaps in terms of influence, meaning and understanding.

Finally, the process of analysis has largely been that of traditional ethnographic description and interpretation (Turner, 1972; Van Maanen, 2011; Watson, 1994, 2011). Although all four members of the team undertook NVivo training in the early months of the research, rather than deploy a qualitative software package, we decided to generate our own grounded criteria relevant to the project. It can be argued that this approach is more closely aligned with the interpretivist assumptions – ontological and epistemological – of traditional ethnographic organizational enquiry and also with those of Critical-Action Theory in particular.

Conclusions

The aim of this chapter is to introduce the research perspective developed and adopted in the course of our investigations into managerial work in UK healthcare. In particular, we describe various theoretical and methodological options that presented themselves vis-à-vis consideration of the formal aims and objectives of the research project. This is based on a largely chronological description of our activities – from early discussions of the epistemological options available to us to developing a formal position on theory and method to operationalizing this perspective in fieldwork investigations.

Central to these considerations is our outlining of a Critical-Action Theory approach to sociological investigation in MOS. We demonstrate how this is based, fundamentally, on the blurring of two sociological traditions – Action Theory and Critical Theory. This sees an ethnographic approach to organizational research joined by consideration of theoretical contributions by, for example, Jürgen Habermas, Herbert Marcuse and Antonio Gramsci in analysis directed at the ideological mechanisms through which actors are habituated to accept the hegemony of an institutional context. Thus an empirical approach is deployed to examine how organizational structures and processes are influenced by overt and covert ideological factors and forces. The result is case analysis that documents changes to managerial practices, but conjoined with an appreciation of how these changes serve to justify dominant political ideologies, such as neo-liberal market philosophies.

Finally, we note how this sociological approach has been employed in field investigations in four healthcare organizations – an acute trust, an ambulance trust, a mental health trust, and a primary care trust. The research undertaken is ethnographic in style and based largely on semi-structured/unstructured interviews and non-participant observation. In total, the research involved over 400 hours of fieldwork. The four chapters that follow explain in detail the forms of ethnographic enquiry undertaken in these studies and the results that were accrued. Here we detail the broad sociopolitical environment for each type of NHS organization studied. We examine the lived experience of NHS managers in those organizations as we draw together macro, meso and micro levels of analysis. We see how these interactions played out in the lives and work of NHS junior and middle managers. Each of these chapters portrays the significant and distinctive effects of the changing legislative and political environment. Ultimately, a picture unfolds of NHS trusts and their junior and middle managers facing the challenges of major organizational change in very different institutional circumstances.

4

READY TO DO BUSINESS

Management and organizational change in an acute trust

This chapter analyses the changing roles, behaviours and experiences of managers in an acute trust, which we will refer to as 'Millford Foundation Trust'.[1] It was the main provider of secondary healthcare services for the large town of 'Millford' as well as some parts of mostly rural 'Millshire' – a catchment area of around 350,000 people. The main site was approximately two miles from the centre of Millford. The inclusion in the catchment area of urban and rural, affluent and deprived areas meant that Millford served the needs of a diverse population in both geographical and social terms. The trust had an annual budget of £200 million and employed over 4,000 staff across four sites. There were 870 inpatient beds and the hospital treated around 300,000 patients during the course of a typical year. We focused our research on the work of junior and middle managers in the first instance. However, a key dimension of our fieldwork developed in an organic fashion, allowing us to explore groups of linked individuals without imposing our own structural preconceptions. Thus we tended to interview and observe junior and middle managers as members of groups sharing such elements as physical proximity, organizational proximity, occupational culture, identities and understandings. In addition, we sought out specific managers at a more explicitly strategic level; for example, associate director and director roles. At times, we were referred to these people by their colleagues, but at director level, we were able to identify potential interviewees through trust documents such as organization charts. The managers we spoke to fall quite broadly into four categories: clinical managers, research managers, business group managers and trust directors.

We interviewed and observed the work of *clinical managers* such as matrons, paediatric nurse clinicians and heads of nursing for a particular service – for example Trauma and Orthopaedics. We spent time also with *research managers* who worked in the audit department or were engaged in research initiatives as a project manager. Spanning the territory between operational and strategic responsibilities were the *business group managers.* This group included both clinical (e.g. diagnostics and clinical support) and non-clinical (e.g. human resources) managers at associate director level. Speaking to *trust directors* gave us the opportunity to hear the views of the most senior NHS managers at the trust; these included the director of communications, the director of nursing and midwifery, and the director of human resources.

Acute trusts are often the focus of health policy and research. As they often operate the local hospitals, they play a prominent part in public understanding of what the NHS is. Therefore, they are, perhaps, the most generally well-understood NHS organizations. Speaking to managers across the organization, both vertically and horizontally, allowed us to understand how local organizational structures and dynamics interact with national policy and prevailing ideology at the macro level. We thus situate managerial roles and behaviours within the ideological, financial and political realities of life at work – the framework for their daily experience. At the meso level, we consider both the formal roles of junior and middle managers and the functional outcomes associated with fulfilling these roles successfully. And at the micro level, we examine how managers work or the strategies and tactics they employ – their behaviours. We explore managers' own perceptions of their role and the related issues of identification and identity. Beyond this, we situate them within the wider organizational structures with which they interact and must negotiate.

Overall, this is a case study in which senior managers anticipated the effects of the global financial crisis and an increasingly commercial environment and were in a good position to respond. As a result, job cuts were made, managerial structures were rearranged and business units were created in order to enable charging per patient to various NHS commissioning and provider bodies. At the same time, the severe financial pressure and the need to make cost savings were imperative. This case study, therefore, concerns how healthcare managers attempted to make sense of their changing organizational roles and behaviours in times of severe financial pressure, structural rearrangement and job losses.

Millford Foundation Trust

Situated in a leafy but socially mixed suburb of Milltown, Millford Foundation Trust could be accessed through a myriad of roads, walkways, gateways and doorways, some open to the public and others restricted to hospital staff, giving the impression that it was physically, as well as organizationally, embedded in the local community. Reinforcing the impression of local embeddedness was the fact that many staff lived locally and could be seen walking to and from work. The hospital is a major employer in the local area. Staff and visitors who must drive encountered hastily constructed steel alloy two-storey parking areas, and at busy times such as visiting hours, private cars and taxis crawled around looking for free spaces. Like many historically established acute trusts, the estate was a mix of late twentieth-century, Victorian and more recent buildings, presided over by the looming forms of the laundry, boiler and incinerator chimneys. The heart of the hospital remained a large Victorian building, albeit one that was mostly obscured by the modern additions that had attached themselves to what was once its exterior; they presented a picture of architectural trends from the 1960s to the 2000s. Following an expansion in government funding for NHS capital projects during the years 1997 to 2009, it was the new buildings that dominated, visually at least, many replete with reflective glass and automatic doors. As the associate director of quality observed: '*It's very common that you have this Victorian core and then all these little pods that grow up*'. For patients and visitors, the hospital was bright, clean and welcoming. In the main building, the oldest part of the hospital, there was a new cafe, a small shop and a popular canteen that was open to both staff and visitors.

Staff offices were predictably functional, even at senior levels. For many middle managers, it was understood that one's office was less than permanent. This was particularly true for managers working on one, or a series of, projects – a managerial group that was expanding. One case in point was Keely – a modern matron during the time we spent at the trust, who was also working on a project to encourage patients to adopt healthier lifestyles. Keely's office, where we first met for an interview, was a bedroom in a former nurses' residence. She had made the room her own by displaying some of her sporting medals and pictures of her family as well as work-related noticeboards. A few months later, we returned to look for her but found her office empty – like the other rooms on the corridor, it was filled with old tables and shelves awaiting disposal. And Lois, head of nursing in the elective services business group, shared an office in an annexe where the heating was turned off at night, meaning she relied on portable heaters to make late working more comfortable. Once again, at a meeting one year later, we had to search her out in another part of the hospital. Lois had been moved to a less senior role (as part of a compulsory restructure) and now occupied a smaller shared office. As we will see as the chapter and indeed the book unfolds, middle managers in the NHS had to contend with constant organizational restructuring. We found that this was manifested not only in changing roles but also in changing working environments. As our project neared its conclusion and the effects of the global economic crisis were realized, we also found that some of the junior and middle managers were no longer employed.

Between the buildings and the people were the cultural artefacts of the organization. Plaques and ornamental gardens provided an organizationally endorsed dimension to the hospital's sense of place, offering both a distinct identity and forming part of the sedimentation of its cultural memory. The same can be said of the display cases of medical devices and historical photographs in the corridors of one of the side buildings – Damson House. Other aspects of material culture tended towards the category of 'organizational kitsch' (Linstead, 2002): the screensaver, the noticeboard, the corporate slogan. Even the apparently mundane poster asking people to '*please turn off the lights*' has some analytical value, speaking as it does to the organization's preoccupation with minimizing waste. Other posters had a more inspirational invocation, with beaches, blue oceans and childhood wonder featuring heavily. They found their natural home in Damson House, the central hub of organizational development, training and conferences. There, one poster, a reflection on the theme of '*priorities*', had somehow made its way onto the floor of the men's toilet; something which had, for us at least, an indeterminate resonance all of its own. Elsewhere, outside the office of a nurse manager who would shortly be restructured out of the trust, a poster of a '*developmental oak tree*' illustrated the value of mentorship and development with the words '*you are valued*' at front and centre.

It would be unfair, perhaps, to overemphasize the significance of this ephemera since for the staff at Millford, they probably made up little more than a faint quotidian backdrop to their working lives. Further, it is appropriate to avoid outright cynicism; inspirational posters and visualizations of mentorship are hardly sinister in either intent or effect. In any case, for us as researchers, the site was saturated with significance, and materiality and textuality took their place in the mosaic of meaning that we sought to analyse.

Stability, strategy, structures and business groups

> *Come into this strange world.*
> (Dawn – Children's Services manager and lead nurse for Paediatrics)

As one of a number of hospitals to become a foundation trust in the first decade of the twenty-first century, Millford was steered by the concepts embodied in the foundation trust model. Foundation trust status was originally intended to extend a number of freedoms:

> [f]reedom from Whitehall control and performance management by Strategic Health Authorities: [f]reedom to access capital on the basis of affordability instead of centrally controlled allocations; [f]reedom to invest surpluses in developing new services for local people; [f]reedom of local flexibility to tailor new governance arrangements to the individual circumstances of their community.
> (Department of Health, 2009)

In return for these freedoms, the trust had to maintain levels of patient care and medical outcomes in order to ensure continued funding and avoid financial penalties. Trusts had to meet centrally set targets, and there was continued tension between local freedom and central control. The monitoring and enforcement framework for hospital trusts was itself undergoing change in the wake of the Francis Report (2013) with the Care Quality Commission, Monitor, and local/regional care commissioning groups taking responsibility for different elements of the governance regime. The Department of Health set policy and acted as ultimate authority or, as they would have it, 'system steward' (Department of Health, 2013: 16).

The trust had six directors, each of whom were responsible for the key strategic elements of the trust. Although not routinely involved in day-to-day operational matters within their remit (in theory at least), they represented the penultimate level in the hierarchical reporting structure with the final level being the chief executive.

The trust board had been unusually stable over the preceding 15 years, during which time the chief executive, operations manager and trust secretary had remained the same. This was viewed positively by many, including the trust secretary, Kevin:

> *It's a team.* [Chief executive] *Tim Fowler and I have both been here as you say since the late eighties. I remember Tim starting here … there tends not to be a huge turnaround to the top team at all. I think that helps.*

For many senior managers, their role was not simply to respond to government policy and resourcing changes – since this is the origin of most of the change in the NHS – but to seek to anticipate them and to shape locally mandated institutional change to their best advantage. For junior and middle managers, constant change had indeed produced a sense of organizational memory in that it had become part of the culture of the organization itself and was seen as something that would inexorably continue into the future. Junior and middle managers described the perpetual cycle of restructuring and policy change at local level with a sense of resignation, but they also acknowledged that it added to the pressures of their role.

The delivery of patient care was organized through business groups and managed through business line management (see Hoque *et al.*, 2004 for further discussion of NHS line management). Reflecting the size of the organization as well as the complexity and range of specialist services it was expected to deliver, actual lines of reporting were often less clear than the business group model might imply. To further complicate matters, organizational structures at the trust were constantly rearranged. For instance, areas of responsibility within the business groups had, in recent years, been expanded to accommodate the removal of significant numbers of middle managers as a result of financial pressures. Ruth, the director of HR, had been with the trust for over a decade. In that time, she observed that it had '*metamorphosed into lots of different organizations*'. This continual metamorphosis had entered the organizational consciousness and had, in Ruth's words, given rise to '*myth and folklore about changes we've had in our organizational structure over, say, the last 10 or 15 years*'. This large and complex organization operating in a highly politicized sector presented managers at all levels with particular challenges. As Ruth says:

> *We like to feel as a foundation trust we are like a healthcare* [organization] *but* [also] *a business. But it's quite difficult because it's unlike other businesses in that it's so political and it's also … they try to control a lot from the centre* [Department of Health].

The senior management team at Millford were not only strategically aware but also had to communicate strategic priorities to managers and thence to staff. While it was the job of the senior managers to mediate between central control and local organizational imperatives, it was junior and middle managers who translated these negotiated local strategies into reality at business group level and, ultimately, ward, department or office level. Operational priorities were outlined by senior managers at fortnightly briefings for middle managers – associate directors and other key individuals from the six main business groups. These operational priorities tended to emphasize a fit with the wider governance and performance strategies of the trust (both financial and in terms of targets). The briefings usually consisted of a presentation from the chief executive, Tim Fowler, covering the trust's present and medium-term financial position as well as issues such as staff sickness (or, as it came to be known, '*wellness*') levels and monitoring procedures, waiting time and infection reduction targets, patient satisfaction levels, and so on. These were elaborated on by trust directors from the relevant directorates. Other events took place throughout the year; for example the '*year ahead*' conference at which priorities for the coming period, and their possible consequences for staff, were discussed.

The ideology of business at the acute trust

One important element of the move to foundation trust status had been the adoption and intensification of an explicitly business-oriented approach. This was despite Millford's, *quasi-business* status (similar to other foundation trusts); it was still ultimately accountable to and financially dependent on central government. Nevertheless, the language and *modi operandi* of business had been thoroughly entrenched, and should acute hospitals in England move to a fully private model, they will find that relatively little cultural shift is required. This cultural and organizational understanding was premised on the notion that 'each [foundation] trust will operate like a private business with limited liability, a board of directors and ownership of its assets' (Pollock, 2003). This understanding, in turn, was framed by the concepts that make up New Public Management (see Chapter 1). Operationally, its watchwords are performance, cost, efficiency and accountability in the sense of audits and beyond (see Diefenbach, 2009). At Millford, people tended not to talk of New Public Management by name, even as they described it. The term they tended to use was, simply, '*business*'.

To achieve and maintain their status as a foundation trust, and in line with their ideological and quasi-statutory status as a business, hospitals such as Millford had to demonstrate that they were financially robust and had clear financial strategies for the medium term. In keeping with this, the organizational – that is to say, corporate – culture at the trust emphasized the need for financial awareness on the part of managers and non-managers alike. We can note here that although finance was an omnipresent topic for managers from executive to junior level, it was embedded in an awareness of patient care. Cost savings were seen as both a way of managing resources effectively in order to deliver continually improving patient care and, concomitantly, minimizing the impact on patient care of already tight and shrinking resources. The issue of diminishing resources came to the fore as our study was underway because of the global financial crisis and the government austerity measures that followed, but this must be seen in the context of a health system in which resources were already running short. Trusts were encouraged both by limitations on resources and by institutional changes – both stemming from government policy – to become more entrepreneurial and to generate, as well as save, money. For Millford, as for other foundation trusts, income could be generated by operating *profitable* services that patients and commissioners actively chose to use. As Shirley (associate director, Diagnostics and Clinical Support business group) put it, '*it's about saying, alright, what are our profitable services?*' Patients were seen as customers, with some services, such as maternity, offering the potential to gain

> a customer for life ... you get that mother to have a really good experience and deliver here. The chances are she's going to choose here for paediatric care. She's going to choose here for her ongoing care. Her partner's going to choose here. You've got a real 'catch them at birth' scenario with maternity services.

Running a profitable service also meant collaborating at times with a neighbouring trust in the style of a joint venture. As Shirley put it: '*I need your resource [...] to help me out, but you're going to get a share of the profits*'. Conversely, others such as Shannon, a former occupational therapist and clinical audit manager at the trust, found that managers were '*constantly told from the top down that we are in competition*'. For Shannon, a form of commercial secrecy was unspoken or '*written between the lines*'. And so the question of whether the consumer-led business at Millford was responsive and transparent or competitive and secretive (Newdick, 2014: 117) lacked a definitive answer. Many staff, including senior managers, were acutely aware of the organizational – indeed, ontological – tensions inherent in a business-led NHS. Evincing the focus on patient care that typified the managers we spoke to, Katherine, director of nursing, asserted the need to make sure business imperatives were concomitant with a focus on delivering care:

> It's my job to stick up for the patient side of everything. And because particularly I think, as a foundation trust, we're much more of a business if you like than we were. That probably sounds a silly thing to say because we've always been businesses. But I think it's thrown it in sharp focus a bit more by becoming a foundation trust. So I think it's more important than ever that the nurse director and probably the medical director to a certain extent are the ones with the patient viewpoint. And therefore, from my point of view, the nursing viewpoint, which is actually – no, let's not do that because we don't have enough staff, or the staff would suffer as a result of it, or the patients would suffer as a result. So I see that as part of my job [and it] is the thorn in the side of some business developments.

Katherine's views were prevalent amongst clinical managers, particularly those who spent most or all of their careers inside the NHS. Nurse manager Lois was typical in that she was '*very much involved with the business stuff day-to-day*'; but as a '*non-business person*', speaking the language of business did not come naturally. This left these managers in a more vulnerable position where '*it's easier to chip away at us because we don't speak that language; we haven't got the business acumen*'. However, many nurse managers and, more predictably, associate director level managers had adopted a set of words and phrases such as '*benchmark*', '*lean*' and '*flex*' – drawn from the lexicon of corporate organizational development. Lois' observation that those who were appointed to senior management roles tended to have business and management degrees and business experience took on a certain poignancy in the light of her subsequent demotion and then departure from Millford. Care, for Lois, had come to be seen as the '*fluffy stuff*' in contrast to the '*stats, figures and finance*' of business management. This stood in further contradiction to the wishes of patients who wanted to know that they were cared for by professionals with extensive clinical as well as management experience rather than those who are worrying about

> *somebody's budget and the percentage of cost cuts and blah de blah. You don't want to know; it's crap … they want to know that they're safe and they're well cared for,* [that] *they're going to come out of hospital and they're going to be better – get back to a normal life.*

To a large extent, speaking the language of corporate business was a strategic necessity rather than a choice. Expectations of adherence to this linguistic form cascaded downwards through the organization, and ambitious managers recognized the importance of compliance. Senior managers faced a similar expectation as they were compelled to present an image of the hospital and its processes consistent with New Public Management; failure to do so would imply some sort of diversion from the path of the 'successfully managed' trust and, indeed, the hegemony (cultural and otherwise) of business in wider society. So it was that Lois wondered whether the language of business was part of a transition to privatization: '*the language is totally different and I can see in a couple of years it'll be private healthcare and that'll be an absolute bloody travesty. Because … if you look at it economically and politically …*'.

Paralleling the entrepreneurial drive at more senior and strategic levels and providing something of an ideological steering device for resource management, managers from ward level up had to make a business case if they wanted extra resources, to expand a service for example. This could be a '*mammoth task*' according to Gabrielle (a ward manager), requiring research and evidence gathering for which junior and middle managers had little time available. Some managers noted a clash of cultures between the commodity-driven model and the traditional care-focused culture of the NHS. For example, performance-related pay for nurses, modelled on what was in place at Sainsbury's and Tesco, was strongly resisted at Millford despite the efforts of HR managers. Elaine (a clinical audit manager) noted a difference between her more business-focused approach and that of some clinicians:

> *They just want to look after their patient and do their best for them. But we are a business and if we're not, if that service isn't making money, we need to look at why not and decide whether it's a service we should carry on or not.*

Confounding the notion of a clear clinical/non-clinical split – if not the impression that managers with work experience in business were more likely to take a business orientation – were nurse managers such as Gabrielle. Despite her misgivings about the scope for nurse managers to develop business cases, she saw '*both sides of the fence*' and understood '*where* [those with a business orientation are] *coming from, whereas a lot of people don't*'. Gabrielle, who had previously worked in corporate IT, highlighted the penetration throughout the trust of the concept of hospital managers as entrepreneurs:

> *the NHS cannot run on pure cost alone. You need some money back. So it has to run more like a business. You have to generate income somehow to be able to fund the NHS going forward and with the current financial climate.*

The fundamental tension between business and care was highlighted by Kay (a paediatric nurse clinician) who acknowledged the need to run profitable services. But she maintained that:

> *There is always a core to the NHS that is different because we have a moral duty of care to everybody who lives in our area. So* [the trust and the wider NHS] *has a business ethos … but there is a big core of this that says it doesn't* [matter] *how cost-effective this is – if someone comes in with a broken leg you're going to fix that broken leg.*

Manufacturing consent: Lean management at Millford

While business approaches to quality improvement may, in previous decades, have been 'something of a "foreign body" in most NHS acute units' (Pollitt, 1996: 107), they had become part of daily organizational life at Millford and other hospitals. Seeking to chart a course between shrinking resources and maintaining patient care, the trust was focused both on the reduction of waste and an increase in *productivity* (number of patients treated by a particular service, for example) as ways of cutting costs and generating income. This was reflected in nationally endorsed but locally implemented corporate initiatives such as the Lean Hospital Program, locally known as the Millford Improvement Programme (for an extended discussion of this, see McCann *et al.*, 2015b). Building on the concept of Lean as a management system designed to reduce waste, increase efficiency and encourage organizational learning, adoption began in 2007; and with the help of outside management consultants, the senior managers sought to embed Lean as part of their business strategy. The trust emphasized the positive aspects of Lean in its internal corporate communications for managers and staff, which included references to Henry Ford: '*who took all the elements of a manufacturing system – people, machines, tooling and products – and arranged them into a continuous "lean" system for manufacturing the Model T automobile. So we know it works*' (*Take a Minute*, trust newsletter, July 2009).

Observing a Milltown Improvement Showcase, as well as other Lean training events, gave us further opportunities to see what the trust understood by Lean and how it was being implemented. In line with the reference to Ford and the production line, Lean was seen as something which had been proven worthy through being used successfully in manufacturing. Companies such as Ford, Jaguar and Toyota were seen in corporate briefings and by those delivering Lean awareness training as paragons of efficiency with much to teach the NHS and the trust more specifically.

Lean was sold to the managers at the trust as something that could offer '*less stress, less work*' because '*things are now in the right place*'. Many distinctly practical examples were given. For instance, the laundry was made more efficient with the use of different types of laundry bags that dissolved at a lower temperature, and a new worktop installed in a treatment area proved a simple solution to overcrowding and led to quicker drawing up of intravenous drugs. These elements were generally positively received by junior and middle managers at the trust, who saw a genuine benefit in new and more effective ways of getting things done. Shannon, for example, liked the systematic approach of Lean and praised its simplicity: '*It doesn't have to be complex, although Lean can be quite complex. And Lean practitioners … I think they probably make it very complex, but it doesn't have to be, and there's a lot of tools in there.*'

This view was widely shared, with Lois noting: '*It's very well supported in the hospital, and I think the nursing staff are really on board with it and see the benefits of it*'. However, as McCann *et al.* (2015b) note, during a training event, some staff did question whether the '*messy*' world of healthcare delivery (sick, distressed, unpredictable people in unpredictable numbers at unpredictable times) could really be equated with auto manufacturing. There was for some, then, rather a sense of detachment and unreality regarding Lean, and this was highlighted during the centrepiece of a Lean training session – a group exercise involving the construction of toy cars out of Lego pieces. The following extract from our observation describes now a detailed training game was played out. There was plenty of enthusiasm for the exercise shown by the trainer and the audience – mostly junior nurse managers – but it was difficult to avoid a sense that the practical applicability of Lean was limited. As our field notes describe:

> *Jenny* [an organizational development trainer] *gets out a large tool box which contains lots of plastic Lego car pieces. She has a stopwatch and a calculator. It is notable that the kit for this exercise is all from* [name of management consultancy]. *She explains that we need one volunteer to be 'Stores Manager' – who looks after the distribution of the Lego pieces – and that we will go through this process three times, each time building 12 cars. After each time, we will assess what's happened and try to improve the process so that we can get to 12 cars more quickly. She puts a bit of Blu-Tack on one of the car pieces so that we can 'track it through the system'. … As soon as Jenny says 'go', a hush descends. The nurses and midwives work intently and quickly. There was a mistake and one nurse jokes: 'Reject!'; 'Shit!' another says. Several cars break up and have to be reassembled. Soon it descends into chaos – pieces pop up and snap off to much laughter and derision. Some pieces went back to the other table, provoking the response: 'Hey we don't do wheels!' Someone says: 'Good job we work in a baby factory, not a car factory!'*

Can such an exercise have any real application to the departments that the participants worked in at Milltown? Much of their work involved patients with diverse medical needs on different wards, requiring different levels, forms, and urgency of care. Generic Lean products can seem superficial and ill-fitting when used in public administration (see Carter [B.] *et al.*, 2013). At an equally fundamental level, where Lean *falls down* for many of the staff was:

> *When you're really under pressure and it's very, very busy, you don't have time to go off and do all the nice ... and that's when things start falling down, isn't it? ... I think where it starts falling down is when you get to the wards and they're busy and they've not got enough staff and [you] say, 'I've not got time to do this'.*

Whilst some were hampered by their existing workload and competing priorities, they thought it worthwhile; others were more cynical and saw Lean at Millford as just another management fad, illustrated by the following comment from a nurse manager at the Lean training day:

> *There is no way in a million years the NHS is going to be lean. There's lots of lip service to new ideas, but they can't actually happen. You get lots of knee-jerk reactions. They go for the next big thing, but soon it'll be something else. It's like wheels within wheels.*

The global financial crisis and Millford

In a team briefing to senior managers at the start of 2010, the trust chief executive outlined the theme of the upcoming year ahead conference. Although government austerity had yet to really bite – a situation Tim Fowler described as a '*phony war*' – the need to save money and get by with fewer resources was to be the focus. Ruth added that the trust had tried to '*get ahead of the curve*' regarding austerity measures, and the year ahead conference would be an opportunity to communicate the trust's strategies for coping with cuts to a large audience of managers (around 100 people) from all levels. The trust would be losing £40 million out of their annual budget of £200 million, which, Kevin, communications director, described as a '*huge cut*'. At the year ahead conference, the audience were taken through a range of cost-saving strategies from Lean management and QIPP (Quality, Improvement, Productivity and Prevention) to the more practical matters of turning off lights and using the correct rubbish bags. Amongst these were hints of possible service reconfiguration: insourcing some services but outsourcing others. This was summarized by the following diagram:

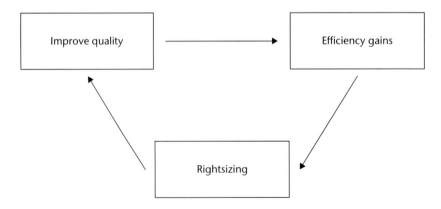

FIGURE 4.1   The way ahead

Perhaps in response to the comment that Ophthalmology, Dermatology and some other services are going to be reviewed in relation to the 'rightsizing' phase of the reconfiguration, one nurse's reaction, spoken with a concerned glance to her colleague, condensed the general feeling of unease in the room: '*bollocks*'. Others were concerned that drastic cuts would lead to a situation similar to that at Mid Staffordshire NHS trust, which had been implicated in reports of high death rates and patient neglect. The trust chief executive was quick to reassure staff that unlike Stafford, where nurses were '*culled*' without concern for patient care, there was '*sufficient waste*' at Millford and savings could be made without jeopardizing patient care. Finally, staff were encouraged to share in his sense of *esprit de corps*: '*look around, because the future depends on the people in this room … I am enormously gratified …*'. It was clear that much would depend on the skills and adaptability of the assembled managers and that these qualities would be all the more important in straightened times. It is to the managerial identities of the people in that room that we now turn.

Managing the acute trust: definitions, perceptions and identities

In broader, formal terms, the role of clinical managers was to manage staff reporting to them in order to deliver good-quality care for patients. Clinical managers' specific job titles spoke for themselves to some extent, but let us explore further the specificities of NHS junior and middle management roles. Beyond the level of formal job titles, the managers often had their own concise understanding. Nurse manager Rose was able to give a summary of her role which covered two levels – that of the manager within the organization and that of the manager of the unit for which she was responsible:

> So I work in a small unit. My day or my diary is made up of … I attend professional meetings based up at the acute sector; I attend workforce meetings; I attend the modern matron's lead meetings; so I get all of my … and that happens within [my acute trust], within that support structure. Then within the unit, I oversee the day-to-day running of the unit, monitor the bed capacity, liaise with my partners in intermediate care and primary care. I manage the budget and I organize staff meetings and support training for the team that I manage. Does that make sense?

Having spoken to a number of clinical managers, we can report that it does. Rose's description of her work was a good summary of the work of more or less all the nurse managers and we can see that it really did place these managers in the *middle* of the organization. Like her counterparts, this NHS middle manager and senior nurse worked to connect the different levels of the organization, both vertically upwards (to senior colleagues), horizontally (to colleagues such as matrons and other senior nurses) and vertically downwards (to junior colleagues – '*the team that I manage*'). The perspective of Katherine (director of Nursing and Midwifery and therefore a senior manager at the trust) reflected this notion of the middle manager as essential organizational intermediary in the transmission of senior management prerogatives:

> *Without them, I miss out a level. I need that structure which is a bit like a tree – tree branches spreading throughout the organization. So those middle managers, heads of nursing we call them here, I meet with monthly and we talk about nursing issues; and if there's anything I need to get out into the organization, I feed it through them. And they're my agents if you like.*

While Dawn's functional role was very similar to that of Rose, albeit in a different area of patient care, in discussing her role, she focused on professional leadership for nursing: '*There are about 173 nurses I think in our service, so it's about making sure they're led clearly, that they know what they're up to; so supervising, managing, and leading the Band 7s that work for me.*'

Although the use of the term *leadership* rather than *management* must be viewed in the light of a semantic shift in NHS policy that favours the former over the latter, Dawn gave another reason for the use of the term: '*I think that might be cultural rather than taught. Do you see what I mean? We don't like to think of ourselves as managers.*' In conversations with nurse managers during observations at the trust, as well as in formal interviews, we found that many clinical managers were anxious not to be seen as out of touch with staff – something that was associated with the stereotype of *manager*. While some other research on management identity features interviews with people for whom the shift away from nurse to manager was unproblematic, indeed desirable (Reedy, 2009: 27), we found that for many of our interviewees, there were negative connotations attached to the latter term. To some extent, this reflected broader views of NHS management in society, which have tended to be negative in the UK; but as we see below, there was also an impression amongst some junior staff that managers were out of touch and '*just swan around*'.

What was striking was the magnitude of complexity inherent in NHS management, adding a further dimension of ambivalence in ontological terms. Lois, working at a similar level to Dawn, was also responsible for nearly 200 nursing staff. For her, defining her own role was made difficult by the large number of functions that she had to perform:

> *I would say in terms of 'who am I?' … I'm a nurse manager, but then there are some people who would define me as an operational manager. The person that's on the ground, doing the stuff … middle manager. Some people see you as a senior manager, but I would say nurse manager, operational manager.*

In the end, then, Lois opted for a definition of her role that encompassed multiple identities. The managers we spoke to (for managers they were) sought to emphasize their concern for, and sometimes proximity to, patient care. John (a consultant and clinical director) '*came into medicine to treat patients. If I wanted to become a manager, I would have gone to do a management course or whatever and gone down that training route.'* Ultimately, however, John did concede that while the key driver of his role was to improve clinical care for patients, *'how to achieve that involves a lot of management'*.

Despite some ambivalence around how to define their roles in terms of identity, we have seen that clinical managers were usually able to give a concise definition of the functional thrust of their role. John, for example, although apparently disdainful of the business of management (in contrast to treating patients), was happy to define his role as *'interfacing between the management team and the other clinicians'*. And notwithstanding her hesitancy over role definitions, Lois described her functional role as: *'Managing my patch. I've got four or five wards, and I've got a group of specialist nurses as well that I manage. I manage the trauma team. So it's quite a big area in terms of nursing.'*

Rather like Dawn, then, Lois' *headline* definition of her role related in the first instance to the numbers of junior colleagues she was responsible for, framed within the organizational units that encompassed them. Interestingly, our paediatric nurse clinician, Kay, chose to define her role primarily in terms of what her skills and qualifications allowed her to do. Following the completion of an MA in nursing, she was able to prescribe and handle the admission and discharging of patients: *'So, effectively, I work like the doctors'*. Our exploration of managers' roles did not, of course, extend only to the level of organizational or individual definitions. Rather, we were able to see for ourselves the roles NHS middle managers had to perform in order to deliver their services.

Managerial roles and behaviours at the acute trust

In this section, we follow Mintzberg in asking '[w]hat do managers do?' (1973: 1). As he pointed out in his classic book *The Nature of Managerial Work* (1973), models of management roles abound, and certainly the proceeding discussion will reflect many of these. We wanted to understand the nature of NHS management as an element of healthcare work. And so our immediate task was to answer the more specific question: what do junior and middle managers at the acute trust do? We detail those roles here and note that they reflect many of the managerial roles at the three other trusts. Rather than repeat these findings in the following chapters, we draw out distinctions and differences.

Leadership (by example)

Leadership was a concept that was recognized and a quality that was actively encouraged in the NHS as a national organization. In this, the NHS was following a global business trend that has seen the rise of the leader and the supposed decline of the manager (see McCann in Edgell *et al.*, 2016). Hence, there was an NHS Leadership Academy explicitly geared towards facing the challenge of institutional change; most notably, that there is limited money available to the NHS (NHS Leadership Academy, 2014). Under the NHS leadership model, managerial staff (including doctors) were encouraged to see themselves as leaders as well as, or perhaps rather than, managers. For managers who wished to advance their careers, many followed the example of Rose: '*I did leadership programmes and I know that the government were very, well, there's been lots of drive for developing leadership and clinical leadership*'. For clinical managers in the acute trust, as for many of us, leadership might be something of a nebulous concept. Managers like Rose were able to conceptualize management and leadership as distinct features to an extent. She used the following metaphor: '*Management is about the nuts and bolts of the movement of the actual whole machine. Leadership is about having that light on the front* [of the bicycle] *and actually knowing where you're going and how to get to it.*'

How was leadership manifested at Millford? Spending time with clinical managers, one quickly became aware of their desire not to appear detached from the work carried out by junior colleagues. This was the case from the most junior manager in this group, Gabrielle, to more senior managers such as Dawn and Lois. We can say that leadership is a key constitutive role – one that, with others, came under the headline role of a formal management position. Put simply, leadership was one of a number of roles that NHS managers had to carry out in order to achieve their overall goals. Dawn, like many of the clinical managers, tried to lead by example.

Perhaps because of negative inferences about managers being detached from the realities of medicine (see the discussion on identity, above), many clinical managers reported that they aimed to be '*hands-on*' when on the ward. Barbara, a matron, would '*go down and make a bed ... and quite happily do bits and pieces*'. Barbara saw this as helping and supporting staff, perhaps practically as much as in terms of leadership and motivation – although these levels were by definition intertwined. Gabrielle, as a ward manager, tried to be as visible as possible on the ward as time for her to engage in hands-on patient care was limited. She rarely got to wash a patient anymore, for example, but this was due to the '*volume of other things you've got to organize*'. Echoing this sentiment, Annette, having recently left her role as head occupational therapist, remembered coming to the uncomfortable realization that being an NHS manager left her little scope to maintain her work, and identity, as a clinical practitioner: '*Well I suppose the stark reality was that I stopped ... to a large extent stopped being a practitioner of my skills*'.

To the tension between carer and business person must be added that between manager and practitioner, and it appears that the scope for making the latter integral to leading by example was sometimes limited. However, many of the clinical managers tried to develop their practitioner skills in formal ways. For example, Lois had completed an MPhil and Kay had done an MA in nursing. These were not unusual cases and may be indicative of a desire by clinical managers to cement their status as a practitioner, perhaps helping to counterbalance the sense of a drift away from their practitioner identity that came with understanding management roles.

While she may not have been able to take on some of the tasks relating to immediate patient care, Gabrielle was keen to stress that she would always support the ward staff by staying beyond her official hours during busy periods. If not literally hands-on then present and visible. Lois concurred on the issue of both visibility and spending clinical time on the wards:

> *I feel that it's really important to be visible and to be seen. Because what I never wanted is for people to say, oooh, Lois is somebody that sits behind a desk and she's at meetings all the time … we try and make a conscious decision each week to spend some clinical time out there.*

In a similar vein, Dawn had recollections of managers as '*ethereal people who kind of came in with a clipboard and in a navy blue suit … and you didn't have any respect for them*'. She tried to challenge this view by incorporating presence and hands-on work as part of her leadership role. An essential constituent of management, a leader can only lead effectively if they have the *respect* of their staff. Thus Dawn asserted that:

> *You couldn't manage nurses without ever stepping foot on the ward, but to lead them and get them to follow you when you make some of the difficult decisions* [then] *you absolutely have to show that you can do their job with them sometimes.*

And yet Dawn felt that the staff would never understand her job and must '*wonder what I do all day*'. Paradoxically, clinical managers were often compelled to contribute to the practical business of patient care on the wards. The day before we spoke to Dawn, she had been '*feeding babies on the new unit because we had no staff*'. For Dawn, this was not management in itself, but certainly of itself:

> *So at that point, you're not a manager at all are you, you know? Other than making the decision that I was the one to go and do that, so making the decision is I think a management decision that you say 'right, actually doing this is more important than doing the thing that was in my diary'.*

We can already begin to see that the roles of middle managers in the NHS were characterized by fluidity, particularly in the sense of how they relate to the identity of the manager *qua* manager. In our discussion of leadership by example, we have seen that managers attempted to fulfil this role through behaviours that emphasized their hands-on abilities and willingness to undertake front-line work. We have also seen, however, that this behaviour was a response to the practicalities of the situation. In some cases, getting hands-on was simply a matter of solving a problem – ensuring patient care was delivered, however 'overworked and under-resourced' they and their colleagues might have been (Hutchinson and Purcell, 2010).

Problem-solving

Lois emphasized the operational element of her role: '*At this level, because it's very operational, we tend to do a lot of firefighting … you've got the firefighting every day*'. By firefighting she meant solving problems that arose unexpectedly as quickly as possible as '*somebody will phone me up with a problem and it's literally down sticks and you have to resolve that problem*'. This on-the-spot problem-solving took up around 50 per cent of her time. We saw that this was a key role for NHS junior and middle managers more generally and (as we see in later chapters) across all NHS organizations.

We should be clear that these problems were usually far from trivial and were in fact symptomatic of stresses, not to say failures, in the systems within which these managers worked. We saw managers plugging the gaps in the system, and our observations provided ample illustrations of this. Walking around the wards with Keely, we came across senior nurses, heads of service, cleaning a linen cupboard on a newly refurbished ward. The reason? The tradespeople were behind schedule and yet the timing of the ward opening remained the same. Snagging, the final stage of the refurbishing, had concluded at 10.00 a.m. The ward was scheduled to open at 12.00 noon. Denise, a head of nursing in the Elective Services business group, at the time wearing a plastic apron and wielding a cloth, noted: '*When you're working with people,* [you get] *crisis*'.

Senior nurse managers were expected to do eight-hour shifts as an on-call manager three or four times a month, and this could be on any day of the week, at any time. The on-call or *9201 bleep* manager is, during their shift, responsible for operation of the hospital as a whole. In practice, this means they deal with untoward or unpredictable events. Our shift with Lois clearly reflected this and saw her attending to a wide range of issues. At one point, we accompanied her as she was called upon to investigate an intruder alarm going off on one of the wards. Not knowing whether we would actually encounter an intruder or not, we were relieved to find someone better suited for that eventuality was already on the scene – a security guard who was, according to his regimental tie, a former paratrooper. Sometimes firefighting takes on a more literal meaning. She told us of another nurse manager who had two fire alarms to investigate on one night. While the culprit turned out to be burnt toast, the manager was not to know that. Lois had been called upon in the past to respond to media as well as police enquiries (which could include enquiries about murdered children who had been brought to the trust in an attempt to save their lives). During one of our observations, she recalled being asked by the police to look at a foetus in a jar to try and determine whether or not a young mother was responsible for aborting it herself. When we suggested that this was a particularly traumatic thing to have to do, she responded that it is all part of the job and that '*you get used to such things*'.

Less emotionally intense, but still calling for pragmatism and professionalism, on-call managers dealt with bed shortages and near breaches of (A&E) four-hour targets. While a potential breach necessitated a hurried meeting with one colleague and telephone calls to various others, solving a bed shortage called for equally nimble organizational footwork. In this latter case, Lois was called into a hands-on role once again, and here we encounter the figure of manager as bedmaker. In order to perform the problem-solving role, the manager must use their initiative and deploy practical skills acquired through experience. Faced with a bed shortage during a Sunday night 9201 shift, Lois opened up a ward usually used for day patients and co-ordinated a group of porters to bring in the appropriate type and number of beds. She then made the beds and checked the relevant equipment (oxygen cylinders, etc.). It is clear that even having moved on to management roles, nurses such as Lois, Dawn, Denise and many others, still saw themselves as belonging to nursing as an occupational culture. In keeping with this spirit, the researcher did their best to help with the setting up of the room, learning how to make a bed *NHS style* into the bargain.

Arbitration

Arbitration and, connectedly, conflict management were also a form of problem-solving. Although this role did not come across strongly in interview discussions, it was clear from our observations of clinical managers that this was a role that they needed to carry out in order to maintain a properly functioning system. Clinical managers, particularly those with operational responsibilities covering staff across different units, were required to deal with conflicts between staff and patients, usually in the form of administering complaint procedures involving individual staff and sometimes between organizational units that were competing for limited resources.

On a 9201 bleep shift, we observed as Lois took phone calls in quick succession from two groups of nurses. The issue at stake was access to a cupboard containing surgical scrubs – one group wanted access and the other wished to retain the stock for their own use. As Lois later recalled, '*it was almost like being the adjudicator in the middle of it all*'. She fulfilled the role of arbitrator by, in the first instance, preventing the conflict escalating any further and, in the second, attempting to find a solution that would satisfy both parties. However, in the end, a direct intervention was required, and we found ourselves once more back on the wards or, in this case, very much in the backstage area of the hospital amongst darkened operating theatres and storerooms with Lois retrieving the necessary scrubs herself. These were handed over to the junior nurse managers who required them, removing the element of negotiation, and thus conflict, from the equation altogether. It should be noted that in some cases, the most appropriate form of arbitration was for the clinical manager to remind junior staff of their professional duty, ultimately, to resolve the conflict themselves; delegation of course, being one of the core strategies of any manager.

Co-ordination and planning

We know from classical accounts (Mintzberg, 1973: 1, 9) as well as conventional knowledge, that much of a manager's job involves co-ordination; and for clinical managers in the NHS, this was certainly the case. We have already seen examples of this within other key roles: the porters needed to bring beds to a ward that needs to be opened, the staff who had to be found, contacted and brought to work on the ward unexpectedly, and so on. Much of the problem-solving role, in a sense, was about co-ordination. There were other contexts, often more structured and formally systemic, where co-ordination took place. Often, this co-ordination had much of the character of planning, and so we deal with these key roles together.

Many important elements of co-ordination took place in meetings, which occurred on both a scheduled and an *ad hoc* basis. A clinical manager tended to have around a dozen or so meetings per week. For example, at the scheduled meeting for key management staff in the Trauma and Orthopaedics unit, problems were raised, discussed and compared; these included apparently mundane but nevertheless relevant issues such as a dentist banging his head on a poorly positioned lamp, someone asking to be redeployed and someone needing a reference. More systemic issues, such as staff sickness, were likely to come up at many of these meetings, as were performance targets including recent *close calls* where a target such as waiting time had nearly been breached (see above). From these discussions, decisions on operational matters were made or at least plans were made for the most appropriate people to follow the issue up, which often involves a further meeting with senior managers. In unit meetings, middle managers worked together, building knowledge of common issues and developing co-ordinated strategies in relation to an organizational reality of which these issues were largely constitutive.

Another scheduled meeting with an on-call manager concerned bed spaces at the trust over the coming busy weekend period, and this was characterized by high intensity and fast pace. The pace was, in fact, so fast that the observer soon lost track of what exactly was being discussed. Numbers, names and places flew back and forth, as our notes illustrate:

'*Gynaecology is OK because you don't get a lot of GP admissions…*'

'*B5 is moving to B2, which gives me two extra beds*'

'*C2 … C5 … Plan E … 8 … identification from medicine or DMOP* [Department of Medicine for Older People] *ward … got a nice "med reg." coming in 9-9 on Saturday … A12 situation is difficult …*'

At the end of this meeting, the associate director for emergency medicine asked: 'Bottom line across the trust?' The answer: 'Three beds over what we need'.

We can see here managers co-operating with others across the trust in order to ensure that patient flow and necessary resources are co-ordinated. This is co-ordination in a very immediate, very focused sense.

In terms of planning as an element of co-ordination, this tended to centre, for junior and middle clinical managers, on two sets of resources: first, HR (staffing) and, second, financial resources in the short and medium term. Often, the two were closely connected. Gabrielle placed the co-ordination of staffing with her given budget at the centre of her role and identity as a manager: '*I'm given the title of ward manager because you get a budget basically. You have budget meetings and … have to make sure the staffing's balanced and so on and so forth.'* Gabrielle was one of the managers reporting to Lois. Lois was responsible for around 200 staff, liaising with junior managers such as Gabrielle in order to co-ordinate resources effectively. Thus these managers at different levels had monthly budget meetings:

> *That is actually to tell us whether we're meeting our budget or not; whether we're overspent, underspent … if we're spending too much on staffing for whatever reason, what we need to do about it and we need mainly an action plan, all that kind of stuff.*

For clinical managers, the issue of budgets and finance was an important one. They had to negotiate, both intellectually and practically, the tension between financial resources, in the sense of material and staff, and care. A quote from Dawn illustrates the difficulties in negotiating this tension when co-ordinating the expenditure of these resources:

> *I think that two years of doing general management makes you see that actually it doesn't matter how much as a nurse you believe in something, if you can't afford it* [then] *you can't afford it. But no, I'm fairly comfortable. It's a constant tension. I would say that one of the hardest things I do is to try and get that message across to my team leaders without them thinking I'm just being mean about money.*

In the case of other middle managers, such as Lois, they not only had to co-ordinate budgets as they currently stand, but needed to plan further into the future. This meant *'putting together a business case'*. With staffing the primary resource issue for clinical managers, these business cases tended to relate to workforce planning: *'So I've just had to write some proposal papers for the strategic health authority because I need some more advanced practitioners'* (Lois). Day-to-day, maintaining enough staff with the correct skill-mix appeared to take up a large proportion of a clinical manager's time, particularly at the more junior level. Even there, Gabrielle felt it helpful to delegate some of the staffing work – constructing what is called the off-duty rota – to some of her staff nurses. For Kay and Barbara, rotas must be done at least two months in advance. It is, according to Kay, a *'nightmare'* that used to take eight hours and now takes considerably more: *'Staffing is the biggest; I think staffing is the biggest one* [issue]'.

Project management

As is the case across the institutions and corporations of the advanced economies, project work was an increasingly significant feature of NHS managers' lives. Positively, project work allowed managers the opportunity to develop their co-ordination and planning skills by applying them in a more self-defined area. In the case of Keely, her role as a matron allowed her the flexibility to initiate and manage a project on improving patients' lifestyle choices. Keely's project also required a certain entrepreneurial instinct since it needed to be *sold* to staff across the trust as their co-operation would be pivotal in making it effective. As well as relying on Keely's well-developed network of contacts at Millford, the project required her to build networks between organizations; for example, liaising with commissioners – the primary care trust as it then was. Lois, by contrast, had moved into project management after being restructured out of the higher-grade nurse manager job that she held during our earlier fieldwork observations. Ironically, she spoke of how her project on electronic rostering was aimed at increasing efficiency but that some staff feared it was part of a wider strategy of job elimination. Whilst making the best of her new role, Keely's mood during our final interview was characterized more by melancholy than by entrepreneurialism. For her, project management was part of a process of being moved out of a role and an organization with which she had identified strongly and had worked hard at doing well. On her move from nurse manager to project manager, she reflected that: '*Yes, there were elements of that job I didn't enjoy. I didn't enjoy disciplining people; I didn't enjoy telling people that they weren't doing their job correctly.*' But in concert with our earlier discussions of managers' desire to retain both the identity and performance of a clinical practitioner, Keely, noted: '*The bits that I enjoyed were patient contact, and I miss that. I really miss being with patients. I miss making a difference.*'

Project management is not the exclusive province of the project manager, of course. For some, like Jason, a senior research manager, their work constituted a series of projects that had to be developed and often funded on the initiative of himself and other colleagues. In a parallel to one familiar aspect of academic life, Jason was always on the lookout for sources of funding from external bodies – something that didn't just help to supplement internally derived resources, but which increasingly seemed to be essential for the survival of the research unit itself.

Many managers had, alongside their day-to-day operational concerns, medium-term goals that they sought to achieve by conceiving them essentially as a project. Given the fact that NHS organizations appeared to be in a permanent state of near financial crisis or trying extremely hard to avoid such a state (Vincent, 2012), it was not surprising that planning and project management sometimes fell victim to organizational caprice. Elaine (audit department manager) described the conclusion to a three-month project that she undertook with the aim of restructuring her department and staffing it according to its needs. Her attitude of resignation is coloured by an intention to continue trying, despite it all; and this is typical of the managers at Millford:

> *I went through 87 applications, interviewed 11 people, picked 2 because I had two posts from it. Because I went from one Band 3 to three, offered the part-time lady hers and she accepted it, and half an hour later I was going to phone the other guy to offer him the Band 3 post and I got a phone call to say it was part of our contribution towards the trust trying to make some savings. I couldn't have it any more, which just totally destroyed everything that I'd worked for [over] the last three months. Extremely frustrating. But anyway, we just get on with it. We've been there before. We'll do it again.*

Managing people and relationships

Middle managers sought to cement their ability to manage the people around them by being visible *on the floor* and displaying their leadership skills along the way. Other behaviours reflected differing approaches to managing relationships with other professional groups, such as doctors. Reflecting the balance of the literature on the subject (see Chapter 2), it is fair to say that the majority of the junior and middle clinical managers had a rather negative view of doctors or at least the attitude of doctors and their willingness to work in concert with managers. This was reflected in what Eddie (associate director of HR) had to say about the perspective of doctors:

> *What all consultants and doctors and clinical directors want is to be left alone. That's what they want. They want to be left alone; they've been trained very well to look after patients; they want to go and look after them. That's all they want to do.*

As ward manager Gabrielle said: '*the amount of time we spend chasing after doctors to do things is incredible*'. Even senior managers appeared to hold limited influence over senior consultants who, according to Eddie, '*have an enormous amount of power*'. Controlling the behaviour of staff in the organization or getting them to do what they are asked rather than ignoring management edicts is one of the fundamental difficulties of management. On this theme, Eddie recalled a conversation with the chief executive who found it hard to enforce his will and that of senior management since the cadre of senior doctors could *bolt him out* – that is, force him out of the organization, should they wish. If this is the case for the chief executive then perhaps it is little wonder that Gabrielle had to '*virtually grovel*', although she did then correct herself to emphasize instead the way goodwill can be created by '*making a cup of tea*' for senior and junior doctors alike. Gabrielle suggested that acts of kindness, looking after junior doctors in this way, was particularly effective in building relationships – they are '*run ragged*' after all. Similarly, Kay saw '*looking after*' junior doctors as a key part of her role. Because of her experience and expertise, it was the case that doctors often sought her knowledge and support. Indeed, this was illustrated by a scenario where, as the researcher walked with her down a corridor, a young doctor pulled her aside to ask for advice.

Our findings on the relationships between managers and doctors are in concert with much of the literature (e.g. see Hoque *et al.*, 2004). This is not to say, however, that all doctors were fundamentally anti-management. Clearly, no hospital could function without co-operation between managers and medics; and indeed many doctors perform management roles, often as clinical directors of a particular service. John, a consultant surgeon and clinical director of emergency medicine, as noted earlier, saw himself performing something of a boundary-spanning role (Currie *et al.*, 2007) at the interface of management and medicine. Reflecting the prevailing view, John believed that doctors who were really interested in management were '*few and far between*'; although we did encounter medical directors at Millford who had developed an interest in the strategy and implementation of Lean and leadership and who appeared to have ambitions to remain in, and progress through, clinical management roles in the longer term. While John noted that he, like many consultants, used his management role to help him pursue interests in a particular field, the fact that his overall priority was improving care for patients in his department suggests a strong commonality, in motivation at least, between managers and doctors.

Most junior and middle managers we encountered shared an underlying philosophy regarding their management style, considering it important to deal with people fairly and '*think about how I can make life easier for other people, how I can help them*' (Gabrielle). We have already noted that some junior and middle managers were conscious of differences between the way management operated in the public and private sectors. Despite some of their frustrations with this situation, managers with private sector experience were at least able to draw on experience that they had gained in private industry of building relationships across a variety of contexts. This experience came into play particularly when they could see that the philosophy mentioned above would not be sufficient to ensure the efficient management of their service. Amongst the managers, it was Elaine – someone with a career history mainly in corporate industry – who drew a distinction between those who had entered management from a practitioner background and those, like her, who had worked in corporate management. The former, according to Elaine, were sometimes less able to deal with '*difficult staff*'.

When relationships can't be managed: conflict and bullying at Millford

Considering that some research suggests that 20 per cent of staff in the NHS have reported being bullied (Carter [M.] *et al.*, 2013), it was discussed in only a small number of our interviews. It may be that Millford was successful in creating a culture that discouraged bullying, and it was also the case that our interviews did not seek to address the topic as one of their specific aims. Gabrielle did discuss the issue but reinterpreted it as one of the necessary functions of the manager's role. She suggested that in some cases, supposed subjects of victimization had misinterpreted the situation and, more specifically, the manager's position: '*I have to do this. I have no choice. And it's getting that across. It's not a bullying issue. It's the fact I am following a process.*'

Of course, for those on the receiving end of a *process* – however dispassionate it may ostensibly appear to be – the experience can be intensely personal, as Annette's story illustrates. In her nine years in post as an occupational therapy manager, Annette felt the culture of the trust change. In contradiction to the aims of the trust – creating transparent and efficient management systems – she reported instead an increase in micromanaging by senior managers, many of whose roles were opaque beyond having '*funny titles*' such as '*director of modernization*'. Annette told how her job '*disappeared in the restructure*' and related the loss directly to both the change in government and the global financial crisis with the fiscal austerity that quickly followed. The trust's restructuring of the organization into business groups placed Annette in a new management structure with an '*autocratic, command and control, Tayloristic* [sic]' manager. The details of Annette's experience from that point forward include the accusations of dishonesty, excessive ruthlessness, and narcissism that often feature in cases of bullying. In a dysfunctional mix of office politics and a push for cost savings, Annette found herself vulnerable after a period of sickness. After further organizational and, in Annette's view, personal manoeuvrings, she was placed on '*gardening*' leave as part of a formal transition out of the trust. Characterizing the senior management culture at Millford as authoritarian and the process of organizational change as equally ruthless, the personal consequences for her had been severe: '*This behaviour over months has brought me to the edge. I need to be at home now, to start … . And also to lick my wounds, because I do, I feel wounded.*' We should note that Annette is recounting and reflecting on the organization from an intensely personal perspective – so intense, in fact, that she became distressed during the interview. As the Thomas theorem suggests, 'if men [sic] define situations as real, they are real in their consequences' (Thomas and Thomas, 1928: 572). The experiences of Shannon and Annette, though clearly not universal, remind us that scarcity of resources, complexity, organizational change, tensions in personal identity and professional relationships are not always simply challenges a manager must face and overcome; their scope and intensity can create a toxic situation that some find impossible to deal with.

Elaine's earlier discussion of the distinction between those with a management and those with a practitioner background came about when she was reflecting on the problems her predecessor had experienced in managing apparently difficult people in the audit department. Elaine said that attempting to manage the audit staff without previous team management experience was almost '*suicidal*'. We spoke to her predecessor, Shannon, who said: '*in clinical audit, the staff were untrained, unruly, nightmarish*'. Here, we encounter the issue of what happens when managers were unable to manage relationships, partly because they faced a level of hostility that they found difficult to cope with. Shannon's experience was different to Annette's in that rather than being on the receiving end of change implementation, she had been attempting to carry it out and faced hostility and resistance. For Shannon, part of the problem stemmed from the fact that when '*people needed to be moved somewhere quickly because there was a case of bullying and they needed a place of protection, they'd put them with me*'. Whether these people were the bullied or the bullies, Shannon did not say; but certainly she found the atmosphere when she joined the audit department to be '*completely dysfunctional*' and '*bullying*'.

Her attempts to improve matters and make working practices more efficient did not go smoothly. Not only did she have to sack somebody within the first four months in the post, something she found personally difficult, but another member of staff took out a grievance against her. Though the grievance was unsuccessful, Shannon reported that the employee then began harassing her. Shannon sought support from the HR department but found it '*neither use nor ornament*'. Similarly, her union was of little help because, according to her, '*they feel you've gone over to the dark side when you become a manager*'. When Shannon sought support from her own manager, the advice she received conflicted with another one of the roles discussed above – problem-solving. Shannon found it hard to follow their advice to avoid taking on other people's issues. She felt that her dynamic approach was not in keeping with a '*stereotypically moribund*' NHS culture, which she summed up with the image of the '*NHS being a really slow ship that you can't turn around very fast*'. She acknowledged also that, as Elaine mentioned, her career in nursing and occupational therapy had not really equipped her with the requisite people management skills. Once again, the disjuncture in identity between practitioner and manager comes into play:

> *And so to have to manage people's expectations and do a hell of a lot of negotiation all the time with people about their objectives and trying to get them, cajoling people and trying to take them forward so that, you know, getting them to see the direction in the department. Things like that. It's alien to me – I'm a nurse you know?*

Clearly, a range of factors were in play, and as researchers, we were only able to hear about this situation from Shannon herself. Whatever caveats we place on this example, the bullying and hostility was real enough from Shannon's perspective. So after one year in the post, she went off sick with stress and left the role of audit manager before moving to another NHS organization.

Monitoring

Managers were required to monitor the performance of their services. Matrons played a key role here, often acting as the '*eyes and ears*' of other managers (until the role ceased to exist at Millford in 2010). The official role of matrons at this acute trust related to quality; what this meant in practice was that matrons had a monitoring role based on collecting audit information from across an area of the hospital for which they were responsible, such as: infection control, hygiene, falls, patient lifestyle, and so on. This information-gathering role, together with their extensive experience and tacit knowledge of nursing/clinical care and the organization as a whole, meant that matrons at Millford seemed able to glean information from colleagues about what was going on across the trust. The following field notes were taken whilst accompanying Keeley as she went from ward to ward checking on the implementation of a project that she had initiated. In the corridor, we stopped and spoke to a matron, Beth:

> *Ward B13, all Sisters have resigned ... no sisters there ... big problem ... but you don't get support from management ... 'disaster zone' ... [!] ... Various people off sick. Nicky back today but looks like she should still be off sick. Builders not very good; job which was meant to take a week has taken eight.*

We have discussed managerial visibility already, but it is worth noting that this also gives managers the chance to monitor, first-hand, both the staff and the patients on the ward. In terms of the staff, monitoring need not be in the sense of surveillance (although it might be – see below); rather, it could focus more on informal discussions with staff in order to hear the issues currently affecting them. Visiting the wards further allows managers to monitor, at least in a superficial sense, the condition of the patients there – clearly an important factor in the performance of a healthcare organization. Lois, for example, visited a ward where the patients looked rather unkempt and perhaps not as clean as they should have been. On other occasions, junior staff reported concerns such as staff members being rude to patients. It was her responsibility to investigate these concerns. This was usually done in two ways. First, she might spend a shift working with junior colleagues in the relevant ward. Whilst this had the advantage of allowing the middle manager to see things first-hand, it had all the obvious disadvantages of overt observation. Another strategy employed by clinical managers was to place a trusted colleague in their place and have them report back.

Information management

While information management has obvious links with a variety of other roles – for example, co-ordination – the central role played by information in the work of the clinical manager bears further examination. Information was gathered either formally in the sense of audit statistics or informally in what Keely called '*gossip pathways*' (e.g. a conversation in the corridor, which was useful only if it was well managed). Thus a key role of the managers was information management. Many elements of information management, in the sense of collection, were mandated by national and trust governance procedures; hence the need to audit for *quality*. Once collected, information was then discussed at scheduled meetings. Managers had to assimilate and make use of a significantly high volume of information; in the case of middle managers with responsibility for large numbers of staff, effectively all of the topics discussed in a meeting such as this were relevant. Even when managers were not expected to remember everything they heard, such discussions formed the backdrop to their work *as* a manager, and they had to be able to process this information in order both to prioritize tasks and to maintain their oversight of their area of responsibility. We can see here that monitoring and information management were intrinsically linked. It was here, also, that the monitoring role of matrons intersected with the role of information management as they fed back both their formal findings and their informal observations. As Gabrielle explained, scheduled meetings served to facilitate a flow of information both up and down the hierarchy of the organization:

> *It's just basically a* [forum] *that gives us a chance to say what we think, you know. And it's also a venue for people like* [the associate director of the business group] *now, who can come in and give us an overview of what's going on in the organization.*

> *So it's a way of the organization being able to get in contact with all the sisters* [ward managers] *together and actually feed back, share information to pass it down* [so] *that I can then pass on to my staff.*

This is entirely in keeping with Katherine's earlier description of middle managers as '*agents*' or communicative intermediaries between senior and junior staff.

Statistics related to governance were often presented in the form of *traffic light* or *dashboard* tables. In simple terms, these were visual management tools where the performance of an organization or organizational unit was represented by colour-coded tables or, literally, dashboard-style dials; these were intended to make assimilation of the information easier and to give a sense of performance against governance targets. Indeed, information pertaining to mandated targets – such as waiting times or infection rates – were a key feature of managers' discussions in scheduled operational meetings. They were, in a sense, monitoring themselves. Targets at Millford were taken very seriously. To quote Lois: '*you get hung, drawn and quartered if you let a patient breach their 18-week pathway*'. Meeting targets could have a negative impact on patient care, according to Kay, who spoke of patients being moved around to accommodate patients in the emergency department who were nearing the four-hour target time. This, according to Kay, was '*heartbreaking*' for the nurses involved, who were aware of the negative impact on quality of care for the patients being moved around (to three different wards in one week, in Kay's example). Yet they had no choice but to move them; such is the power of targets to influence behaviour. Barbara captured the essence of many colleagues' concerns about the use of performance targets in healthcare in an inherently unpredictable environment and in the context of already stretched human resources:

> *It's just, we're talking about people here. We're not talking about machines and, you know, so you can only reach so many targets. People can do better in some areas but some days, like in the emergency department, you can have three* [cardiac] *arrests coming in, road traffic accident. Where are all the doctors? Where are all the nurses?*

In the wake of the Mid Staffordshire scandal, the government promised to review the use of performance targets; although managers we spoke to at Millford noted that, in practice, they remained in place. Indeed, since they had become institutionally embedded in management systems, they were likely to do so indefinitely. In contrast to some of the negative attitudes, Lois, having noted some of the pressures around targets, did point out that they had facilitated a transition from the '*bad old days*' of very long waits in the emergency department or for a life-changing operation. Information was a crucial resource where the need for monitoring had greater significance than was the case in many other organizations. In other words, this is information relating to matters of patient care and, sometimes, life and death.

While many middle managers must be able to assimilate and manipulate data effectively and understand its significance in the round, they, along with junior managers and medical and administrative staff on the ward, were also responsible for the actual collection and inputting of patient data. Many managers complained, in simple terms, of an excess of paperwork. Much of this related to collecting audit data (including information on individual patients) and inputting it either on paper forms or onto a computerized database. Other elements included governance around risk assessment, for example. This paperwork was said to be ever increasing. Illustrating the challenge that audits and related paperwork posed to ward managers in particular, Kay offered some examples:

> *We do … the environmental audits … you do infection control audits, the MRSA targets … and then you've got nurse care indicators, which they've got to do which is nutrition, falls, pressure areas, safeguarding children …. We've got various slightly different ones in women's and children's but, you know, it's all …. And medication and things like that; they've got to do all different audits for them.*

Managerial challenges and organizational change at Millford

> *The banks can be bailed out; they can find trillions for that, but not for us.*
> *(Nurse manager at a Lean training event)*

We were able to conceptualize the broader role of NHS middle managers as made up of a number of individual, though not fully discrete, sub-roles (Anthony and Reed, 1990: 28; Oroviogoicoechea, 1996: 1275–6). Acute trust management therefore was highly diverse across the range of different managers and within each formal role or job title, and this was particularly the case for clinical managers such as nurse managers. All managers were expected to be both operationally and, increasingly, strategically aware. Acute trust managers were managing information, people and resources in a unique, challenging environment. Whilst managers in other sectors of the economy doubtless face similar difficulties, rarely must they seek to balance these limitations against the needs of the most vulnerable in society – people facing illness and life-changing, sometimes life-threatening, events. At times, the operational challenges caused by limits to resources created a sense of low-level crisis. Senior managers at the trust suffered severe financial pressures on a no less immediate basis, and this provided the backdrop to much of what they did. They were able to respond strategically by developing new management processes and initiatives. They also attempted to gain a greater awareness of future policy developments – an organizational clairvoyance communicated by the chief executive through metaphors of the '*phony war*' or the '*gypsy's warning*'.

Though Sergeant (2003: 37) has argued that NHS management and, in particular, middle management remains 'untouched by the commercialism that transformed business in the 1980s', this was far from true at Millford. For acute trust managers, the market is the 'horizon' against which organizations must operate, and managers are its navigators (Parker, 2002b: 3). Managers at all levels understood the business pressures. This was reflected not only in their language but in their ontological negotiation of their role – their identity.

For clinical managers, Duffield's observation holds true: 'the transition in nursing from the role of a clinician to a manager can result in role confusion and conflict' (1991: 1248). We saw this in two primary senses: the conflict between business and care; and the conflict between manager and practitioner identities. Be this as it may, managers were keen to engage with development opportunities (should time allow) and showed an often entrepreneurial approach to negotiating sources of funding and even to the path of their own careers. They were explicitly motivated by the chance to be of service to patients and, often, wider society, though they increasingly found themselves attempting to fulfil their role from within the iron cage (Weber, 1930: 181) of economic rationality. Thus there was a broad though sometimes wry acceptance of new management strategies such as Lean management. If programmes such as Lean appear to the reader, as they do to some staff at the trust, as '*management gimmicks*', it could be argued they are a logical response to pressures at the highest level of the NHS and national government to be seen to be doing 'more with less'. Efficiency savings is a concept – or at least a phrase, since *concept* suggests some sort of logical coherence – that now permeates policy pronouncements from government. Managers are effectively obliged to respond to this hegemony of efficiency in a manner that is culturally compliant with the notion of the NHS as a corporate business. Senior, middle and junior managers are unlikely, indeed unable, to resist the imperatives of the market and their ideological expressions through direct protest. Resistance to such a dominant ideology would have the character of utopian fantasy, and those espousing it would risk being perceived as dangerously unorthodox, as impractical and unrealistic (Parker, 2002b: 3). Trusts are also encouraged to appear *proactive* rather than *reactive*, and so they seek strategically to anticipate future developments and mould the organization accordingly. Thus the trust itself collaborates in maintaining the momentum of neo-liberal change or in the idea of acute trusts as businesses with their own strategy and vision for the future cemented. Performance targets, similarly, were something that Millford acute trust, like others, had no choice but to comply with. They were seen as having some benefits for patients in terms of waiting times, but alongside other audit-type data, they placed an ever-greater burden on managers' workload.

Dissemination of strategic priorities took place, as we have seen, through training, events, and at the level of organizational symbolism and material culture. If acute trusts such as Millford were compelled to continue to seek efficiency savings, they also faced the fundamental contradiction that these savings must be made without harming the quality of patient care. The metaphysical infrastructure of corporate culture must also serve to hold out the promise that this is achievable, in effect operating to suspend organizational disbelief. Perhaps it is possible to maintain patient care under conditions of constant organizational change and severe resource pressures. Such organizational change, as already noted, is a response to an environment where new policy arrives without warning and White

Paper follows report follows five-year plan; where visions for the future rise and fall even within the same parliamentary regime, each one appearing to offer solutions to our now familiar contradiction. Junior and middle managers occupy a central role in attempts to square this circle. While work intensification for nurses and doctors is a more or less well-recognized phenomenon in the public imagination, the same cannot be said for NHS managers. And yet our findings are broadly in concert with those of many other researchers (see our discussion in Chapter 2) in that they do point to intensification for them also. Managers were often required to work at high levels of pace and intensity in often emotionally and interpersonally challenging circumstances.

One way of coping with increased demands but static resources was for managers to work longer than contracted hours as well as taking work home. Many, though not all, of the managers we spoke to did this. While for some senior managers like Kevin this was seen as a positive element in a dynamic executive role, for others it was simply a necessity – Gabrielle, for example, who is supposed to start at 7.30 a.m., actually starts at 6.45 a.m., accepting long hours as part of being a manager; or Shannon who worked from 7.00 a.m. to 7.00 p.m., five days a week – something which had an adverse effect on her health. Our findings parallel those of Buchanan *et al.* (2013) in that healthcare management seemed to take on the character of extreme work. *Wicked problems*, interpersonal tension, high stakes, fast pace, long hours, and emotional intensity were all elements that we observed at Millford. Our characterization was borne out to some extent in a follow-up discussion with Lois – by then, on her way out of the trust for a new job in private healthcare.

> *This is, this is an extreme. I honestly think, as an operational manager, you would class it as an extreme job because there isn't any other job, I don't know of any other job that would expect you to deliver on so many levels and, you know, just keep going, keep your sanity, keep being professional, but just keep going.*

What we saw was the human cost of austerity with redundancy for some managers and increased uncertainty for others. This had an emotional impact on people who had dedicated their (professional) lives to the NHS, including Millford specifically. Keely expressed sadness about the loss of the matron post, which had only been created a few years earlier. Curiously, given the commonly observed nature of project work as contingent itself, she worried that her new role as a project manager would be perceived by others as a secure berth in turbulent times and already felt tension in the air at meetings with colleagues whose positions were less secure. For her part, Keely was aware that she was, in fact, vulnerable following the demise of the matron role: '*once it's gone, that's when you sort of inwardly sort of think, panic. What happens when this job goes because I actually haven't got a job to go to?*'

The analysis of the NHS as part of a system of political economy is not the preserve of academic researchers. Gabrielle, for example, considered the recent financial crisis as part of a cycle:

> *So, ultimately, I don't care what anybody says; and this is just from a business perspective now because I've seen it so many times. In business, what they do is they get to a point and there's a squeeze on money, they make cuts … they will do that until they get to a point, till we reach … until money then becomes more freely available and then it will expand again. And it's a cycle. It's happened before and it will happen again because that's how business works and that's how the NHS will work.*

Others such as Lois were less phlegmatic, and foresaw a deep systemic change in secondary healthcare with mergers of trusts and the outsourcing of various services:

> *It's interesting, the migration of people, senior people, moving into the private sector and I just think that's where people will go and I think that suits the government's agenda … all of a sudden, before you know it, you turn around and we'll have to pay for our healthcare.*

Managers sought to cope with the challenges, and sometimes the extremity of their roles, through a sense of professionalism. Proving oneself able to solve difficult problems was seen as a rite of passage, which the manager had little choice but to endure. On a social level, managers found support in being part of a community of colleagues working together and often sharing a common history. Thus we might speak of a 'community of coping' (Korczynski, 2003) in that managers did support each other as much as possible. Ultimately, however, organizational changes tended to be experienced at the level of the individual.

Professionalism and an appeal to an (albeit sometimes compromised) identity as a practitioner was, for our managers, the most effective form of resistance to what they perceived as a drift away from patient care and towards the domination of a business rationale. This was the case from the director who remained a '*thorn in the side of business developments*' to the nurse manager who remained true to the '*fluffy stuff*'. Beset by a mercurial policy environment, where the only certainty appeared to be dwindling resources and increased demand, managers at senior strategic levels were also doing their best to keep patient care at the centre of the trust's priorities – whatever administrative, cultural and ontological contortions had to be performed as part of this endeavour.

People join a profession or take a management role for a wide range of reasons, and clearly the NHS offers some extrinsic rewards to managers. But acute trust managers' motivations can hardly be viewed as mercenary. Finding themselves caught between resource pressures and maintaining patient care, the acute trust managers faced both strategic and operational challenges with a sense of professionalism and a commitment to their role and to patients.

Conclusion

On the surface at least, the acute trust can be seen as the most stable and least affected of the four NHS organizations in terms of the effects of government reforms and new healthcare ideologies. Throughout our time there, the organization received excellent quality ratings from the CQC. The stable and long-standing team of directors had largely come up through the ranks and were confident in pushing back against national pressure to outsource services. Consequently, the introduction of private suppliers under an NHS badge was less obvious at this organization than it was at NHS hospitals nearby. They had not entered into costly Private Finance Initiative (PFI) arrangements and, with the exception of national-level service contracts, had succeeded thus far in maintaining their in-house NHS service provision.

However, following the Health and Social Care Act 2012 – which legislated for competitive tendering – and the national austerity programme, the organization faced serious and worsening financial challenges. In the face of increasing cost pressures, the trust was shifting away from patient and public service values and towards a more commercial business orientation. Departments were organized into business units. The consequent emergence of internal charging between and beyond departments took up time and effort while larger companies were negotiating for whole service contracts at both a national and regional level. In contrast to many NHS acute trusts at the time, this hospital had ended contracts that outsourced cleaning and hotel services and brought them back in-house. Where possible, it sought to retain direct control over its own services. Managers attempted to retain a focus on patient care whilst adopting the language of business, competition and commercialism. To some extent, the strength of the medical profession in acute services meant that doctors, managers and lead nurses continued to work in a triumvirate relationship reminiscent of earlier phases of NHS evolution.

While senior managers hunkered down in the face of increasing demand and decreased investment, they dealt with severe cost pressures by delayering the management and nursing hierarchy. This delayering intensified the daily work of the remaining managers – contracts were changing and those in the middle reaches of the organization were regularly reapplying for their own jobs, experiencing downgrading and being transferred to temporary contracts related to short-term projects. This internal restructuring, regrading and reappointing combined with interdepartmental charging distracted attention away from larger businesses looking for profitable regional contracts to provide discrete services. These contracts were beyond the control of the hospital senior managers who used the resources they had to rapidly build tendering and business acumen.

Note

1   The names of places, organizations, departments and staff have all been changed. We use fictional names to maintain anonymity whilst carefully maintaining an accurate depiction of situation, circumstance and experience. Any resemblance to names, job titles, departments, documents and organizations is entirely accidental. The name Millford is used in three of the chapters to indicate the overlapping health economy for these organizations. To explain, the acute trust occupied most of the geographical area covered by the primary care trust. However, Millford was only one of five areas covered by the mental health trust and a small part of a much larger region for the ambulance trust.

5

CONTESTED CULTURE

Managerial work in an ambulance trust

This chapter explores managerial work at our second NHS trust, 'Combined Counties Ambulance Service NHS Trust' or 'CCAS'. This organization played a critical role in the healthcare economy of the region of England where we conducted our research. CCAS emergency vehicles were highly visible in urban and rural areas, threading through traffic on blue lights with sirens blaring as they responded to emergency calls. Nationally, ambulance trusts represent the only NHS services that are genuinely available to any person 24 hours per day, 365 days of the year. Anyone in the region can call 999 and expect a CCAS vehicle and emergency crew (in various configurations) to respond quickly, according to nationally mandated target response times (eight minutes from the time the call is connected to arrival on scene for the most serious, potentially life-threatening conditions). This theme of highly demanding, immediate, mobile, often unplanned and always-on-call work emerged regularly within the distinctive *emergency-focused* culture of this organization.

Yet, paradoxically, despite its importance, CCAS occupied a rather low profile in policy development in the NHS region and seemed to have little influence over debates that affected it. Ambulance services in general were under-represented among the higher-profile NHS occupations and, despite its undoubted social importance, CCAS was a somewhat overlooked organization. In contrast to the acute trust, this organization was also highly geographically dispersed; its mobility and spatial fragmentation meant that it had a less grounded *feel* in terms of the anthropologically informed research design of this study. Fieldwork at CCAS took us to many different research locations, from a well-equipped headquarters and large new facilities on industrial estates to small, out-of-the-way, sometimes run-down ambulance stations. We also, at times, accompanied staff going about their duties in emergency response and planned care episodes out on the road, which sometimes gave us access to the back stages of NHS organizations and work; hospital waiting rooms and patient assessment cubicles, ambulance-only entrance areas to hospitals, patients' homes, remote accident sites by lonely roadsides, or highly public scenes inside workplaces or shopping centres. While scattered across a large area, we quickly came to recognize familiar visual and behavioural cues: blue NHS signage and yellow-and-green emergency vehicles parked on otherwise nondescript trading estates, the grouping of CCAS staff in their bottle green uniforms in office buildings or corners of hospitals, and the swapping of 'war stories' (Orr, 1996) about work and management in this highly mobile occupation.

The first location we visited to conduct preliminary interviews with managers was the CCAS HQ, about which we provide some field notes:

> The HQ is surprisingly large and sits alongside two to three other outer buildings of more modern construction. From the outside, there was no clue as to what this organization might be, other than a couple of ambulance rapid response cars parked across the way. The use of the term 'HQ' gave the workplace a 'uniformed' feel. This was reinforced as we entered the building and glimpsed some very large canvas bags lying in the hallway, containing manikins of human torsos for CPR training. Staff in uniform bustled down the stairs. Seemingly younger-looking students were in a group being led by a senior paramedic with pips on the shoulder. It gave the impression, to some extent, of a drilled organization, the way they sort of 'trooped' down the stairs.

CCAS provided emergency and planned care and transportation across a population of approximately seven million people and a geographical area of 5,500 square miles. This made it one of the largest ambulance services in the UK and, by extension, one of the largest 'free at the point of need' ambulance services in the world. At the time of the research, it employed over 5,000 staff and owned and maintained nearly 1,000 vehicles operating out of 114 ambulance stations. It had one headquarters and four regional offices in addition to three paramedic emergency control centres. It responded to around 780,000 emergency calls per year and typically completed around 2.4 million planned patient transportations per year. CCAS was formed ten years earlier by the merger of three separate regional ambulance trusts.

CCAS provided several vital services to the public, and it often operated under extreme financial and temporal pressures. We came to learn that it was also facing considerable organizational challenges. Demands on its front-line and managerial staff were growing in their complexity, variety and intensity. In a somewhat ambivalent fashion, it was becoming more sophisticated in its clinical and logistical capabilities while also struggling to fulfil all of its basic duties and responsibilities; it was also hemmed in by the incessant pressure of performance targets. This chapter explains why this is the case, focusing in particular on the daily working lives of junior and middle managers across three distinct parts of the service. It focuses on the themes of intense work pressure amid a quite strongly entrenched *uniformed* culture and demonstrates how organizational change is contested and complicated. The managerial culture of CCAS closely resembled the type of work that the organization itself handled: emergency and unplanned care is often demanding with sudden surges of demand; stresses, strains, conflict and resource shortages further complicate matters. While management and front-line work had powerful intrinsic value, working life for many at CCAS was stressful and sometimes fraught.

It is important to note that ambulance clinicians are essentially para-professionals (Freidson, 1986; McCann *et al.*, 2013) and do not enjoy the forms of recognition or professional power that other occupational groups (e.g. doctors, surgeons, nurses and midwives) have traditionally held (see Willis, 2006). This sometimes meant that ambulance clinicians had weaker forms of potential resistance to, or influence on, general managers or administrators than other more powerful occupational groups in the NHS. Ambulance practitioners were therefore often more closely *managed* than other clinicians. However, in keeping with broader medical norms, ambulance staff and managers were long-serving staff who had come up through the ranks and held hybrid manager/clinician roles rather like the nurse managers in the preceding chapter. At CCAS, they were often area managers or clinical team leaders who were both paramedics and managers and often wore a uniform rather than managerial office clothes. Again, like the hybrid managers of the acute trust, they tried to place 'patient need' above all other priorities wherever possible (McCann *et al.*, 2015a). The constant juggling, (re)prioritizing and contesting of needs was a dominant theme, as was the interesting (and somewhat problematic) identity of managers in the service. On the one hand, *management* had more power and traction here than it might have in, say, a hospital in terms of the well-known issue of weakly qualified general managers trying to micromanage highly trained, motivated and autonomous professionals (Mintzberg, 1998). This was partly because of the relatively low prestige of ambulance services in the medical professions hierarchy. On the other hand, managers were often experienced ambulance service personnel who had worked long years out on the road or in control centres, wanted to keep their clinician identity, and were anxious to avoid being pigeon-holed as 'management' – just as we have seen among the acute trust nurses. Moreover, the emergency-focused culture of the organization meant that front-line employees would sometimes be critical of managers and would try to assert their own authority and identity as clinicians, using their own discretion and common sense based on working semi-independently *out on the road* and away from management intervention.

The chapter begins by providing a brief overview of the historical and contemporary backdrop to UK ambulance services in order to contextualize what CCAS does, the problems it faces, and how it is trying to adapt and modernize to face increasingly complex and challenging environments. We then move on to explore, using our observation field notes and interview data, precisely what junior and middle managers in CCAS did, how and why they did it, and how they felt about it. We explore their roles and behaviours in great detail in order to provide a detailed account of the realities of managerial work in a vital and under-researched organization. It is towards an analysis of the background to the trust that we first turn.

Ambulance trust background

Ambulance services in the UK (as well as ambulance services in other countries, such as Australia, that are based largely on the US-derived *rapid response* model) have traditionally occupied a rather marginal status in relation to the core organizations and professions of medicine (e.g. hospitals, nurses, physicians). The emphasis in ambulance services based on an Emergency Medical Services (EMS) model has traditionally been on rapid response, basic life support and transportation to 'definitive care', rather than medical treatment on the scene. Ambulance services historically emerged from military settings, which instituted the practice of urgently evacuating casualties as quickly as possible to more advanced clinical settings. The most well-known example of this process is probably the rapid transport of casualties to the US Army's former MASH units (Mobile Army Surgical Hospitals), as popularized in the iconic TV series (Caroline, 2008; Vuic, 2009: 32). Donald Metz (1981), in an early ethnography of ambulance work in the USA, described how in the everyday urban setting, the model was traditionally one of speedy collection, assessment and transportation of patients with strictly limited amounts of clinical care being delivered by responding crews. Practically speaking, a large part of the work under this traditional model was about preparing the patient for arrival at definitive care – i.e. a hospital. The blue symbol of the Star of Life originated from the US Department of Transportation as an international marker of ambulance services and contains six points: 'Detection, Reporting, Response, On Scene Care, Care in Transit, and Transfer to Definitive Care' (US Department of Transportation, 1995). This implies that the clinical scope of EMS crews traditionally does not extend much beyond calming down and *managing* the patient, learning basic details about what the illness or injury is, taking a patient history where possible, immobilizing the patient if necessary, cleaning and bandaging any wounds, taking basic measurements such as blood pressure and oxygen saturation, all so that the patient is then *packaged up* ready for *presentation* to the core medical professionals – the doctors and nurses at hospital emergency departments (Metz, 1981).

Historically, ambulance responders received somewhat rudimentary training and low pay (Kilner, 2004; McCann *et al.*, 2013; Metz, 1981), and ambulance trusts have not had a clinical research culture because their work and professional scope has essentially been defined for them by more senior clinical professions. In the UK, paramedics were widely referred to as *ambulancemen* or even *ambulance drivers* – terms that still circulate among the general public today and the mistaken use of which tends to annoy today's paramedics and Emergency Care Assistants (see Brent, 2010: 13). As one of our interviewees, a senior HR manager at CCAS, explained about prior practice: '*We used to hire van drivers*'. Indeed, pay for ambulance staff was traditionally so inadequate that many used to 'moonlight' on other jobs on break days to supplement their pay. Ambulance workers have traditionally been heavily unionized, and ambulance trusts have a legacy of a uniformed culture with low levels of trust between road staff and management. This has often been manifested in a *blame culture* when care episodes go wrong, and a *them and us* culture in relation to front-line staff versus managers.

For at least the last 15 years, a management-driven *hit the targets* culture has dominated ambulance services – a culture that is typically resented by paramedics as not genuinely patient focused. Indeed, it is seen as an impediment to the development of a genuine medical culture and more highly trained clinical roles for ambulance responders (McCann *et al.*, 2013). Research on the work culture of ambulance services is fairly limited and has often highlighted troublesome relationships between line management and front-line paramedics (Boyle, 2002; McCann *et al.*, 2013; Metz, 1981; Tangherlini, 1998, 2000; Wankhade, 2012). An official report into a failed adoption of a new IT system at London Ambulance Service, for example, blamed some of the failings on 'a climate of mistrust and obstructivism' (South West Thames Regional Health Authority, 1993: 3).

Although working relationships may have improved to some extent with the gradual upskilling and 'professionalization' of paramedics since the early 1990s (McCann *et al.*, 2013), a somewhat hostile industrial relations climate has tended to persist in UK ambulance trusts. Pay remains low with paramedics on NHS Agenda for Change starting salaries, being (at the time of writing) on Band 5 (£21,000–£28,000) with little room to move above this – unlike other professions, such as nursing, which also starts at Band 5 but where it is possible to rise through Bands 7 to 9 (£30,000–£98,453). New ambulance service roles have been introduced, such as Critical Care Paramedic and Paramedic Practitioner (at Band 6), but these roles are in short supply and highly sought after. Ambulance clinicians face either continuing in a Band 5 paramedic role until retirement or moving up into management roles, which many find unattractive. The last major work stoppage by ambulance staff represented by COHSE (a predecessor of Unison) was back in 1989 (Kerr and Sachdev, 1991); and more recently, ambulance staff represented by Unison took part in strikes and demonstrations as part of the TUC's *anti-austerity* industrial action of 30 November, 2011. As we see below, many CCAS managers spoke of the intense difficulties of handling certain staff and occasional breakdowns of trust and communication. Discourses about a deep rift between road staff and managers who have *lost touch with the realities of the road* circulated widely at CCAS, and such war stories were part of the organizational folklore (Orr, 1996; Tangherlini, 1998, 2000).

Though widespread, this discourse was only partially accurate and often seemed unfair on management. Many of the junior and middle managers we interviewed and observed at CCAS were, like the nurse managers and midwife managers at the acute trust, often close to or on the front line. Many at CCAS remained registered paramedics who would at times attend serious and complicated emergency scenes in uniform in rapid response vehicles. In a fascinating example of the kind of unexpected development that can emerge from target-based cultures, if the organization looked likely to miss its monthly objective on response times, CCAS would put managers in uniform and back on the road in order to '*blitz the target*' for a short period. Many of the managers enjoyed this, as they got to do some '*real work back out on the road*', and some of the front-line paramedics and technicians without management responsibility also respected this in that '*the managers*' are '*finally doing something useful*'.

This hands-on element to managing was quite common in the service with large proportions of the managerial staff at CCAS being former road staff with little career experience outside of the ambulance service and little formal management training. The boots on the ground, rapid response *feel* of managerial work at CCAS strongly reflected its emergency-focused operational culture – it had to deal with things '*as they come in*' and just '*take it on the chin*' when workloads were heavy and intense. Like the paramedics themselves, many of the managers at CCAS perversely seemed to enjoy being '*the last line of defence*' and often told self-deprecating stories about being at the bottom of the heap in the NHS hierarchy (and the lowest status in the emergency services).

Despite the mistrust, conflict and gallows humour, the traditional model of emergency ambulance care has been changing toward something more sophisticated and professionalized. The old EMS-derived *scoop and run* model of taking the patient to the hospital has been changing amid an all-graduate intake for paramedics and a national drive towards increasing the scope of practice of emergency crews. A new practice of *bringing the hospital to the patient* has been nationally supported; theoretically, a reversal of the traditional emergency care model, which emphasizes rapid response, basic care and transfer to hospital. The sheer scale of unnecessary ambulance transfers is one reason why hospital trusts have such overloaded emergency departments. The thinking behind bringing care to the patient was to allow ambulance responders more leeway to treat and refer on-scene and thus obviate the need for hospital transportation and admission. In reality, however, this model has been hard to realize; despite the emergence of a professional body, the development of a research base in the field of pre-hospital medicine and graduate-only intake for new paramedics, the professional status of paramedics remains relatively low in the NHS (McCann *et al.*, 2013). Many argue that insufficient training and a lack of management support prevents them from taking the additional risk and responsibility of non-conveyance (McCann *et al.*, 2013; O'Hara *et al.*, 2015; Porter *et al.*, 2008).

In addition to providing the emergency 999 response and in keeping with the nine other ambulance trusts in England, CCAS provided a large non-emergency service for transportation of patients to and from scheduled outpatient appointments (often in hospitals but increasingly in specialist treatment centres such as renal centres). While emergency response was clearly the more visible and better-known part of CCAS operations, planned care was also a major part of the service and an important source of income to the trust. Non-emergency patient transport provided a vital service to patients who had few or no means of travel to and from appointments, which were often regular (perhaps weekly) treatments.

Based on our field notes, CCAS was, at the time of our research, contracted to undertake emergency and planned transportation of patients for a combined annual total of £250 million. This contract was negotiated centrally by a primary care trust which acted as the *lead commissioner*; in effect, a sole customer which acted on behalf of the hundreds of thousands of possible organizations and members of the public who may at one time require unplanned emergency care. The planned care contracts added up to around £60 million and all were negotiated separately with individual contracts from across primary care providers in the region – a total of 79 individual contracts. One immediate issue following the Health and Social Care Act 2012 was that CCAS was nearing the end of the negotiations to make one new contract for the next three years across all the primary care trusts. Instead, it had to be put on hold as the primary care trusts were scheduled to close in 2013. CCAS was forced to redraw the contract to one year, waiting to see how the system changed before negotiating a wide array of new contracts with the new care commissioning groups and all the customers who wanted CCAS services. Eventually, a large contract was awarded to a transport company that was a subsidiary of a major multinational corporation. CCAS managers expressed little hope of being able to compete with contractors of this size and power, especially on the non-urgent patient transport side of the business. There were signs of the emergency side of the CCAS operations also being opened up to competition with private sector ambulance vehicles increasingly operating on blue lights and responding to calls on a contract basis to ambulance trusts across the country.

Similar to the other case studies in this book, CCAS faced severe and growing financial pressures. It also tried repeatedly to gain foundation trust status. CCAS was an extremely important NHS organization that operated within the network of dozens of other NHS and local authority care providers in the region. In so doing, it functioned within a kind of inter-organizational web that connected many disparate parts of the regional health economy. In the CCAS region during the time of our research, there were over 40 local authorities and over 60 NHS organizations (comprising e.g. 20-plus acute trusts operating over 50 main hospital sites, 20-plus primary care trusts, 9 mental health trusts). Although CCAS connected with all of these organizations, sometimes the interactions were fraught with conflict. As noted, ambulance services, when compared to the other professions of the NHS, are substantially under-researched. Paramedics and Emergency Medical Technicians (EMTs) appear almost nowhere in the sociology of professions literature; the service enjoys weak levels of political advocacy and is probably the NHS service most abused by patients in terms of needless callouts. On the other hand, it enjoys considerable public interest with *reality TV* documentary series about ambulance services aired frequently, and some highly popular books based on workers' experiences. The *Blood, Sweat and Tea* books (Reynolds, 2006, 2009, 2010) have been particularly popular, based originally on a somewhat controversial blog by Tom Reynolds (the pen name of a London Ambulance Service EMT).

Early in our research, we came across a similar kind of writing. We were given a heartfelt complaint and plea from a recently retired CCAS paramedic who wrote a six-page letter to the then chief executive expressing his deep dismay about how the organization was being run. Below we include a few excerpts:

> *I have been an employee of the ambulance service for the past 38 years and I do feel that I have a right to inform you of the shambles that we call CCAS and how it is being run. If any major company, employing a large group of individuals like ourselves and responsible for the welfare of such a large community of people, was to operate as we do, they would be out of business and bankrupt. … I would appreciate it if you could take time to read my most comprehensive letter and see the way the service is being run, for everything that I state is the truth. I do believe that your most valuable assets are our road staff, and yet they are regarded almost like cannon fodder in the goal to achieve targets with no consideration for their health and welfare. … It would appear that the computer system does not allow for control managers to use common sense anymore, and therefore a computer is now running the ambulance service and, as a result, chaos prevails. Call prioritizing is a joke, and as a result, control managers never seem to have any spare capacity, i.e. vehicles available, and so we get to a situation where members of the public are waiting (because there are no vehicles available to send) anything up to 50 minutes or maybe longer for an ambulance to arrive. This is unacceptable.*

The issues raised in the letter (and the distinct themes of dedication mixed with exasperation and a hint of militancy) would be instantly recognizable to managers and road staff in ambulance trusts. Work pressure and operational frustrations were endemic in this field. Resource constraints and time famine (Perlow, 1999) bedevilled CCAS. While researching the trust over two and a half years, we often found it hard to arrange interviews simply because CCAS managers were so busy with their existing workloads. Practically everyone we contacted said they were happy to take part in our study, but finding a spare hour proved extremely difficult in most cases and impossible in many. What often happened was that a manager would say that he or she cannot arrange a definite hour for a meeting, so instead they would invite us to their workplace to meet them, observe what they do and maybe catch a few minutes to talk where possible. We took up these invitations readily, resulting in some fascinating, vivid and immediate observational data about the realities of managing in sometimes stressful and often literally life-or-death environments. This severe lack of availability and time was particularly common on the emergency side of the organization, which by definition involved unplanned work where overstretch was common and the peaks and troughs of demand are not always predictable.

Throughout our time with various managers and employees of CCAS, we were constantly impressed with their dedication and effort and sometimes wondered among ourselves how they managed to cope with what was, at times, 'extreme work' (Granter et al., 2015). While emergency crews clearly experienced high risks to physical and mental well-being, many managers were also exposed to high levels of work-related stress. Indeed, many managers were themselves at or near the front line of NHS emergency care, working on ambulance stations and paramedic emergency control centres, facing constant interruptions, and having to attend some of the worst and most complex emergency incidents (such as road traffic accidents where patients are trapped inside vehicles). In addition, they often had to advise and support road staff and, in many cases, take part in investigations (both internally and for external authorities such as the police or coroner) about serious incidents. At times, listening to managers recounting some of these gruelling stories of emergency and planned care incidents, often with barely adequate resources, made researching at CCAS a humbling experience. The picture of middle management at CCAS was far from the tabloid-style attacks on bloated and cosseted public sector 'fat cats'. In certain areas, the organization was in some distress, but workers and managers were highly dedicated and capable of delivering very effective care on a daily basis. Rarely did staff receive positive recognition from the public, from other NHS professionals or from the government.

We chose to explore three groupings of managers in CCAS. The first cluster included managers working in Paramedic Emergency Services (PES), which provided the unplanned emergency care (e.g. 999 call handling, dispatching of ambulances, liaison with hospitals, emergency preparedness). The second was constituted by managers in Planned Care (PC, also known as Patient Transport Services or PTS), which provided scheduled transportation of patients to and from medical appointments. And the third was the Organizational Learning and Development cluster. Part of the HR directorate, this section of CCAS tried to play an important role in the ongoing attempts to change the culture of the organization, primarily by running a wide array of training courses and events. As we shall see, organizational change in such an overstretched and culturally entrenched organization was a considerable challenge. We begin our data analysis with a discussion of the daily responsibilities of managers across these three clusters.

'Anything we can do to secure the contract': what ambulance trust managers do

One of the most immediate findings was that the middle managers interviewed from the PES and PC were largely involved in managing people. A significant amount of their time involved handling staff rotas, accounting in minute detail for the hours worked and jobs completed of crews on the road, and attempting to make cost savings wherever possible. It was often a difficult task to cover all the patients and areas for which they were mandated, and much time was spent juggling crews and vehicles to cover sickness absence, vacancies, mechanical breakdowns and vehicles requiring cleaning as well as coping with a large number of legacy issues inherited from the large-scale merger of 2006. Managers in Organizational Learning and Development (OL&D), by comparison, had fewer people management issues to deal with. Their roles were more to do with handling projects and initiatives – providing more of an overview of policy changes, encouraging many other managers to develop and change their opinions and behaviours.

Neil, an operations manager in Planned Care, was a particularly useful source of information about the kinds of task involving managing people. Below he explains his span of control and the tasks his job entails:

> [I have] *four CSM's* [customer services managers] *reporting to me and 110 road staff across the north, central, south and 24-hour services. Primary responsibilities are ensuring we have sufficient resources out on the road, we're meeting our rota requirements, we're doing that within budget … resource – both staffing and vehicles are available to us. Monitoring and managing sickness within defined parameters so our sickness at 5 per cent or what have you … offering support, advice and guidance to customer support managers … liaison with the hospitals; dealing with complaints, queries from patients, carers, hospital trusts … investigating…*
>
> *From our point of view, our responsibility is to ensure that we have a rota which is fully staffed, and we aim to put out 98 per cent of our staffing resource on a weekly basis.*

He explained that he was in direct individual contact with the four CSMs that report to him on a weekly basis and monthly as a team. CSMs are based around the region, mostly at hospital sites and some at ambulance stations. Organizing rotas and handling absences, family-friendly policies and sickness would form just part of these meetings. An impression was gained of managers having to continually juggle resources (human, financial and physical) in order to keep to CCAS's contractual obligations.

In keeping with all of the case studies, managing sickness absence was an important issue for junior and middle managers in the ambulance service. Once again, clear and strict procedures (including targets) had been put in place with the aim of aiding managers in dealing with this often difficult and contentious issue. Targets were in place to monitor resource usage, and cases of staff being frequently absent were '*escalated through the management structure*', as Neil explained:

> *Within our Key Performance Indicators we have a target around our resource at 98 per cent. One around our annual leave … no more than 15 per cent of our resource off at any point in time on annual leave. And the sickness is less than 5 per cent. We're working to 5 per cent or less as a sickness target. So that's what we're working to … from a service point of view, I think that is something that we are becoming stricter with. … [B]ecause obviously on the other side of that, the disciplinary route if you like. So, people at the point at which they have three periods of sick within a 12-month period, they will get a stage one sickness disciplinary, sickness hearing … a further one will trigger a stage two disciplinary hearing … those are escalated through the management structure. So, the customer support manager will do the stage one hearing. Stage two would be myself and HR. Stage three would be onto either [names senior managers in the service].*

Sickness absence was a serious matter in CCAS. Injuries from carrying and moving patients in cramped or awkward spaces were especially common in both the PES and PC road operations, leading to a lot of difficult long-term and recurring problems such as back strain. In interviewing and observing one of Neil's direct reports at work – a CSM called Amanda – we learnt more about how these issues manifest themselves at ground level. A day observing Amanda and her colleagues revealed seemingly ever-present staff and vehicle absences, amid an increasingly complex and ever more demanding caseload of patients to transport to and from a wider range of locations. In the following field note, the researcher is in Amanda's very small office with Darren, another manager, in a corner of a major city-centre hospital:

> We are in a small room, with no windows, and walls painted yellow. The room is cramped, probably about 4ft by 10ft, with two desks along one wall and with very small desktops and monitors. The desks are squeezed in between several filing cabinets containing manual records. There is a noticeboard above the desks with lots of paper pinned to it, including a document displaying 'the CCAS Wheel' which looks remarkably similar to the Millford Trust Wheel [a diagram of strategic goals stated in general terms]. On the right-hand wall, someone has stuck drawings of three birds, mimicking the kitsch household ornament of a trio of Mallard ducks flying up the wall. Only these look like seagulls. Each has a speech bubble. One says 'I miss Amanda', the next, 'So do I' and the trailing bird, 'Who is Amanda?' It is hot in this room. The electric fan blowing the whole time fails to offset the stifling heat.

> [O]ther bits of paper stuck to the wall include sheets of phone numbers for NHS organizations, all over the place, including several outside the CCAS regional area. There is a sheet explaining details about different kinds of child seat that can be used in the various vehicles. I read a handwritten sheet that contains the following info:

> **Study day 1** M/ Handling, Vul adults, Paperwork IRFs, Litigation, Scene Management of an Incident

> **Study day 2** BLS and o2, Communication, Prepare for new tech, Airwaves

> Another document contains information about infection control procedures. There is a WH Smith monthly calendar with all the days crossed off until today. On the PC keyboard in front of me is an incredibly old plastic ruler which has somehow survived – it is from British Rail and British Transport Police and has a picture of the 125 train on it, the pride of what was the state monopoly rail fleet. One carriage has text on it reading 'I've been train trained'. The other says 'I'm aware that I must take care'. I am struck by how the endless trivia and sloganeering I've seen all over NHS organizations is by no means exclusively an NHS thing and is not necessarily new; this looks very mid 1980s …

> Amanda and Darren, in green ambulance uniforms, are sat close together hunched over computer keyboards and paperwork, deep in administrative chores. They are working through overtime spreadsheets. Amanda picks up the phone: 'Frank, it's Amanda. Have you got the mileage from last week? Are you driving? Can you pull over and

give me your mileage? I don't need the forms, just the figures now is fine. 147? Ok, thanks. She puts this number into the spreadsheet and turns to me to explain what they're doing:

'I'm doing all the figures from last week's work. I've got last week's rota [a printout from Excel], *which has everyone's hours that they're supposed to have done and then this, the OCT240, which records what actually happened. Things run over; people move into unplanned overtime. Doing all this is standard for Monday mornings. We no longer hold the budget for taxis, so doing it has got a bit easier. One frustrating thing is that we do duplicate some paperwork. Having filled in the OCT240, we then have to upload it to the Dashboard Tool. So it's duplication, from Excel onto the dashboard.'*

As the intranet is accessed, there is a bit of a wait. Amanda says 'the computer's on a go-slow'. Darren: 'the IT is slow – it's a nightmare. It's connecting to a remote server.' The details from OCT240 are then manually entered into the intranet dashboard tool. It is a process of Amanda reading down through the names and numbers of the OCT240 using a ruler and calling out names and numbers to Darren who taps them in. So that's what the rulers are for.

The extensive use of manual and ITC systems, dashboards and numbers/targets was time-intensive and seemingly rather alienating work for managers for it took them away from people management, task management and front-line interaction with patients. Karen, a supervisor in charge of scheduling Planned Care journeys, explained:

What concerns me is the way we treat patients now – it's like they want them to be treated like we're transporting boxes. Patient care has gone out of the window. There's so many people to transport, so much to do; the human element gets lost. You have to make recommendations in your report – more money!

Why did 'they' – the senior managers – want the staff to treat patients like 'boxes'? It seemed to come down to cost control. Like all public sector organizations, the trust was constantly striving to extract maximum utility from its assets and to demonstrate cost effectiveness and transparency while meeting a wide range of reporting commitments. If CCAS was unable to do this, it ran the risk of losing some of its care contracts to private sector competitors eager to move in on its former monopoly territory. On top of that, the service was also compelled by changing government policy to attempt to deliver a wider, more efficient and more diverse and flexible service. Karen gave us a clear overview:

'Postcodes fit into either "north" or "south", and from there, I can schedule them to appointments anywhere in the country', *explains Karen. Obviously most of them are* [City] *hospitals, and I recognize many of the abbreviated places on her computer screen. The display shows that she has 73 inbound patient journeys in 'north' region to sort out for tomorrow. But there's 'south' also. So in total for tomorrow she's got 139 inbound trips and 141 outbound trips to organize. 'The vehicles can take three patients at a time. So I have to juggle around and try to work out how to do this in the most efficient way. I currently have 18 wheelchairs; these take up more space on the vehicles. Sometimes, it's a strangling day.'* [She makes a gesture of having hanged herself; head to one side, tongue hanging out].

'Is this normal?' I ask. *'140 trips?'*

'Yes, it is. The load has grown steadily in recent years, but we don't have an increase in resources to cope … it's also complicated by more power being given to patients.'

'What do you mean?'

'They have much more choice about where to go these days, and that can mean going much further away than simply your closest hospital. People chose to go to some quite faraway places and that means bigger distances to travel. Choose and Book does mean a better service for the patient, but it makes life harder for us. We have set higher standards, but then these standards are not achievable. Let's say you've got five patients in north, they might all chose to go to four or five different places rather than just around the corner, so I might have to put them in four or five separate vehicles. The service hasn't expanded to cope. At times, I'm down on vehicles too for repairs or cleaning, or down on crews with sick leave or whatever'.

She has a piece of paper stuck to the side of the monitor showing today's 20 crews. Four have lines through them.

'I'm four down today – sickness mostly. There's always long-term sick, maternity leave, and often vacancies. The other day, I had four for north and four for south, so just eight vehicles. Also there used to be a cut-off point whereby if you've not booked in your journey by 2 p.m., there's a cut-off and you're moved to next day's scheduling. But now I'm taking bookings up 'til 6 p.m. Anything we can do to secure the contract is good for us, but then we have to make the best of it'.

'*Anything we can do to secure the contract.*' Such talk was common throughout the study. Managers were acutely aware of the need to make their service as attractive as possible in the face of increasing competition. Yet the promises being made could not always be achieved easily, or even at all.

On the PES side, pressures associated with resource overstretch, incomplete information, and physical and emotional exhaustion were intensified by the unplanned nature of the managerial work. Their work sometimes involved life-threatening accidents and medical emergencies, so the consequences of errors, bottlenecks, information failures and delays were potentially calamitous. Their work, like that of the operational road staff on the ambulances and rapid response vehicles, was becoming ever more complicated and demanding. The volume of callouts continued to rise year on year amid an emergency and unplanned care system that often defaulted to ambulance callouts simply because no other service was available. This was taking place on top of new initiatives designed to increase the capacity of the service in the realm of *emergency preparedness* and *resilience* in the face of the seemingly growing risk of *mass casualty incidents*, such as acts of terrorism or disease pandemics. The organization was struggling to adapt while also keeping itself going.

Like their Planned Care colleagues, managers in PES also had to cope with substantial volumes of paperwork, dealing with a large and growing burden of information collection, interpretation and reporting, sometimes (to use the words of one former PES operations manager) '*at the eleventh hour*'. This was coupled with the need to explain what had happened out on the road and in the office, to be accountable, to produce narratives for various auditing bodies. Indeed, the managerial workload for many PES managers seemed to border on the 'extreme work' end of the spectrum (Granter *et al.*, 2015). One operations manager moved from PES to Planned Care partly because the intensity of PES managerial work had become extremely burdensome, mentioning in particular the demands of being on call for one 24-hour period per week on top of the normal working week:

> *I was probably the unluckiest manager. All sorts of incidents really. It ranged from, say, medical gas incidents to large-scale RTAs or RTCs, which [is what] we call road traffic accidents. The first time on call, at 9 p.m. in the evening [I get a call]: 'Naomi I think you better go out to this' … it was an RTA with an ambulance and a car and the car ended up in someone's front garden. So you get called out for lots of incidents. Some that you can deal with quite quickly, but in the main if you're called out, you're probably three or four hours in the minimum, and if there's paperwork needs doing … you know, statements off staff, etcetera. I've worked all day, been on call, been called out and then met my senior managers … with part of the investigation, part of what's gone on.*

PES managers also had to liaise frequently with local hospitals regarding delays in handing over patients. This could involve issues such as low bed capacity and knock-on problems where ambulance crews had to wait at emergency departments with their patients on trolleys. Sometimes this would tie up emergency ambulance crews for 30 to 40 minutes or more when they were supposed to be *clear* and back out on the road ready to respond to the next emergency call. Many managers were exasperated by the ways in which the ambulance service seemed to have little power to influence other parts of the NHS health economy. This seemed to replicate a broader occupational culture issue in ambulance services whereby front-line crews and middle managers felt they were at the bottom of the heap of the NHS hierarchy. This engendered a somewhat hostile approach to management in general, reminiscent of classical conflict-ridden British industrial relations in which grievance proceedings (or their threat) were common.

While low morale was understandable, complaints and conflict were read by some in the trust as a tactic for weaker and '*disengaged*' staff to try to mask their poor performance. Pressure, conflict and behavioural issues kept the OL&D team very busy at CCAS. Below, a manager, Tara, explains the them and us culture that was endemic in ambulance services. Interestingly she linked this culture to what she perceived as broader failures of middle and senior managers to adequately manage the performance of those staff who were 'crap':

> It winds me up actually – anyone who says 'it's crap here'. Well, leave. Go and get another job. See how long you last in the private sector with that attitude … honestly, it boils my blood 'coz I just think, 'You've been here 20 years. Why don't you just go somewhere else?' 'Oh, well, I'm not going anywhere' and 'I've got a right to be here'. Yeah, of course you have, but we've got a right to say, 'Well you need to meet the standard of working practices and you need to be able to do … '. As well … it's quite scary going into stations … you go into a station, you are met with suspicion and 'Why are you here?' and 'What are you looking at?' I feel quite disappointed about that side of it. But it is clearly not managed well. I had an incident where I went to a station and I was sat in one of the chairs just talking to somebody and they did not like the fact that a manager [was there]… they didn't even know who I was, but a manager or what they perceived as a manager … This guy came in and he threw his keys on the table, and he went, 'Oh!' and stormed out in this big huff, and I was just like, 'What's wrong with him?' Completely oblivious. 'Oh, it's probably 'cause, you know, you're sat here and it's … it's our room! We can't come back here. How are we supposed to come back and have a rest if you're sat in it having a meeting about work?' And it's like, 'This is our away-from-the-office-type approach'. And I was absolutely horrified. And the manager did not deal with it at all. I actually said to the manager, 'Why have you not dealt with that?' 'Oh, it's him. He's always been like that.' Now I'm sorry! That was very intimidating, and I felt like putting a grievance in myself! You know, I was like, 'I'm going to put a grievance in!' Just playing them at their own game! [Laughs.] But I didn't. But I was really, really disappointed about how it was all handled. And we've got that going on at senior level. … I witnessed a conversation going on the other day with the chief exec. – a couple of, you know, senior managers, and somebody made a flippant comment about, 'Oh. Oh it's him. He's always been crap.' And one of the directors turned round and said: 'Well you used to manage him for six years didn't you? So why is he … why have you not dealt with that?' 'Oh well he's always been like that.' And that's exactly the attitude that we've got to try and change. Actually, that's not good enough, you know? You need to manage it. So … that's what I feel my role is. To kind of re-educate! [Laughs.] You've got every right to say: 'You are crap. You are not …' you know, 'you need to improve or get out'. But it's a massive shift from what they're used to, you know, where it's just 'put up'. And it's accepted.

People management issues were difficult as many staff were overloaded, conflict was common and morale often low, as reflected in ambulance trusts' typically poor scores on national NHS staff satisfaction surveys (McCann et al., 2015a). Managers in CCAS had wide spans of responsibility and in many cases very wide spans of control. The work itself was becoming increasingly complex and demanding, and it sometimes wasn't possible for CCAS managers to meet all the demands made of them. The demands of the emergency response targets were so great that other targets (such as staff training, career development or performance management) often '*fell by the wayside*'. Information demands were growing in their intensity, and IT systems weren't always adequate for the job.

Given this context, the next section explores how these managers behaved under such trying conditions. What emerges are distinct coping strategies of using informal means to prioritize work though a tough-minded dedication to duty and appeals to traditional forms of identity. These forms of behaviour took place amid a culture that was under substantial pressure to change, but the direction of change was unclear and contested. For many managers cultural change was proceeding frustratingly slowly, yet the *traditional*, uniformed, *patient care before business* culture also possessed some elements that could be mobilized by managers as they navigated the tricky pathways of their management duties.

Management behaviours: how do managers handle their workloads?

Chronic shortages were a fact of life for junior and middle managers in CCAS. Managers, many of them retaining front-line duties, tried to find time to attend staff training and development but got used to being *knocked back* or refused to go to other sessions which appeared to offer little or no value. While staff development events were advertised widely, sometimes they were impossible to attend due to the demands of keeping rosters fully staffed and with the aim of hitting service targets. Many middle-level managers were studying part-time for additional qualifications in the hope of career advancement. They frequently complained about operational blockages and failures in co-ordination between NHS organizations (such as hospitals) and private sector providers (such as independent urgent care centres). Management staff were encouraged in training events to look for creative ways to get around blockages and delays. Clinical team leaders told stories of their struggles to get themselves and their road staff together at the same time in order to complete various management duties such as performance management or appraisals. Occasionally such stories morphed into complaints about senior management, who were often described as not prioritizing training. Instead, meeting the targets was the dominant priority and innovations emanating from the ground floor were often disregarded, as these notes from a reviewer training day suggest:

> *Simon mentions the idea that people on his station had to set aside a specific training vehicle to use for clinical training. 'But this was pooh-poohed. Our idea was just bombed out by management. It's now a core vehicle on the roster for callouts.'*

Inadequate resources time and again prevented CCAS operators and managers from making improvements they might want to – which exacerbated the them and us culture. Control managers, especially, were often perceived by road staff as having little real contact with the *realities* of the road. However, from the point of view of control staff, the problems they faced were also clearly visible. We observed the daily work of managers in two of CCAS's three Paramedic Emergency Control centres and this extract from our field notes describes the scene at one of them:

The next building along has a blue and white sign on the front which looks like an NHS logo. This can't be it, surely? Then I notice aerials and a radio mast mounted on the roof, so I guess it must be. Sure enough, as I get closer I can read the sign – Paramedic Emergency Control Centre. It is a grotty-looking old brown brick building. Two storeys, an A/C unit mounted on the outside. There is a tiny car park, which is jammed with small cars – Ford Ka, Toyota Yaris, Peugeot 106. A couple of cars are sat on the pavement amid the slush and dirty snow. A few staff arrive and buzz themselves in through the garage gate. A group of young kids wander by. It feels a million miles away from the plush HQ. … We sit outside in a corridor for a while where we notice two little orange signs that read:

The Area is currently operating at Level 4	The Trust is currently operating at Level 4

The duty manager mentions that the recent freezing weather has been a major challenge. He says he's driven 500 miles in the last few days, going around in a Nissan Navara picking up staff to bring them into work because the conditions have been so awful. He's been out all night driving around – 3 a.m., 4 a.m. I mention the volunteer mountain rescue guys I saw on the news and he says: 'They were here yesterday looking to see if we've got any fuel. They've been great.' He mentions the 4×4 Skoda Octavia RRVs have been surprisingly good on the icy roads.

The little reception office is quite messy – lots of boxes and files lying around. No one seems to have the time to file anything away. Eventually Bill comes back with three headsets and he starts to explain how the place works. He ushers us through a door and into a large garage area. A couple of ambulances and a few response cars are parked inside. Bill shows us where the fire exits, mess room and toilets are. There are a couple of drinks machines and a snack vending machine. Recharging power lines hang from the ceiling. On the far side of the garage are a few steps up to a keypad-controlled door that leads into the control centre proper.

Once inside, the place looks and feels much newer and cleaner and actually seems quite a nice working environment, probably built from scratch as an addition to the old ambulance station. I'm lucky enough never to have worked in a call centre, but I had a decent idea of what one looked like – rows of desks with computer screens, operators with headsets and large wall-mounted TV screens displaying operational performance stats. It's just as I've seen on TV news and read about in sociologies of call centre work. Except that it's very small. Each of us is struck by how few people seem to be working here. Bill explains that the centre is split in two with the left side working on inbound calls and dispatch on the right. There's about 20 people handling inbound calls and probably around 12 on vehicle dispatch. The workstations in the dispatch section seem completely occupied. About four workstations in the inbound section are empty. Despite the dreadful weather, the atmosphere is calm amid the busyness. Several staff throughout the day mention that it could get much worse than this and that 'we're quite well staffed today'.

Bill explains that this control centre covers the whole of [City] – well over a million population. It seems very 'lean' to me. He has rustled up three spare headsets for us. He also grabs something from a nearby table – it's a set of plastic cards that connect together in a manual tree of knowledge. He explains that, in theory, every emergency call scenario can be worked through via these cards, which are exactly the same as the on-screen prompts. This serves as the script for the call handler to follow. It is immensely detailed – probably about 30 initial entry points, which then cascade via decision trees. They cover a bewildering array of possibilities: cardiac arrests, drownings, RTCs, hangings, sinking vehicles, burnings, electrocutions, falls, etc.

We're told that they usually receive about 1,000 calls a day, of which up to four-fifths will be unplanned emergency (999) calls; the remainder will relate to planned episodes such as patient transfers. He says that things have been incredibly busy over the Christmas period, and on Boxing Day they received 1,400 calls.

I listen in on a call: a female who has fallen on the ice and has a suspected leg fracture. It all happened pretty fast – the whole call I'm guessing maybe 90 seconds. Sharon [a manager] explains that the decision tree takes this as a green call – i.e. not life-threatening – but she escalated it to amber (19 minutes target response) as the patient is lying on the ice and obviously in distress. She shows me on her right-hand screen that the dispatch has gone through and there is an ambulance on the way – the vehicle shows up as a little box with numbers (presumably its radio call sign) moving down the road. 'They'll probably turn off here and go down the dual carriageway here.' That's exactly what happens: we watch the little numbers-box make that turn and head down in that direction. From this vantage point, I'm impressed by how efficient the service seems to be. … Throughout the time we were there, there was a zero in the top-right window of the targets screen, meaning that no emergency calls were stacking, so it seemed to be working well. 'That is the only number on the screen that matters', she said.

Our observations included spending time at another emergency control centre site, during which one of the authors accompanied Paul, a middle manager responsible for co-ordinating emergency ambulance response across a diverse area that encompassed two counties and hundreds of thousands of people. Paul's role was senior middle management and carried wide responsibility. In what follows, and in contrast to the excerpt above, the reader gets more of a feel for the intensity and high stakes of the work as the level of management responsibility rises with seniority:

> *Large LCD screens are mounted on the walls of the dispatch room showing statistics on call handling performance targets in real time. Paul, like those around him, uses a number of advanced computer systems to monitor staff performance, ambulance response times, and a range of other metrics; he switches regularly between different screens. ... The phone rings approximately every 120 seconds. When not on the phone, Paul is walking around the office helping colleagues with their decision-making choices and offering encouragement. At 10.23, Paul is dealing with ten vehicles off the road due to mechanical faults; at 10.24, possible criminal proceedings against an ambulance crew; and at 10.25, conflict between ambulance crews and hospital staff. Throughout the day, disjointed accounts come over the airwaves and on the computer system of a 'double fatal' car accident. At around 10.30, Paul notes that 'it's starting to build up'.*

> *In the time we have to discuss organizational issues, Paul says that change has been 'non-stop' since the trust was reconfigured in a merger some years ago. ... At 10:40, I ask him to place this level of work intensity on a scale of 1–10, and I am surprised to find that we have reached only 5 or 6. Something appears on Paul's screen which catches his attention: a junior colleague is dealing with a case where a doctor has apparently called in an MI (myocardial infarction) and then left the scene. 'Fucking hell!' ... He offers guidance to this colleague. Someone needs to go to [city] and there is no one to take them. Elsewhere, a situation is developing which may call for the air ambulance to be scrambled.*

> *By 11.45 ... Paul no longer has time to walk across the room to talk to a colleague, so he phones her instead. Throughout, Paul remains calm and professional, and tells each person he's called to 'have a nice day'. Still, the intensity level has risen to 7/10 Paul tells me, unprompted. ... Someone is trapped and injured in their car but the ambulance is struggling to reach them because of ice. Elsewhere there are reports of a member of the public hit by a train. Another patient is caught in an industrial saw. By now, when Paul puts the phone back on the hook to make another call, it immediately rings with an incoming call. While he is on the phone, a junior colleague approaches his desk and asks about overtime. ... By 14.10, Paul tells me that the intensity level has reached 9/10, but 'sometimes we go up to 11!'*

While gallows humour was often prominent and was perhaps a coping mechanism, the seriousness of the managerial work had to be '*shelved*' in one's mind; according to Bill, '*it's playing God to some extent*', but you just have to make that decision:

> *Bill goes on to describe how decisions are taken: 'Usually you go with whoever's nearest the scene, but sometimes you've got situations where there are two crews equidistant, where there's always something for them to do, and you just have to make that decision, which is the more urgent? One is a cut leg; one is a red call. It's playing God to some extent, but you just have to make the best decision that you think.'*

Workplace duties for operational managers, rather than control centre managers, took them closer to the emergencies and the crews who responded to them. Naomi, an operations manager, joined the ambulance service aged 18 under what was the Ambulance Cadet programme. At the time of the interview, she had built up 27 years of experience in the service. She had recently moved away from PES to Planned Care and, reading her story, one can easily see why as the demands of the PES job seemed potentially overwhelming. Hers is another example of a manager who is working very close to the front line, handling a wide array of operational and people management issues, accounting for costs and tasks, and investigating incidents in a stressful and emotionally demanding environment. Negative media accounts about public sector managers who *have it easy* seemed far removed from this kind of working reality. She mentioned that she was '*the only real-time manager for 150 staff*'. She provided a rundown of the multitude of stressful things she had had to deal with in this post:

NAOMI: *I did find the PES job stressful because I was the only real-time manager for the 150 staff – high workload – senior managers requesting detailed information at the 'eleventh hour' – responding to emergencies. There is a big time lapse since putting clinical knowledge into practice and no time for refresher training, and this is not put as a priority by senior managers. Resource issues are created by high levels of staff sickness – for example, there was a long-term sickness of* [an] *administration officer for our group.* [You're] *constantly required to attend A&E departments due to delays for ambulance staff as A&E departments are 'full', you're told. Even with good planning of your day's work, it would be constantly interrupted by demands of Paramedic Emergency Control and PES Staff – you know, attend incidents, deal with staff issues, station issues, liaison required.*

INTERVIEWER: *Roughly speaking, how many hours per week do you tend to work?*

NAOMI: *At PES, I'd say ten hours at least per day and sometimes six to eight hours at* [the] *weekend. This would be four to six hours taking work home which needed concentration to complete because while at work, there were constant interruptions.*

Bear in mind that these 150 staff were paramedics and EMTs who deal with some of the most stressful and exhausting work done in the whole of the NHS. This is a working population with a history of troublesome industrial relations with management. Some managers had very wide spans of control in this complex and high-stakes field. The workloads were so heavy that it was common to come across staff in managerial roles who could not find time to do the *management* work, because of the immediacy and unpredictability of front-line demands.

The following observed discussion, at a reviewer training day at CCAS HQ, highlighted this issue. This session was run by the OL&D team and was intended to encourage junior managers to find ways to complete the performance appraisal and staff development processes. While friendly and relaxed, a considerable range of practical issues were raised by the front-line team leaders, many of which bordered on *resistance*:

Nathan comes straight out with it, 'I'm a Clinical Team Leader, but I'm not really leading a team. We're all out all the time on two-man crews. Really, I'm a paramedic with admin. duties. This won't ever change.' Tara [OL&D manager running the event] says, 'No, it will. Team leaders are the key to sorting this whole organization out. So that you're no longer paramedics with admin. duties. We devolve things like appraisal to the line, and we get it moving. We can then behave as a team.'

Nathan says, 'Yeah, Tara, but we've done that. I'm in the real world. It's not gonna change. It always comes down to pressures. The situation won't change.' Tara replies, 'No, if I thought like that I'd have gone mad! I'd have checked myself into the Priory![1] *[Lots of laughter!] You can't say it will never change.'*

It was most instructive to hear Tara trying to assert that '*[y]ou can't say it will never change*'. From a managerial viewpoint, it must have been disheartening to hear staff having given up on the prospect of organizational improvements. Things can change, but few seemed to expect them to. The demands of the targets culture seemed to consume all available time for staff; both managers and front-line road staff – and of course, the significant population that occupies both identities at various times.

Nevertheless, there were many such training and organizational/career development days, usually run by the OL&D managers, and we were invited to attend several of these. Topics included handling difficult people, commissioning, and Knowledge and Skills Framework (KSF – pay progression rules) reviewer training. These were cancelled from time to time due to small numbers of delegates, but sometimes were attended by anything from 5 to 15 mid-management staff from across CCAS. The following is typical of the kinds of discussion that junior managers often engaged in during such meetings. Again we see a situation in which overstretched staff will essentially chose what they think is *really* essential. This relates to professional norms and registration, while other – typically more management-driven – duties will '*fall by the wayside*' as this extract from the training day illustrates:

SIMON: *The thing is, it's reactive work. It's hard to put new stuff in. In [my former Council-based work in] youth offending, we had ten staff and four shifts, but we had monthly reviews and so you could get round the table together regularly. You can't do this in the ambulance service.*

GARETH: *The demand has gone crazy. It's nowhere near covered as it is.*

RHYS: *You can't maintain this level of demand; the morale will collapse.*

PATRICK: *It already has, yep.*

KEN: *We try to think of what we can actually do. Certain troops won't come in for appraisal – it falls by the wayside. So you split up the crew, try to get it done, but they get sent to a call in [town] and you never get 'em back. But for mandatory training, you do get them to come to that. You do get people on these. Once a year, you make a point of it, with allocated time slots.*

Tara, the manager in OL&D, described herself in an interview as '*a Pollyanna*' and in '*cloud cuckoo land*' with her optimistic efforts to effect organizational and behavioural change. By the end of our research in CCAS, she had, with apparent regret, moved on to another employer in the private sector. In a rather sad conversation we had in a corridor, Tara hinted that the new HR team had '*no time for*' what OL&D was trying to do. She had an uphill task, not to mention a thankless one.

In short, CCAS junior and middle managers demonstrated huge commitment to their operational roles while sharing sometimes deep concerns about how the service was being run. As the next section shows, there was concern about whether this commitment and effort would help them handle current demands and forthcoming changes. In recent years, change has enveloped the organization, and further attempted transformations – some radical – were on the horizon for this ambulance trust.

New organizational forms in the ambulance trust: responding to the challenges of new competition and new policy demands

Although culture change often seemed to proceed at a glacial pace, other forms of organizational and structural change were near constant. This section explores managers' views about the ways in which CCAS was changing and adapting. In managers' discussions of daily work challenges, the ambulance trust was portrayed as threatened by commercial operators that had more flexibility, freedom and financial power than overstretched and under-resourced NHS organizations. The pressures of competition weighed heavily on CCAS, reflected in a well-rehearsed discourse about the imperatives of being able to adapt and respond to them, as witnessed from observation notes from another management training session:

> Ken (PES manager) says: 'We're up against the private sector all the time. We are tendering against so much other stuff out there.'

> One of the Planned Care managers talks about the growth of new specialist centres for renal or oncology that are springing up. At present CCAS Planned Care provides contractual services for patient transfer to and from these centres, but 'they might want to offer private sector transport services of their own, or contract from elsewhere'. The facilitator explains that these providers are called Independent Specialist Treatment Centres and that we now have to think of them as essentially commissioners; they will only commission services from CCAS if the price and the service is right.

> Ken again: 'We don't have a monopoly any more. Who can do it for the best price, best feedback, reliability? We have to be accountable for all that we do.'

> The facilitator puts something up on PowerPoint about 'Challenge Vested Interests'. 'We can't afford to be unresponsive', she says.

> *A range of commercial providers are mentioned – British, European, even South African companies. The facilitator notes that the new government White Paper mentions 'any willing provider' being given the opportunity to bid for care contracts. 'People are dying to get these contracts.'*

> *Ken: 'At the moment, there is no obvious threat to A&E, but a threat is possible in future.'*

The rise of commercial competition was worrisome for CCAS and usually discussed with suspicion. Arguments were regularly made that commercial providers could compete at a national level for contracts, would put financial goals ahead of patient care, and introduce yet further clashing incentives and conflicts of interest into an already complicated environment for service provision. Complaints were made, for example, about a private operator that had won the contract to run the front desk at a hospital that CCAS vehicles often use. This company also ran Independent Specialist Care Centres and their management was putting pressure on NHS crews to take patients to that unit rather than the nearby A&E – something that ambulance crews were hesitant to do because of patient safety concerns (see McCann *et al.*, 2015a). Concerns were also raised as regards the competence of some of the private operators, as this extract from a commissioning training day illustrates:

> *Anne tells a sad story about a particular innovation that went wrong. 'It was there where we had the disaster of the new electronic patient record forms. We trialled it at that hospital and it was a disaster. Paperless PRFs. The project manager cried. There was a lack of research into what was needed. We were running [IT system] and [another IT system] – there were basically four systems running. The one supplied by [major communications multinational] was supposed to be a paperless PRF, but it didn't work with the other three systems.'*

As public service professionals, many CCAS managers were deeply sceptical about the value and logic of private sector intrusion into NHS operations. Their complaints were seemingly a form of attempted resistance to change that they felt was unnecessary and not in the interests of patients or the ambulance service. Other changes driven by central government policy were more substantial in nature and perhaps less opposed in CCAS. However, concerns existed about whether these new developments were a sensible use of government resources. The introduction of new Hazardous Area Response Teams (HARTs) was a major innovation in ambulance services, influenced by a government drive to improve the capacity of ambulance responders to access patients in potentially dangerous scenes (e.g. fires, floods, chemical leaks, large accidents or even terrorism-related CBRN[2] incidents) and to prepare for major crises such as mass casualty accidents. A member of the research team visited one of CCAS's new HART facilities, as the notes from the following observations describe:

After about ten minutes of aimless wandering around the industrial estate, I find a much more modern-looking facility than I was expecting. It looks rather more occupied than the older, more run-down parts of the estate. There is a DHL[3] sorting facility here, and a large HGV is reversing, bleeping noisily. Just across the way is the now-familiar CCAS logo on one of the buildings. It looks very new – I think the place has been open only a few months.

I'm passed through the security gate into a completely full car park and end up outside a door with a buzzer. A friendly staff member takes me inside and says that the manager I am due to meet (Sharon) is in a meeting but will be available soon. We walk upstairs. There are several mounted photographs on the walls of the staircase – posed images of terror attacks and disasters: personnel in murky green pressure suits and gas masks shout instructions into bullhorns; streets are sectioned off with warning tape; an ashen-faced man lies prone on a stretcher, heavily strapped down – he is being evacuated from a building.

We walk into the open-plan office of Emergency Preparedness where I wait for Sharon. I look around a bit. I notice a bookcase with a binder saying 'Civil Nuclear Accident Protocols'. There are two large LCD TV screens. One is switched off; the other shows different views of the facility – different CCTV shots of the car park and entrance, the vehicles in the outer section of the garage. I see on the TV a specialist vehicle I'd not noticed before – a big articulated lorry in CCAS yellow and green; I guess this is some kind of decontamination unit or 'Hazmat truck'. Everything is brand new; big new HP printer, monitors, keyboards.

'Where's Pete today?

'Glasgow – he's on a Gold Command exercise.'

We cross into the ambulance garage and it is considerably bigger than others I'd seen. The place smells new – the concrete underfoot is grey and unblemished, there is a smell of new rubber, and the entrance doors have that sticky, pulling back sensation when opened. There is some very expensive looking gear lying around. There is a mobile command unit parked inside, and a couple of RRVs. There are four new trucks, all with brand new number plates.

On the way back into the offices, I notice an upper level inside the garage where a young woman looks as if she's being trained to use the high-access harness. She is accompanied by two big men in uniform. It seems as if most of the staff here are highly experienced ambulance service men. Women seem to be outnumbered about 15 to 1. The place is very well staffed; the car park is jammed, and I see about 20 or maybe 30 people milling around, mostly in uniform, some in suits. Clearly this facility is a major investment and quite different from many of the other facilities we've seen, some of which were small and quite run-down in comparison.

With HART, the ambulance service seemed keen to demonstrate its indispensability, effectively upgrading its capacity to compete with other providers, notably, in this case, with Fire and Rescue Services who have tended to dominate the emergency preparedness/mass casualty field. Government policy is increasingly looking at shared response and co-location of fire with ambulance and is developing its 'joint doctrine' of interoperability (JESIP, 2013). But when discussing such matters, ambulance service managers tended to consider their organization under-resourced in relation to Fire. In an interview that we quote from below, two highly experienced ambulance area managers joked about the Fire Service's comparative riches of time and money. It was suggested, for example, that the Fire Service can arrange school visits 'with a vehicle taken off the roster and a member of fire crew dressed as the Welliphant', whereas the Ambulance Service cannot spare the time or resource for it is at full capacity all the time. Light-hearted at first, the discourse became almost fiery as James started to reflect on the seriousness of financial pressures:

CHRIS: *You don't go to an airport firefighter at the end of a shift and say 'You've had a rubbish day today, you've fought no fires and I'm paying you x amount of money!' Because they* [Fire Service] *live or die – literally – by that one Jumbo that crashes, and an ambulance trust should obviously work on the same principle, you know: 'You've not turned a wheel today; well, that's because everybody's well'. But we don't … we are very good at what we do and I just think, managerially, we just need now to get a bit of extra help from outside. It's funding, … or the GP consortia not sending everybody to hospital. You know, since the doctors signed out of not responding to their own calls, we went to a centralized* [geographical area] *medical centre and they're busy, so if you ring and* [it] *defaults to 999* [you get] *'ring an ambulance'. It's all that.*

JAMES: *I think now – and I've pretty much, you know, I've not got as long as Chris in the service, I've been doing it 15 years – now, seven out of ten people we go to don't need to go to hospital; that's the top and bottom of it. But I know things are in place with Pathfinders and Care Pathways and this, that and the other; but until someone makes the decision and says to the ambulance crew, 'if you go to this individual, and in your professional opinion that patient does not need to go…'. But on the flip side of that, the staff need to have confidence in the management that if they do that and something does happen, they won't be hauled up in front of the HPC.*[4] *Because that is the staff's mindset: it's easier and simpler to wrap a blanket around someone, take them down to A&E; they don't need to go there, their vehicle didn't need to go there, they didn't need to go there, but their mortgage needs to be paid at the end of the day. So it's a fine line, really. And the thing is with the NHS – ambulance services, everything – there's too many people taking out of the pot and not enough putting in. … It's not a finite resource. And unfortunately, with the four per cent cost improvements from the government every year, that equates to ten million. All right, this year we might squeeze through, but then we've got ten million to find next year, and the year after, and the year after. And it's not beyond the realms of possibility that the fiscal year starts April, you get to January of the next year … you haven't got any money left. 'We haven't got the money to send an ambulance to that individual.' And then ultimately who suffers at the end of the day? It's you, me, Chris; because when you do need that resource and when … you're struggling for breath, there's nothing there. Although we've paid into it, there's nothing there for us. That's the scary thing. … It's gonna come to a point soon where this pot of money that the NHS have isn't enough. … But the people are gonna have to pay more. The NHS is basically exhausted. Since 1948, it's run out of money. I'm passionate about it!*

Clinicians and managers have long described the NHS as being in deep financial trouble. Ambulance EMT and blogger/author Tom Reynolds described the NHS back in 2006 as 'on the point of collapse' (2006: 275). A group of A&E doctors, in an open letter in May 2013, portrayed A&E units as 'on a cliff edge' with 'simply unmanageable' workloads (see McCann *et al.*, 2015a: 777). Somehow it seems to struggle on, but for how long and in what shape? Resource shortages are nothing unusual for NHS organizations. But ambulance practitioners and managers described CCAS not only as the least well resourced emergency service but also as largely neglected by the rest of the NHS, which was, by implication, better able to look after its own interests. Resource shortages, lack of managerial support, a traditionally weak professional identity, and passionate beliefs about the need for a fully funded NHS care system tended to re-enforce the siege mentality that characterized much of the front-line and junior/middle management behaviour in the ambulance service (McCann *et al.*, 2013). As we see in the next section, the combined effects of these phenomena created a strong impetus towards reproducing the norms and features of CCAS's traditional uniformed and *emergency-focused* organizational culture.

Organizational culture in the ambulance service

This section explores the relationships between managers and front-line staff in more depth, focusing in particular on the contentious issue of organizational culture. Throughout our research at CCAS, we encountered considerable strains and tensions between and across certain management and staff populations. Moreover, relations *between* organizations were not as concordant as they could have been. The hybrid roles and identities of the NHS mid-manager, as both business administrator and carer/clinician, were often apparent; the latter was often emphasized by these mid-managers wherever possible. When patient care is at stake, NHS organizations and managers typically did not act commercially in that they couldn't refuse patient needs even if the organization might not get paid for the service it renders. This point surfaced when observing a management training day on commissioning:

The facilitator gives the example of eligibility criteria for PTS: 'What if there's a situation where, technically, we don't provide outpatient transport home if a patient is discharged [from hospital] *early – say, a Bank Holiday Monday – but we were contracted to take her home Tuesday.'*

> *A manager in the audience replies: 'Technically, we can't do it. Financially we're not contracted for this. But we do it, don't we? Are we actually commissioned for this? But it will be "Mrs Smith denied transport" in the local newspaper, so you do it.'*

The conflicts that arose between the needs of patient care and the rationing of resources and lack of support meant that the culture of road staff versus management could sometimes manifest itself as obstruction, rudeness, and even militancy and aggression against managers who were perceived not to be putting patient care first. This arose in interviews and more informally during observation of managers at work. While observing Planned Care managers at work, one customer support manager, known as Emma, was very outspoken on this issue; and her outburst seemed to reveal deep levels of frustration:

> *Emma goes into a comic but serious rant about workplace politics and I miss most of it as it was obviously inappropriate to sit there making notes about it. 'Amanda's been out on the road; Darren's been on the road; I've not. There's a real difference to it, in how you're seen.'*
>
> *She says something about going to an ambulance station and people 'looking at you as if you were an alien with three heads – they're here!' she laughs. 'You go out to another site and it's like "who's that?!"' Amanda agrees, mimics the reaction with an accusatory 'Who's she?!' Emma goes on to say that once she was at [District] Ambulance Station and someone left notes on her car. '"Don't fucking come here telling us what to do". It was like the mafia!'*

She went on to give an example of where she has felt the need to respond in kind. Stories such as these, of slanging matches among managers and between managers and road staff, were not uncommon in our study:

> *'But I can kick off when I need to.' She describes how she had 'a right old go' at Ken; 'do you remember?'*
>
> *'Ken was the stuff of legend!', says Darren.*
>
> *'I went up to him [starts to re-enact the scene, takes two strides forward, bends forward, jabbing the finger] and shouted: "Don't eff-ing well tell me how to do my eff-ing job, ok?" I then rang HR and said: "I've gone off at someone. Don't worry, I've not hit him!" They said: "Don't tell me any more on the phone. Come and see us … !"' She turns to Darren: 'You've had lots of rollickings from me. Were they justified?' 'Yes!' says Darren.*

Tara, a manager in OL&D, while clearly stating that most staff were committed and approachable, described a significant minority who act out of what she described as *'a mob mentality'*, and she drew attention to the need to change this toxic culture. Describing it as '*crazy*' and '*venomous*', changing this form of behaviour was one of the main goals of her department. The traditional 'macho' uniformed emergency services culture was quite distinctive among our four NHS case study organizations and was well known in prior studies of ambulance service culture (e.g. see Boyle, 2002). A paramedic by the name of Laura, a former nurse, who was just moving into a supervisory role at CCAS, had this to say:

> *I used to be a nurse and one thing I can't get over is the attitude of some people in the ambulance service. They seem to think it's OK to simply refuse to do things. We'd never do that as nurses. You'd never react like that – 'I'm not doing it'. If a manager says you do it, you're doing it!*

Several other junior and middle managers had police and military backgrounds, contributing in some way to the traditions of a uniformed culture among many of the people we met. It was common to hear ambulance road staff referred to as '*troops*'.

Some road staff complained quite bitterly about management and often felt undervalued and ignored by the organization. A *crew room culture* existed in some parts of the organization, and certain front-line employees had built up a defensive attitude whereby they felt that managers who came '*down*' to ambulance stations were '*invading their territory*'. This organizational culture perhaps derived from the high stakes and the mobility of the work that CCAS carries out and the tendency for management to appear remote and out of touch with reality.

However, obstructive and quarrelsome relations were not the norm for all CCAS staff. Some gave much more sanguine views and mentioned that it was possible to get on well with management. Karl, a recently recruited PES clinical team leader – a US-born paramedic who had previously worked in firefighter and lifeboat crews in America – offered an explanation of this phenomenon in relation to HART. Although these new HART teams were well resourced and a major contribution to the upgrading of the ambulance service's capacity, he noted how they were often looked upon with jealousy as '*elitist*' among many other parts of the service as they had much larger training budgets and were sent out to far fewer jobs than standard crews. As he explained:

> *There's a lack of staff awareness of what HART is. We're seen as elitist. I think there is more openness to change in the US than here in England. Old hands here don't like change; they see it as being stuffed down their throat. Younger or less experienced staff accept it more. They're more eager to try new things. Willing to accept them more. Others see it somehow as an attack on them. I've worked in emergency services for 25 years in different organizations, and I've listened to a lot of moaning. But I often think: 'Why are you complaining? Maybe change is good?' People are passionate and that's OK, but sometimes they get aggressive. They react so funnily, and sometimes I'm like 'what was that all about?!' It's a weird response, a disproportionate response.*

He went on to describe his identity as being closely tied up in emergency ambulance work:

> [Being a paramedic] *It's a hard job. There's no doubt it's a hard job. But I wouldn't want to do anything else. If I got injured and couldn't do this job anymore, I'd be destroyed. My life would be destroyed.*

The stakes can be very high and ambulance clinicians do not take kindly to what they perceive to be ineffective management systems and behaviours. But again, where resources are spread so thin, the effects of such emotional intensity are likely to be higher than they perhaps need to be. Road staff, who typically work 12-hour shifts (and with the strong possibility of enforced overtime) at times encounter stressful and draining episodes on the road. For their part, managers, in charge of large numbers of operational personnel across their section or area, have to handle the repercussions of such problems. The intensity of work for all employees meant less time to discuss and work through problems among managers and front-line staff. A lack of 'face time', or 'development time' appeared a major problem – one that was preventing members of the organization from looking out for each other, keeping each other informed and helping each other with problems and frustrations. This was also becoming an issue for CCAS in that the smaller, locally based ambulance stations were being closed and their areas of responsibility merged into much larger facilities that were opening on edge-of-town industrial estates.

Our ambulance trust data featured many war stories, some of which have stuck in the mind of managers and road staff. One was told by Amanda, a mid-level manager in Planned Care. Changes in the service reflected developments in wider society and, in this case, the calamitous growth of obesity among the UK population. This was creating more complex and demanding work for PC in having to plan for the transport of patients whose size and weight can make them extremely challenging to move. Speciality bariatric ambulances had been developed which were capable of transporting morbidly obese patients. Stories such as this gave interesting insights into the moral ambiguity of healthcare in that in some patient transport episodes were effectively just changing the location where a death occurred. Amanda recalls:

> *One of the first jobs I did with a tail-lift vehicle was a 24-year-old man who was morbidly obese. The fire service had to assist us. They attached straps to his mattress, had him wrapped up in the mattress and lifted him out the window. We carried him onto the vehicle, on the floor of the vehicle strapped up in the mattress. He died a few days later – his organs collapsed under the weight of his body. There's so many obese people around now. I can't say 'obese'; its 'bariatric patients' now.*

Such stories were often 'emotionally laden' (Boyle and Healy, 2003) in that ambulance services (for both emergency and planned care) were regularly involved in duties which involved a mixture of rewarding yet, as Darren told us, often saddening and humbling work:

> *It's good that you're looking at PTS as we tend to get ignored. OK A&E is more frantic and they see all the gruesome stuff, but in many ways, PTS is more emotionally draining. A lot of A&E, maybe 70 per cent of it, is alcohol related. The people we get are really sick. We get a lot of anti-coags coming in. You get to know them. They come in for regular anti-coag treatment ... then they die. The worst is when you've taken people to [Cancer unit] and they've been told they have two to three weeks to live. You take people back home; they've just had a new kitchen put in. Or you see they've had the bedroom done, a new bed – and you think to yourself 'well, you're just going to sleep in that a few nights', you know? The next time we see you, we'll be carrying you out dead. I had a cancer patient ... didn't really expect it, all very sudden. Sometimes things stay with you. We were taking her home from a cancer appointment. Soon after, she was dead ... Christmas Eve. Or sometimes you get reassigned elsewhere. There was this lovely lady who'd come in for anti-coags and we saw her for years. But one day I got reassigned and we don't take her any more. She got us a pewter mug tankard with our names on it saying 'the best ambulance men in the world'. It was the nicest thing.*

While the 'direct' culture was often constructed as a problem and something the organization needed to fix, there were core elements of the traditional 'no nonsense' style that parts of the service did not want to lose. For many staff, the latter represented a straight-talking approach: the emphasis was on retaining workplace dignity and an anti-managerialist culture where *management* is constructed in terms of cost-control and remoteness from the *real work* of treating patients. An appreciation of the importance of these discussions, conflicts and controversies is central to a deep understanding of the complexity of CCAS as an organization and, by extension, issues that are at the heart of what the NHS is, or should, be.

Conclusion

The overall impression we gained from our in-depth immersion into managerial life in this particular ambulance trust was of a vital and, in many ways, advanced clinical organization doing its best to survive amid recurrent waves of change (notably increasing cost pressures) that crashed over it. CCAS faced repeated demands to become more commercial, more efficient and more transparent, but often lacked any proper resources to help it achieve these often ambiguous and morally contested goals. Many junior and mid-level managers expressed concern that patient care was being compromised due to resource pressures and the conflict around and between NHS trusts. Hybrid managerial identities existed here, just as in other NHS case studies, with a large number of those interviewed and observed trying to maintain a clinical identity that reasserts the socialized model of patient care wherever possible. There was pride in the service and genuine efforts exerted to try to keep it going and to improve performance. Many on the front line complained bitterly about shortages and conflicted work relationships, but also claimed to love the work and described life out on the road as the '*best job in the world*'. The desire to put patients' needs first and to try to establish and assert professional identities were central to the road staff versus management discourse – a discourse that was often unfair in that many junior and middle managers had wide responsibilities and severe challenges of their own. Many of these managers were also quite close to the front line, such as clinical team leaders who – given ever-increasing patient demand – weren't really given adequate time to do the specifically *management* parts of their workload.

The lack of a traditionally powerful professional body or identity in ambulance services meant that many clinical staff had little career headroom and that a move into management was the only realistic route for career progression. Except in certain areas that were well resourced (e.g. HART), the targets culture swallowed up much of the time that might otherwise be spent on staff training and career development for the organization, and its middle managers were heavily preoccupied with daily firefighting.

Amid the concerns and conflicts, it is important to note that CCAS generally provided a very high-quality service with extremely positive satisfaction scores reported from patient surveys. According to a document on the CCAS website, as reported from a survey with almost 4,000 responses, 95 per cent of patients rated PES as eight, nine, or ten out of ten for 'overall care' and between 76 per cent and 89 per cent rated similarly for various parts of PTS. CCAS was seen as especially good at providing fast emergency response in urban areas. Its levels of clinical expertise were growing, especially in terms of new emergencies for life-threatening conditions such as myocardial infarction and stroke. However operational overstretch was severe. Stress and anxiety were, to a degree, accepted as part of a sense of commitment and duty, but there were also serious and widespread problems. Managers and front-line staff were becoming burnt out, which contributed to, and in turn was partly caused and reinforced by, sickness absence.

Meantime, broader changes in the health economy of England were creating deep challenges. CCAS will probably struggle to respond to suggestions that it become 'more businesslike' and 'more commercial' when the pressures of meeting its daily challenges are so heavy. The direction of travel for health policy seems to be towards greater fragmentation and competition – a direction that managers participating in this study were strongly opposed to. CCAS front-line and middle management staff were committed to a public service model of professional performance and monopoly provision, of solidarity and equity – all taxpayers 'putting into the pot' and 'taking out' when necessary. They were sceptical of the move towards sector fragmentation and 'any qualified provider' logic and were concerned especially with the prospect of ambulance services being in competition with commercial providers and ultimately becoming privatized. While passionate supporters and advocates of the NHS, they were largely pessimistic about the prospects for an embattled ambulance service to adapt and survive in an increasingly challenging environment of inter-unit billing, cost control, rising patient demand, clamour for ambiguous culture change, increasing visibility of private operators, and the ever-growing intrusion of commercial imperatives into what should be a public service occupation devoted first and foremost to patient care.

Notes

1   The Priory Group is a private sector mental health provider.
2   Chemical, Biological, Radiological and Nuclear, pronounced in a quasi-military style as See-Burn.
3   A major German-owned global logistics corporation.
4   HPC refers to the Health and Care Professions Council (HCPC). This regulatory body governs ambulance workers and other allied health professionals.

6

STAYING AFLOAT

Negotiating change at a mental health trust

This chapter details the rapidly changing environment for middle managers in a mental health care organization: 'Millfordshire Care Foundation NHS Trust' or 'MCFT'. The organization provided community and inpatient mental health care. It was based in the north of England and its territory was extensive, covering that of the acute trust (Chapter 4) and four primary care trusts (one of which is described in Chapter 7). It also sat within the even larger area covered by the ambulance trust (Chapter 5). Our study of mental health managerial work encompasses all areas of service provision and back office support. We also examine the environment in which the study took place. Planned as a study of managerial work in changing economic times, not long into the study we found we were also analysing an organization under severe financial pressure in an environment where many non-mental-health community services (formerly provided by primary care trusts) were coming up for tender. Specifically, the organization could not remain viable by providing mental health services alone. This made the case study of MCFT one of significant organizational change, reflecting expansion into areas of service provision outside of mental health and ultimately the stripping out of management layers to reduce costs and ensure survival.

The Health and Social Care Act 2012 ushered in many organizational upheavals for the NHS. Significantly for MCFT, alongside major structural changes, it mandated the integration of health and social care services – meaning that the trust had to link with community organizations whose staff were either being made redundant or having their employment contracts transferred from the NHS to local authorities or to the trust itself. Primary care trusts were being abolished and the competition clause meant that contracts previously awarded to provide extensive community care services would come up for tender by newly formed commissioning groups and, according to the new legislation, were open to 'any qualified provider'.

We found that MCFT was in a state of almost constant change as it pursued an expansion strategy aimed at increasing the size and volume of contracts (and, therefore, income), achieving economies of scale through reductions in management numbers and diversifying the services provided. By the end of the fieldwork, MCFT was about to double in size again by taking on short-term contracts for further non-mental-health community services from disbanded primary care trusts. New mental health developments were targeted at high-value services such as secure inpatient services, and new units were being built to house these patients. The demands being made on managerial and front-line staff were increasing in variety, intensity and complexity with the result that many of the remaining managers were working long hours.

Millfordshire Care Foundation NHS Trust

The remainder of the chapter illustrates why this was the case by examining the daily lives of junior and middle managers. It demonstrates that organizational changes included attracting new business, management restructuring, devolving management responsibilities and centralizing and streamlining services such as Human Resources and Finance. Furthermore, it argues that these changes were affecting management roles, leading to a disconnected hierarchy – notably as new business management roles impacted on historic clinical managerial roles. We provide details about the main organizational challenges facing MCFT managers and illustrate how they were trying to adapt and modernize. We then explore management roles and behaviours in greater detail, thus providing an account of the realities of managerial work in mental health services, an under-researched type of NHS organization.

This is a case study in which senior managers, new to the harsh financial realities of a business orientation, were at once restructuring the services along business rather than geographical lines and rapidly expanding the business to stay afloat. Mental health services on the whole were still organized by block contracts for provision to particular geographical areas. Such contracts paid for chunks of service and rarely accounted for variations in demand. MCFT, like other NHS mental health organizations, could not move entirely away from block contracts and begin to charge for services per person until they could itemize treatment by type of service and per person. This was far from simple in mental health, not least because of the unpredictability, variety and extent of input patients may require. At the same time as making these structural changes that moved from area-based general services to service lines across the whole trust, MCFT was also bidding for various large area-based community service contracts. The dominant strategy was to expand their way out of financial constraint by gaining large contracts and making cost savings from stripping out layers of middle management. This strategy brought with it similar problems to those faced by corporations and their middle managers in recent decades (Hassard et al., 2009). The changes taking place during our time at the trust saw the major income of MCFT move away from mental health care and towards short-term, high-volume community service provision as contracts were won that began to overshadow the former specialist mental health purpose of the organization.

In spite of the complex and, for some, long-term needs of patients, mental health services have continually struggled to maintain funding even during times of increased health spending. The mental health case study therefore concerns how mental health managers made sense of their place in the organization and what happened to their work behaviour in times of rapid change and expansion into new areas of business. The experience of this trust reflects the influence of marketization on non-profitable services; which represents most of mental health. It shows a stripped-out management function, struggling, sometimes reluctantly, to adapt to new entrepreneurial roles.

Managing mental health services

We've never had good times. We've had reductions each year. We've shut loads of stuff in the last five years. We've never had any more money. … We've got a lot of expertise in bed reduction; we've reduced our beds by about 30 per cent in the last four years.
(*Robert, director of operations, MCFT*)

Mental health services were designed to treat people who developed a mental illness with the aim of making them better and therefore able to resume their normal life. Like the ambulance service of the previous chapter, mental health services were often referred to as '*Cinderella services*' because of the low status of mental health professionals and difficulties they had in attracting funding and attention. However, unlike the ambulance service, mental health services also have the triple challenge of: a poor public profile (only coming to the public attention when things go wrong); shortage of resources to draw upon; and working with patients who do not necessarily want the care on offer, sometimes leading to forced admissions.

Consequently, mental health services in the UK (as well in Australia, the US, Canada and Europe) occupy a somewhat marginal place in the health economy. They are perhaps less well known to the public than ambulance and acute hospital services, and rather than serious attention, they more regularly attract sensationalist reportage (perhaps in the wake of an enquiry into a murder by an ex-patient or the suicide of a person receiving mental health services) than serious examination. Academic research on mental health care is sparse and can again tend towards the sensational. Notable exceptions include studies of the patient experience, perhaps most famously, Erving Goffman's (1961) sociological study of the condition of inpatients, *Asylums*, which was closely followed by Rose Coser's (1962) *Life on the Ward*. Both of these studies drew attention to the poor living conditions and treatment of psychiatric patients. Studies of mental health work are thinner on the ground and largely originate from the US. They include T. M. Luhrmann's (2000) anthropological study of psychiatrists in training and at work, *Of Two Minds*;

Hinshelwood and Skogstad's (2000) psychodynamic exploration of various UK mental health departments, *Observing Organisations*; Lorna Rhodes' (1991) ethnographic study of emergency psychiatric units in the US, *Emptying Beds;* and Teresa Scheid's (2004) sociological analysis of US mental health care work, *Tie a Knot and Hang On.* What these studies describe is the problematic nature of the work for managers and clinicians in mental health services. Their many difficult and competing care roles are broadly aimed at removing and eradicating madness and containing threats of disturbance or violence to self or others. In the process, as well as receiving care, this meant that patients may have been compelled to accept services, restrained or forced to take treatment against their will (Bott, 1976).

Indeed, even in the best of circumstances, management of mental health services has been described as an impossible task because the explicit undertaking is to 'import madness' and apply 'rational processes' to deal with it (Willshire, 1999). As a result, mental health services have been described as the repository of emotional unpleasantness not only for the hospital but also for society (Barnes *et al.*, 1999). Clinical staff can feel torn between a desire to help patients and a fear that patients may go on to commit harm. The real difficulty this poses lies in the fact that clinicians have to predict whether or not someone may go on to kill someone or to harm themselves at some future date. Once a patient has been seen by mental health services, the service could be held accountable for their actions. As these acts are not fully predictable, mental health service managers, like ambulance managers, find themselves involved in life or death decision-making about where, when and how to use scarce resources, such as inpatient beds.

Mental health services have been reorganized several times in recent decades in an attempt to improve the quality of care and to enable mental health services to have a specific call on financial investment. A brief review of mental health service restructuring indicates how these services have been regularly rearranged, often being split off before being combined with other health services in order to effect a change for the better. Prior to the creation of the NHS, services for people with serious mental illnesses such as schizophrenia were provided in large county asylums (Freeman, 1998). Since county asylums were closed and wards opened on acute hospital sites, mental health services have grown to closely resemble other hospital services. In the 1970s, with the emergence of psychiatry as a medical profession and in an effort to decentralize mental health services from large state institutions, small mental health units were created at general hospital sites (Gournay *et al.*, 1998), asylums were emptied and the provision of community services was instigated (Peck and Parker, 1998). Subsequently, mental health services were subjected to a modernization programme along with the rest of the NHS (Department of Health, 1998, 1999, 2000a, 2000b). Around 2002, mental health services provided by acute trusts were separated off and merged with other neighbouring mental health services to create specialist mental health trusts which also provided some community mental health services. These structural changes were often a change only at an organizational level. It meant that although a separate board and NHS organization were created and the name and signage of the trust changed, front-line services were largely unchanged; the same staff continued to provide the same services from the same hospital and community locations. Indeed changes in mental health organizational structures are said to have had little impact, especially for patients (Hyde and Thomas, 2002; Walton, 2000). However, the general trajectory has been one of reducing inpatient capacity, limited availability of talking therapies, rising community appointments and, more recently, increasing the number of beds in (higher-income) secure units.

The relative inability to attract resources is compounded by the fact that mental health treatment is unglamorous and possibly unwanted by patients, who can experience distressing side effects and may perceive no benefit; for example, antipsychotic medicines may cause muscle stiffness, impotence, weight gain and slurred speech (BNF, 2002). Talking therapies, such as cognitive behavioural therapy, counselling and psychotherapy, are less readily available and the majority of mental health treatment involves monitoring the effects of medication. For longer-term conditions, cures are not available and so success has been judged by an absence of violence to self or others, or by the avoidance of readmission to hospital. Both of these are *negative* goals that only become visible through failure. Success, in many cases, involves maintenance of the current or a steady mental state (Hyde and Thomas, 2002, 2003).

Like other NHS services, mental health services could be accessed through the general practitioner or emergency department; but, in contrast to other services, patients could also be admitted by the police, the probation service or the courts. Patients may be forcibly detained under sections of the Mental Health Act 1983; and if they were voluntarily admitted, there may have been considerable persuasion from staff and relatives. Many people recover from acute episodes of mental distress; however, much of the work of MCFT concerned people with serious and enduring mental illnesses. These illnesses often followed a chronic course, including episodes of acute illness and remission. Unlike other chronic problems, the effects of prolonged mental illnesses do not cause death, although mentally ill people were more likely to commit suicide or in rare cases they may kill someone else. Patients could continue in a chronic state until they died of some unrelated physical cause (Hyde and Thomas, 2002).

In contrast to the acute trust and ambulance service, MCFT managerial roles were less clearly defined. This lack of role definition may arise from the fact that psychiatric assessment and some forms of treatment are based solely on conversations with the patient. As we see below, these types of *professional talk* – undertaken by a doctor, nurse or psychologist – were more difficult to categorize than other medical interventions. Another difficulty of the work was that mental health staff were very likely to have been involved in restraint of patients and, in some cases, administering forced treatments. Almost all staff at the trust received training in *control and restraint*, signalling a potential, if not always likely, danger from patients. Involvement in forced treatments included giving of medicine against someone's will or via the signing or writing up of section papers that sanctioned such interventions (documents detailing which part of the Mental Health Act was being applied to enforce admission and/or treatment).

Managing MCFT: doing *'more for less'*

At the time MCFT was created, around the turn of the twenty-first century, a framework for the provision of mental health services was in use that enabled health and social services to offer joint care by allowing them to combine their budgets (Department of Health, 1999). At this time, *The NHS Plan* had provided for a ten-year programme of investment in the NHS under the Labour government of Tony Blair. Mental health services did not benefit from significant increases in income as their services were organized by block contract (i.e. to provide a service to a geographical area regardless of demand). As a result, MCFT had not gained during the period of investment and was worse affected once austerity measures were introduced. The move to service lines at MCFT and other mental health trusts was intended to enable charging per item or charging per person for services, putting the trust in a position to gain from the more profitable areas of work – specialist services such as children's services and secure inpatient units. In spite of this, at the organizational level, MCFT had managed to expand year on year by acquiring additional services and reducing overall management costs.

As noted, MCFT was formed at the turn of the twenty-first century at the time that national mental health services were spun off from acute services to form specialist mental health trusts (see above). The organization was formed by splitting off inpatient mental health services from acute trusts and combining them with community mental health services in the same area. For MCFT, this involved the merger of five inpatient mental health services and five community mental health services. MCFT was the main provider of mental health services for five large towns and three surrounding rural areas. In reality, the services continued to be provided in the same places by the same staff and largely with the same managers in place, but the name of their employer changed along with the signage. Many managers had worked at the trust since its formation and had been employees of the original mental health services that formed the trust. In 2008, MCFT became a foundation trust giving it freedom to raise capital and exercise some managerial and strategic autonomy (see Chapter 2). As the chief executive explained, when opening a junior managers' training course, they had to *'make a profit'* – services were important but they had to find a way to do *'more for less'*: *'We're becoming a successful foundation trust … we have to make a profit … how we deliver services is important … but the organization is not just about patient care … the key phrase as always is "more for less".'*

At the time of the study, MCFT covered a population of 1.2 million people in five heavily populated towns in the north of England. The trust had an annual income of £140 million and employed over 2,600 staff. The work involved offering the full range of mental health interventions, protecting patients and others and containing patients who were a danger to themselves or others. The trust encompassed 40 square miles and covered affluent and deprived, rural and urban areas. It provided services from four hospital sites (one site had closed) and many more community locations, and it offered services to people who had serious mental illnesses (e.g. schizophrenia), common mental health problems (e.g. anxiety) and dementia.

To give a broad overview of the working environment, the trust headquarters (HQ) was located in a town centre towards the middle of the area covered. The modern, glass offices stood alongside the headquarters of several other NHS and charitable organizations and opposite other institutional buildings such as the local courthouse. The HQ stood in stark contrast to the older hospital and community service buildings; the trust modernized a number of inpatient buildings on two of the five hospital sites. Nevertheless, the estate still included Victorian inpatient buildings and some dilapidated community buildings. As with the ambulance trust, there was no real centre to the organization as its services were spread across a wide geographical region with each area apparently having its own *'distinct culture'*. This extract from early notes of arriving to meet a ward manager gives a feel for the nature of the (purpose-built) MCFT site at one of the acute hospitals:

> *As I drove into* [town] *hospital it was hard to find signs for the MCFT building or* [building name]. *I guessed it would be at the back because we were told a joke about acute hospitals putting mental health services next to the mortuary when they were relocated from county asylums. All the signs are blue NHS, the writing is tiny and it's hard to pick out where to go.*

> *I arrived at the unit in the dark and an hour early, having set off at 6.30 a.m. It's half term so the traffic was light. I was not expected until 8.00 a.m. Fortunately, the door to the unit opened electronically and I was able to get in. The reception area was empty. The glass window to reception was covered by a white metal blind. Nevertheless, I signed in to the visitors' book, which was left open outside the reception window. ... I sit in reception to wait until 8.00 a.m. ... I sat opposite the ward doors and two night staff came out, absorbed in conversation. There are lots of notices on the ward doors – 'STOP make sure the door is firmly closed after entering the ward THANKYOU' – some notes on preventing infections and 'Please note protected therapeutic time 2.30–4.00 p.m.'. There are some PALS (patient advice and liaison) leaflets on the table and part of a yellow sick note for a staff nurse. ... Jane comes out of the ward with a set of notes in her hands and crosses over to the stairs. She spots me and says 'Hi, I'll be with you in a minute'. Her shift was scheduled to start at 8.00 a.m. and she has clearly been here for some time.*

As noted, we were told by several of the senior managers that each geographical area had a distinct culture, and the first sign of this was the fact that every site was distinct in physical style; for example, different wall hangings, posters, ceramics, notices, furniture and staffing. In addition, it seemed that HQ also had its own distinct character. At that site, there was a staffed reception office and the artwork in reception was imposing and featured portraits of middle-aged, smartly dressed men – presumably, previous leaders in the field of mental health. More importantly,

HQ had a distinctly corporate look and feel. We met managers there by appointment and the reception staff were always expecting us; we signed in and out. Reception staff provided access through a locked door and managers came to meet us in the hallway on the other side.

In contrast, at other sites, the ambience was more consistent with our experiences in other NHS organizations – more of a public sector look, where no one but our appointed manager expected us, sites were hard to find, and physical access was difficult to negotiate. However, rather than representing a state of disorganization, our impression was that this downmarket image was symbolic more of the high-volume, low-resource and essentially burdensome nature of junior and middle managers' work in such locations. In addition, the facilities for staff appeared poorly maintained, as the following extract from observations of a divisional management meeting at a local area community site suggest:

> *The meeting takes place in a basement room – a former canteen, we are told. There are six pillars in the room with gaps filled by tables put together and chairs around and in-between the pillars. No one around the table can see everyone. It is so cold that a fan heater in the corner is left running at the start of the meeting. There are no windows and it is cramped. Heating pipes run round one side of the room. At one end of the room is a large flat-screen TV and a projector.*

What was distinctive about this trust was the hostile managerial environment – described at various points in our study as: '*bullying*', '*paranoid*', '*mistrustful*' and '*coercive*'. One reason, perhaps, was the fact that the trust, like other mental health organizations, experienced regular investigations from the national regulator when patients had come to or committed harm. (It should be noted also that the trust was rated as excellent for service provision.) This hostility was said to be reflected among board members as tensions between the senior management team played out in public. It was exemplified in what became known as '*the snow email*'. Following extended bad weather, a brief email was sent from board level that reportedly said: '*Thanks to all the people who managed to get in during the snow period – an example to those who didn't bother*'. Even though a quick response had been sent, from another board member, thanking '*everyone equally*', the '*snow email*' had entered the oral history of MCFT as an indicator of the contemptuous view senior staff held towards its employees. These tensions extended further into the organization and played out in blaming between operational departments dispersed across the trust as well as support departments such as HR, Information and Finance, centralized at HQ. The blame culture involved attempts to find out who was at fault when significant mistakes were made, but it also extended to other seemingly more minor mistakes; as Tanya, a service line manager explained:

> *We have a really blame-oriented culture. … This is a tiny example but it just seemed quite symbolic. A member of staff tried to help a service user. They had some dirty clothes so they'd washed their suit for them. It was done with the best intentions.*

Unfortunately, the suit turned out to be a designer suit. So washing it wrecked the suit, and then a claim was put in against the trust. That went to our director of finance. I had four emails. It was £600! I could have easily solved it from my own budget. Then I had a letter from him asking about what the disciplinary action would be for the individual. We have to blame somebody ... the question for me was: how can we prevent this from happening again?

The managers we studied included service directors, unit or business managers and ward managers. The managers fell into two categories: on the one hand, managers with a clinical background who either had managerial responsibilities added to their clinical role or who held wholly managerial posts, what we term 'hybrid managers'; and on the other, those who were dedicated managers of, for example, HR or Estates departments. These latter managers had different backgrounds: those who had progressed through the NHS often at the same organization and a newer group of managers with commercial backgrounds in retail and other private sector businesses. In the following section, we detail the management challenges faced by junior and middle managers at the trust.

Preparing for business: managing service lines

As we began the study, the trust was moving away from a management structure based on geographical area, although it quickly reverted to North and South divisions because of the sheer scale of geographical coverage. The North area had a more unionized culture and a history of difficult industrial relations. The South area was said to be more harmonious. Across these two area divisions there were five service lines that would provide sources of regular income for the trust. The catalogue company Argos was a used as a comparator when the director of operations defined service lines. He described the need to increase standardization and indicated the difficulty in identifying mental health service lines:

Think of the Argos catalogue, then you get all your toys, then that would be a service line. Then you get your home furnishings and then there's your outdoor equipment and camping equipment. The reason business does that is that by grouping those products together, they can get the best quality for those products. The people leading them understand those products that they're trying to sell and they can get more efficiencies along that way.

Within healthcare, I think it's slightly different because it cannot just be a business paradigm for the sake of generating financial profits ... it's evolved in the NHS. It's become very much about making sure you get the best quality and the best productivity you possibly can by running similar services together ... to try and get a currency and then a tariff. ... And it works on the premise that you should be trying to improve standardization, so if you write the care pathway ... you try to reduce variation ... what's happening is benchmarking between services ... we weren't going for a big bang, let's get all services organized together ... we don't understand enough what the service lines should be in mental health to do that.

As a result of being unable to categorize service by type of problem or intervention, service lines were largely organized by the age of the patients, other than for addiction and intensive care, where they were grouped as follows:

- Adult mental health – inpatient and community services for adults of working age including crisis resolution, home treatment, assertive outreach and early intervention;
- Older people's services – inpatient, day services and community mental health services for older people, including assessment, care and treatment;
- Child and adolescent mental health (CAMHS) – inpatient, outpatient and community services for children and their families;
- Drug and alcohol services – information and treatment for drug and alcohol users and training and consultancy for other agencies;
- Psychiatric intensive care – secure units, non-secure intensive rehabilitation and prison mental health services.

Our investigations at MCFT revealed five main challenges that provided the context for managers within the organization: i) regular expansion of mental health service provision, ii) management restructuring and delayering, iii) business and clinical management arrangements, iv) emergent centralized management roles and disconnected hierarchy, and v) attracting new business.

The first management challenge we encountered was the difficulty faced in managing new and unfamiliar services. MCFT had expanded rapidly to provide a diverse spread of services from over 60 locations. The growth of the trust was almost matched by the increase in diversity of employees, their management arrangements and the number of locations from which services were provided. For example, some services were jointly provided by MCFT and council services whilst others were taken over entirely by MCFT. Each service had a distinct local culture and MCFT had struggled to find a simple management hierarchy to cover the disparate services. They released cost savings by removing layers of managers across the entire trust, including newer services. Nevertheless, rating scores for the trust, awarded by the Care Quality Commission, were consistently high and it was one of the highest-performing foundation trusts of its type.

Second, and following on from the first challenge, the trust had undertaken several rounds of management restructuring in recent years. For example, in 2009, it reduced management costs by over 30 per cent. As such, this trust had cut management costs significantly before national austerity cuts were announced. The management of services was being reconfigured during the study and no clear structure emerged during the three years of the study. Rather than being organized by geographic area, the management hierarchy was reorganized to identify service lines (see Figure 6.1).

FIGURE 6.1 Reconfiguration of management hierarchy from geographic areas to service lines

The move to service line management arrangements was, at least partially, driven by the fact that performance data related to service type rather than area and that future arrangements for payment would be by service type rather than in the form of a block contract. This was the latest of many management reductions in recent years and, in common with restructuring in other industries (Hassard *et al.*, 2009), it left managers with rapidly increasing spans of control; larger geographical areas to cover; and managing different people under two simultaneously operating management hierarchies.

For most of our time at MCFT, there was a dual management system in place, with individual managers occupying a role in both hierarchies. Thus, at all times, the organization chart showed many more positions than there were actual people. Managers occupying these dual roles therefore carried extensive responsibilities. For example, Tanya, who held a dual role across locality/area and specialist services, had 600 staff to oversee, an existing budget over £23 million and an income target of almost a further £13 million. The new income had to come from opening new services and competing directly with private/charitable providers:

> *I cover three specialist services. They generate £25 million worth of income to the trust. I oversee a budget of £23.1 million. There's over 600 staff within the three directorates. I also have an income target of £12.8 million. We directly compete, all my services, just to both retain them and to grow them; directly compete with the independent sector and other organizations.*

Carole, who also held the dual role of service line manager and locality/area manager, covered a service that was subject to year-on-year cuts. She struggled to cover both roles and appealed to the trust board to:

> *[m]ake a decision about whether we are going down an area structure or service line structure because I think the boundaries are really blurred and I think things kind of get lost in two parallel universes and then never come together.*

Third, reductions in overall numbers of managers meant that management tasks were being devolved down the hierarchy. In many ways, these devolved tasks were supplanting traditional clinical management responsibilities as, for example, clinical supervision began to be replaced by performance management reviews. Hamir, a community services manager, explained:

> [Name] *who did my job before me was more like an expert clinician … it would have been alright three or four years ago whereas now you're calling on a whole range of managerial skills. In a way, it's a different personality type as well as a different skill set.*

The need to achieve income targets for new services and to make savings from cutbacks was also being devolved down the managerial hierarchy. Once a service line or service was isolated, income targets and/or cost savings were attached. These income targets were part of clinical (or what were termed *operational*) service line managers' performance objectives. The targets were rapidly drawn up and regularly described as '*back of a fag packet*' or '*back of the envelope*' planning. The issue for service managers was that once they accepted the objective, any problem in reaching the target was interpreted as a problem of personal managerial ability. As Carole, a service line manager with cost-cutting targets, put it:

> *It's seen as: 'This is your target; this isn't a corporate problem. So if you're saying you can't deliver this target without closing wards and we don't agree to you closing wards, go and find the money somewhere else.' Then you end up saying 'the money isn't anywhere else', and it's very much seen as your problem not an organizational problem. … How that translates into '… and what this means for your division' is often almost on the back of a fag packet planning; and when you get down to 'well how have you come to the conclusion that making this change will release this efficiency?' the detailed planning and thinking behind it often isn't there.*

She emphasized the difficulties she faced because the only cuts allowed were to managerial capacity and the loss of managers meant that much of the additional management work fell on an increasingly small managerial group:

> *Almost by default, managers are seen as an unnecessary cost and management costs have got to be driven down. But at the same time, we are expecting managers to deliver on the government's agenda, the HR agenda and every other performance management agenda and every agenda under the sun. You can't have your cake and eat it. You can't take managers out of the structure and still expect all the management to be done because it doesn't happen … when something goes wrong then it's got to be the manager to blame and we don't look at: 'Well hang on a minute. As an organization, we've reduced our management by x amount over the years.' And yet we're still expecting more and more management-type activities to go on.*

Senior managers said that the trust lacked a body of trained managers at the middle and lower reaches of the organization and had instituted internal management training programmes for team leaders and for middle managers. This training was aimed at increasing professional management skills and developing a group of managers who could be called upon in the future. Alongside the rapid expansion of the trust and reductions in management costs, ongoing initiatives included national programmes to introduce Lean management ideas: an initiative known as

The Productive Ward and efforts to improve the comparability of performance information – service line reporting. These initiatives drew upon national NHS programmes and derived from business management ideas.

The years of restructuring opened up gaps in the management hierarchy, especially from first-line manager to full service manager (the level immediately below the board). These posts could not be filled by promotion as Bob, a service manager, explained: '*You can't get managers of a good grade. You can't get people who make the grade to make the leap to service manager level … the bar has been raised for long-standing nurses too.*'

Operational managers were crucial in keeping patients moving through a vast network of interdependent services, and interpersonal skills were a key component for any manager of a clinical service, as Carole explained:

> *Our business is the interpersonal skills or the clinical skills of our staff. We don't have big machines that do scans and bring in income. Our staff are important. If they're not equipped to do the job that they need to do and make a difference, we don't have a business. Simple.*

In the centralized support services at HQ, the trust had appointed managers from outside the organization. They instigated their own leadership programme for aspiring middle managers to try to build up the business management abilities of their operational staff. Although a national NHS leadership programme was on offer, this was not highly thought of. Those managers who had been brought in from industry and were based at HQ had a scathing view of NHS home-grown managers. Sasha, the new research manager who had a private sector background, echoed a widely held media view that contradicted our observations when she said: '*NHS leadership programmes have been a void. A repository for those who can't do it in industry. It's a safe culture; there's no real performance management.*'

Fourth, management roles were changing. There were emergent corporate and business roles. As the trust expanded, new corporate management roles developed whilst other more traditional activities were being passed down the management line, adding to the pressures faced by more junior managers (Hassard *et al.*, 2009). Alongside the rapid changes to management structures (noted above), there were few linkages in the middle of the organization. One Human Resource manager, Jenny, asked: '*Can I be the only manager who's not in charge of anyone?*' She was responsible for organizational development across the trust yet held no real authority. Whilst those offering front-line services answered to a line manager and those in the upper reaches had clear lines of accountability, there were disconnections in the middle, leaving some business managers with no direct authority and/or many lines of accountability. One service director, Anthony, explained that management roles were clear at the top and bottom of the organization but were much more opaque in the middle:

> *You go a layer or two below* [the board] *and that will become vaguer, and then it becomes clear at operational level because they know what the targets are. … You've*

got the management hierarchy and you've got the business partners that come in from headquarters. … So you've got IM [Information Management], HR business partners, finance business partners. So it's more opaque.

Our time at the trust suggested that, at least for clinical managers, there was effectively no middle. Those in full-time junior roles covered middle-managerial roles part-time; and those in senior roles had some middle-managerial roles attached to their duties.

Finally, MCFT was undergoing so many rapid changes that it was difficult to present a robust account of managerial work at the organization at any point in time. By the end of the study, MCFT had virtually transformed its business by taking on services from disbanded primary care trusts. As the research ended, mental health work accounted for less than half of the income of the newly expanded organization. The latest addition of community services both doubled the size of the organization and diversified the operation to include services outside of mental health, such as community nursing.[1] This led to a paradoxical situation where front-line services were largely unchanged, albeit with reduced numbers, whilst the organization itself constantly mutated, taking advantage of opportunities for growth and trying to limit the effects of spending cuts through reductions in management costs. The trust was remarkably adept at winning contracts despite the lack of any clear business focus. The sense that the organization would continue to reconfigure rapidly in response to circumstances was widely held. At the same time, it was argued that the front-line work barely changed. As the head of facilities, Peter, explained:

Reorganization's been almost constant since I joined and at the lowest level we have domestic staff and portering staff who've been doing pretty much the same job for 20 years, and they're working for their fourth organization by now.

To summarize, MCFT was facing a wide array of management challenges, and its governance structures were regularly being rearranged in line with anticipated changes in funding. Such simultaneous management structures had significant effects upon the way managers went about their work. To add to the managerial challenge, MCFT services were fragmentary; many types of services were provided in each of the five main towns and through numerous locations both on and off hospital sites. There was no main centre to the trust and each of the five locations had a strong local culture. Each had mental health services that had evolved locally, and many of the staff had worked in the same buildings for many years whilst the organization was expanded and reorganized. The remainder of the chapter examines, first, the formal roles (the responsibilities) of managers, and then their behaviours (the actions they took).

Rapid expansion alongside regular restructuring

Given the diversity of junior and middle manager roles at the trust, we focused our study on three interconnected managerial groups operating at several MCFT sites. We found that whilst many management roles were common to most managers, aspects of the role differed between clinical/operational services and central services. Managers of central services formed two groups – dwindling management groups (such as Estates) and rapidly expanding groups (such as Human Resource Management). In Estates, we spent time with the director, deputy director, head of Estates and heads of Facilities. In Human Resources we spent time with associate directors, heads of Human Resources, head of Organization and Development (OD), HR managers and OD managers. Both of these groups were located at head office, with junior managers based at the five main trust locations. In addition, we studied the work of managers of clinical services in the acute mental health service. These included locality managers, community service managers, unit managers, service managers, team leaders, therapy managers and ward managers. The acute services group of managers covered three geographical areas and involved managers from community mental health services, therapy services and inpatient, acute ward services; in effect, forming three subgroups. We therefore explored the roles and behaviours of three distinct groups of junior and middle managers who were variously affected by the organizational challenges described above.

The previous section outlined the predicaments faced by locality/area/service managers whose line positions entailed extensive spans of control. In particular, there was a wide gap between these managers and unit managers. There were numerous examples of hybrid managers who came from a clinical background and were now working at a service manager level, combining what they saw as the best of business ideas to fulfil public sector values. However, there wasn't always an easy fit between these two competing demands. Paradoxically, it made business sense, for example, to keep certain patients (notably those from out of the area and who attracted additional payments) in longer to improve occupancy rates. As Tanya explained:

> We [specialist services] *have an income target of £12.8 million, so if I don't maintain certain bed occupancy levels and I don't make the £12.8 million, I would be underperforming. We've had to get really good systems about capacity and flow and managing throughput. … If I'm down on income, I'm really going to get it in the neck. … It's a constant pressure to make sure that you're maintaining occupancy and you're developing new business, but people are coming in and going out. You can't have any gaps. It's also making sure that you get the balance between not losing your compassion and your value base. … It's not that I'm being uncaring. I'm just practical in thinking through what has to be done. My added pressure is also maintaining the business perspective in terms of bed occupancy and new business in, new business out … we always have new services to develop and to grow and deliver. This year, we have three new services opening between September and October, so it's kind of spinning the plates. … Targets for occupancy rates used to be 100 per cent but I negotiated them to 93 per cent … it's a perverse incentive to keep people for long periods of time. But we get people through the system because we've not lost our NHS ethos about wanting people to recover and move on.*

There was a wide managerial gap between service managers and unit managers. To compound the problem, there were few unit managers in post. There had been many recent cuts and few clinical managers held permanent posts as ward manager or unit manager. Cuts had been achieved by offering ward nurses a temporary full-time ward manager post with some additional pay for part-time responsibilities as a unit manager (as we see below). This left inexperienced and poorly paid clinicians holding unrealistic managerial workloads. This was exacerbated by the complex management arrangements for services as they were provided in co-operation with many other partner organizations: six local authorities, three acute hospitals, general practitioners and independent sector organizations. As noted above, the delivery of mental health services across the trust also involved complex co-operative arrangements between NHS and other public sector and charitable bodies. The mental health trust had close links to social care, housing, police, acute hospital and community services, and mental health charities. As many patients required a co-ordinated treatment plan, junior and middle managers had to liaise often with several services at a time for each patient as well as having to liaise with the police. In this extract from an observation of an acute ward manager, Sue, the liaison is with the police:

> The police were giving Sue advice about a patient who wanted to leave against medical advice but wasn't sure if she could go home as she had beaten her partner and wasn't sure whether there was a restraining order. She wanted Sue to check. The police liaison officer said there was a warrant out for the patient's arrest for assault, car theft and aggravated burglary, so the police were on their way to arrest her at the unit. Sue told me about another patient who had stalked a staff member and who was awaiting trial. The patient had been transferred from another part of the country where they had stalked and intimidated another health worker. 'She got the person to burn down [names hospital building]. She's really dangerous. We had another patient who burnt out her room. The patient was finally charged but it was awful for everyone.'

Dangerous incidents such as these were an ongoing concern and junior/middle managers like Sue were in increasingly isolated positions as managerial posts around them had been cut. Sue, for example, had been in a temporary ward manager post for two years and was also 'acting up' part-time in the position of unit manager. She was under intense work pressure, which she attributed to doing 'extra stuff' like knowing something about the patients on the unit:

> I'm not sleeping at night. I never sleep well … when it's busy, I wake up at 5 and start running through my list of what I need to do. It's hard to know how much to do as a manager. I was told I shouldn't have done this, but I took a member of staff to the GP. She had arrived and she couldn't stop crying. I saw her through her first appointment and went and spoke to her husband. My manager said I didn't need to do that. So I know it's my choice to do all this extra stuff – knowing all the patients.

The pressure was to make service developments in areas that attracted better payments such as inpatient secure units and to '*divert patients*' where possible. The trust were making savings through *ad hoc* temporary arrangements for managerial cover such as the arrangements made for Sue. In effect, Sue was holding a junior and a middle managerial position, leaving her in a poor position to fill vacancies, for example. Many management responsibilities had been devolved to junior managers. At the same time, there was an increase in centralized control, sometimes delaying relatively simple tasks. So, for example, Gail, a full-time ward manager and temporary unit manager struggled to fill vacancies as each stage of the process had to go through a centralized HR system, which had replaced the local administration and was not running smoothly. All the pressures resulting from these delays were experienced by the clinical managers as they continued to work with staff shortages. The following summary of observation notes illustrates the many simultaneous management tasks undertaken by Gail as ward manager. She had come to work two hours before her shift officially began:

> *Gail arrived at 7.00 a.m. All morning, she was trying to complete the off-duty rota but was constantly involved with liaising with outside authorities such as the police. She was talking about patients with outstanding warrants. She spoke to HR about a post that had been empty for three months as the paperwork relating to a replacement had been lost. She had to start from scratch with this. She had three further vacancies to fill. She organized the off-duty so that willing nurses would be free to do additional shifts. 'I'm cunning. I schedule the staff who will do bank to be off for shifts where I'm short, so I can ask them to cover later.' She booked in performance reviews with some nursing staff. She worked a ten-hour shift and in that time was involved in all the roles and more than the nurse managers at the acute trust – firefighting, leading by example, arbitration, co-ordination, communication, planning, negotiating.*

Whilst the service managers were under pressure because of increasingly devolved management tasks and demands to reach income targets, the HR managers were also operating under strain as they had to work with many disparate groups of staff, many of whom did not recognize their authority. The HR department was expanding as HR services from newly contracted services were brought in, but it could not keep pace with the expansion of the organization. New staff had been recruited from the private sector, and Tesco in particular (mirroring appointments at the Department of Health). The department was introducing private sector policies that were much more aggressive about sick leave, absences and the limiting of recruitment. New HR staff were struggling to deal with a rapidly expanding organization that was changing its way of working. They had little direct control within the organization and HR were offsetting responsibility to already overloaded team and unit managers, leading to difficult relationships outside of head office. The HR department was a very unhappy workplace, and middle managers were experiencing stress-related illnesses and sickness – except at the level of HR business manager where the problem was having no one to manage and therefore being unable to achieve much, if any, influence. HR managers were responsible for supporting many service managers but had no hierarchical relationship within the organization, forming a disconnection in the system. The impact of this intense pressure that HR service managers faced was brought home to us when, on a visit to head office, we saw one of these managers, Paige, for a second time, with a colleague, Sarah (an information manager):

> Paige, the young HR service manager, comes in and starts to talk rapidly [with Sarah] about how annoyed she was yesterday. They both agree that this is out of character for her. She shows a heart monitor that she has had fitted: 'This is how it has affected me; I can show you. I am having my heart monitored for five full days.' She covers the heart monitor on her chest with a grey/silver shawl and clasps it tightly to her chest. She seems very edgy and talks about how everyone else gets office space 'but we are just squeezing people in'. The problem yesterday had been to do with an internal audit that Paige hadn't known about. Sarah explained: 'We have lots of these auditors from [Big 4 professional services corporation]. It was a communication breakdown between finance and HR – they didn't feed through to Paige.'

Such was the deterioration in Paige's health from work-related stress that just two months after we last met her, we did not recognize her. It was only later that we realized who she was. The transformation was shocking. Formerly composed, businesslike and smartly dressed, she looked much older, dishevelled and under the weather. She took us aside to a far room to tell us how unmanageable her role was: absorbing hundreds of new staff into the organization at unpredictable intervals and always with urgency. As well as the contracting arrangements for these transfers and the inevitable job cuts, there were basic practical problems of where to put the new people:

> There is limited space and we aren't sure yet where people will go. ... No one at trust HQ is saying they are crushed because they are afraid they will get moved out ... that's why I'm not kicking up a fuss. ... We may have a disjointed team ... [but] we'll just have to breathe in and make the most of it. We need to think about it politically.

Sarah was an information manager based at HQ who had worked for the NHS for 40 years. When we observed her at work, the auditors had arrived, and they came in many times with various queries for which she had to find answers. Sarah was at the epicentre of increasing demands for information and the pressure was intense. All this information had to come from embattled junior managers, and she worked calmly to get what she needed:

> The auditor comes in with a query about various pay anomalies – notably a three-quarters-of-an-hour discrepancy between the SMART system and a time sheet, plus similar queries about pay slips and hours. Sarah is very calm and sends the auditor away while she starts making calls. She explains quietly what the auditor is asking

and that the numbers need to tally. One manager explains that she has inputted data before having the time sheet and Sarah asks to attend one of their meetings to review the process with them. She feels that this will correct things and that the difference can be explained as a genuine error. She has streams of people coming in with questions and her work seems to be spiralling. Her colleague phones to say that his train didn't arrive and he will be late. She remains calm as people call in at couple-of-minute intervals. She rings the domestic manager who offers to come in on her day off to fax the time sheet over. Sarah says: 'That's all goodwill, it's her day off but she'll go in to clear it up. That's how things should work.'

An hour later she is still on the phone about the three-quarters-of-an-hour discrepancy. Eventually, a manager explains that they can balance it out. The auditor is back in about another query and says that the genuine mistake will have to be reported as a serious risk as it involved data input. Sarah argues that this is an underpayment but it cuts little ice. The auditor is young and very serious. Sarah says: 'It's not a normal week. God, I hope this isn't going to be normal anyway.'

In turn, junior managers were under increasing pressure as management tasks were being devolved. The removal of middle managers in previous restructuring exercises meant that junior managers had to step into the gap. The OD department had organized two training courses: one for middle managers called the Aspiring Leaders Programme and the other for managers in their first managerial position and working at the first rung of the ladder. Observations of the junior management training programme offered considerable opportunity to understand the challenges they faced. These managers were responsible for managing small teams of staff (or a particular function, like complaints, for example) as well as having a substantive clinical or functional role. Job titles included team leader (for a clinical service), ward manager, therapies manager, human resource manager, finance manager and complaints manager. The training was taking place at an out-of-town hotel and involved ten days of study over the course of six months (six days of teaching, action learning sets and a feedback session). The managers were asked to describe their roles – what they expected of themselves, what their team expected of them and what MCFT expected of them. Their descriptions of their roles were similar to those seen at the acute trust and were characteristic of what we observed and were told at interview. Their answers to the three questions were captured on a flip chart and are reproduced in observation notes:

The junior managers shout out answers to the question: 'What is a team leader?' The answers given are: leads by example; good communicator; organized; responsible; confident; professional; sets standards; supportive; loyal; fair. The words are shouted out rapid-fire and there is no disagreement.

These answers, echoing the roles of nurse managers in the acute trust, showed that the managers had a clear idea of the roles they expected to fulfil. These roles resonated with the answers to the second question. However, they made a notable addition – their role in challenging senior managers and thereby protecting front-line staff:

> *In answer to the question 'What does your team expect of you?' the answers are: mediate, listen and consult; have answers so that you can guide and clarify; be honest and straight-talking; explain how changes will happen; be both supportive and firm; challenge senior managers; be consistent and fair. This set of answers brought with it lots of stories about team leaders who weren't like that.*

The third question generated quite a different set of answers and clearly indicated the business orientation of the trust:

> *To the final question about what 'MCFT expects of you' the answers are: balance the budget; use resources effectively; provide a safe, quality service; deliver on strategy and apply MCFT policies; promote services; supervise and recruit; reduce absenteeism; act as a small ambassador.*

They not only had to be emotionally and visibly available to front-line staff, but they were also advertisers and promoters of mental health services, balancing the books and managing resources effectively without any impact on patient care. These themes were all too present in the previous chapters and this trust was no different in that respect. What is interesting is that first-line managers were involved in drumming up new business, finding business opportunities and deciding where savings could be made. This was borne out in our observations and conversations with junior managers. This first-line manager role was recognized as being particularly difficult, not least because these managers rarely had any previous specific management training or experience. As Brian, one of the Estates managers recalled: '*I mean, first-line managers, it's the worst job in the world … I remember being one, but it's not something I'd want to go back to.*'

There was no doubt that morale was low among junior managers. The trainees were drawn from across the trust and included clinical and central service managers. They used the sessions to develop management skills and to focus on particular problems they were facing, such as dealing with a difficult staff member or implementing a change programme. These first-line managers were taught about situational leadership, learning styles and change management and encouraged to develop their own management style. The training included opportunities for coaching, which was used as a development tool throughout the organization. The training programme was opened by the chief executive who emphasized the importance of being profitable and, as we saw earlier, added that '*the key phrase is more for less*'. He described how he liked to recruit from within and asked who wanted to be in a senior management position in five to ten years? None of these managers did. Instead, they answered the question about where they wanted to be in five years as follows: *no idea; doing something I enjoy; managing a bigger team; have a better IT system; be a ward manager.* The junior managers were attached to the front-line aspect of their work and offered this attachment as explanation for their lack of managerial ambition. They also understood, very clearly, that these junior management roles seemed less precarious than those higher up.

There was a significant division between junior and middle/senior managers generally. This was exemplified in the Estates department where the battle between old NHS and new corporate managers was playing out. William, the deputy director of Estates, explained:

> *I don't like to think of 'us and them', but it still works like that. Whether we like to think it or not, at certain levels, it stills works like that; and the supervisor is in the middle, if you like, of what you would call 'us' and 'them' because they don't see themselves as being, sort of, well up the management chain but equally they don't see themselves as one of the tradesmen and the people doing the physical work.*

The Estates department was one of the shrinking departments. The trust had brought in a new director of Estates, Brian, to see through the restructuring. He had worked for another mental health organization in the UK where he won an award for Estates strategy. His temporary appointment was for two years and his role was to see through the restructuring and removal of several layers of management. When we arrived, there was an extremely flattened hierarchy. In addition, he reduced the estates costs of the newly contracted services by incorporating responsibilities for the new sites, which followed new contracts, within the existing team. As far as possible, the trust avoided taking on old buildings with the new service contracts. Where they did and where it was possible, they moved quickly to try and close/sell the buildings and move the services into existing trust properties. He also brought hotel services (portering, catering and domestic services) into the Estates department. Thus he was able to radically increase the size of the department and remove further managerial posts. This strategy was effected across the trust in Human Resources, Finance, Catering, Portering, Domestic Services and Information departments to rapidly strip out management costs.

The previous head of Estates, William, had worked for the NHS for 40 years and was approaching retirement. He was made deputy director on Brian's arrival and effectively demoted. He retained the unenviable responsibility for the performance of the department. Their work was target driven, and they normally dealt with requests in seven to ten days and received 150 to 170 requests per week. Work was classified as immediate, urgent or routine and repair targets were set by the organization. The urgency was driven by potential harm to patients, staff or the public. William explained:

> *What we do is we classify work in terms of immediate, urgent or routine. Anything that is immediate has a response target of a response within three-quarters of an hour and completion within two hours. If it's urgent, it has a response within four hours and completion within eight, and if it's routine, it has a response within three days*

and completion within five. Those are the targets, and then what we set ourselves is to meet those responses in 85 per cent of the cases for the routine, 90 per cent for the urgent and 95 per cent on the immediate.

This classification system obscures the important role Estates played in making sure that patients could not harm themselves or others in any part of any building. Any new danger had to be repaired or replaced at all sites within strict time limits. Once Estates were aware of a problem – perhaps one that had been found at another UK mental health trust – they were held responsible to resolve it before anyone came to harm. For example, this happened when a patient in the UK committed suicide in NHS premises and new, safe equipment or furnishings had to be installed across the trust.

As the span of control of the Estates department expanded, several of the remaining managers were effectively demoted as they were doing more demanding work with larger spans of control at a lower management grade and with lower pay within the organization. The only other middle manager who remained was Peter, head of Estates, who had worked for the NHS for 22 years in Estates departments. He was in charge of catering, portering, linen and domestic staff – a significant change from his expert background managing an Estates department. Estates managers were extremely pressured, not least because of the constant demands associated with acquiring new sites and closing some of them down to reduce Estates costs. At the same time, senior staffing had been slashed by 75 per cent. William, the deputy director, outlined the ups and downs of recent restructuring episodes:

[MCFT] *had more than quadrupled in fact, in terms of size. You had four organizations then at senior level that had to squash into one. So you ended up with one chief executive. And you lost three-quarters of the senior staff. And a similar thing happened in Estates. You still ended up with four people doing what previously probably 16 were doing.*

As we saw earlier, for acute service middle managers, the pressures were different. This group of managers included inpatient and community service managers, nurse managers, managers of other services and specialities, and service directors. Many service managers in this group were working in two roles at once (covering both a service across the entire organization and a locality). As the organization was operating two management structures – one geographical and one by type of service – the management job was almost impossible. These service managers negotiated with each other to offset workloads. A further level of management was being removed whilst more management responsibility was being pushed down the line, not only from HR but from all corporate functions. Several of these managers had been demoted in recent restructuring or had taken on vastly expanded spans of control. The emerging management roles for each level of manager were as follows. *Service directors* were now directing large, dispersed businesses and responsible for income targets, problem-solving, planning, creating and bidding for contracts for new profitable services, and protecting junior managers. *Unit managers* were responsible for all day-to-day management requirements for their unit and, with the exceptions of holidays abroad, were always on call or on duty. They dealt with complaints, breeches of security, bullying, suicides, staff sickness and arbitration with doctors. At the same time, they were concerned to be seen to be 'hands on' in order to lead by example. *Team leaders, ward managers* and *HR managers* had different roles. They were at the receiving end of responsibility within a disconnected hierarchy. This meant that the HR manager, for example, had no one to manage but had to influence organizational development across the trust in co-operation with other team and unit managers. Ward managers carried responsibilities for day-to-day staff management – appraisals, return-to-work interviews, and organizing staffing rotas and replacement posts for new staff. All of this management had to be balanced against a requirement to fulfil a clinical role.

Our time spent with ward managers found them working at many levels. For example, Gail was clinician, team leader, stand-in for the unit manager and leader of a management project for the board. These jobs were highly fragmented and no one occupied a fixed managerial role. Ward managers were seconded into position and then asked to lead projects for the board. There was a move towards project work so that each task was graded and paid on different pay bands. This task-based work did not recognize clinical expertise. In addition, managers were given partial promotions as they were paid on different grades for different aspects of their work. At the same time, and as noted in the previous section, performance management replaced clinical supervision. Long-serving managers sustained vast networks of contacts across this dispersed organization, and this allowed them to find shortcuts and to get things done through informal routes. At the same time, managers were introducing national initiatives from the private sector, such as the Productive Ward. which was derived from Lean management principles. Ward managers were largely uncritical of these initiatives, being more concerned about how they might use them to gather more resources to their area of work (for outstanding repairs and basic equipment like bed sheets). By arguing for resources using current parlance – *'it supports the Productive Ward initiative'* – they were occasionally successful.

Managing the unmanageable: where *'going beyond the deadline isn't really an option'*

In order to fulfil these roles, there were common patterns of behaviour. Peter, the Estates manager, described the culture as being one where: *'going beyond the deadline isn't really an option. You have to do the best you can within that deadline.'* As a result it was common for managers to work long hours. He expanded as follows:

> *We routinely do nine to ten hours a day. That's the normal day. Occasionally, it can be longer than that. But nine to ten hours a day is the normal day. ... I would just prefer to stay here 'til half seven and get it done.*

Ward manager Gail suggested her long working hours were due to poor time management (although our observations did not support this):

> *I probably still spend quite a bit of time with patients, but that's because my time management's really poor. ... At the same time, there's the requirements from the trust perspective and from legislation that, you know, we have to be achieving certain targets, and audits have to be completed, and the documentation that goes with that and the administration. So you're, kind of, you're very much split, really.*

These long work hours extended across the trust and for all levels of manager. While clinical staff had the advantage of fixed working hours and overtime payments, managers from ward level up had no such limits. Their responsibility was to '*get the job done*' no matter how long it took. Brian, director of Estates, seconded for two years to the trust, travelled quite a distance to work, stayed in hotels and worked at home one day a week:

> *It's stressful because of sheer volume of work. ... I usually work here until 8 o'clock at night when the security locks it up; I go to the hotel, grab a bite to eat and then start working probably until 11 o'clock, but I try to make sure that it's only three nights a week. So when Thursday night comes, I travel home; I don't do anything Thursday night. I work from home on the Friday. Once Friday 5 o'clock comes, I make sure I don't do anything on Saturday or Sunday and that's a hard thing to keep to.*

In common with many managers, working long hours was described as a choice. Managers felt that they were not compelled to work such hours but that it was necessary in order to fulfil their responsibilities. For managers occupying dual roles, the pressure was intensified still further and work was made more burdensome by requirements to provide on-call managerial cover out of hours. With only a small number of managers and many units to cover, unit managers were often on call for almost the whole trust and for services they barely knew.

Observation notes from a services meeting showed that rapid, large-scale changes were being implemented by this active group of middle managers. At this meeting, there were 14 managers including service, HR, Finance and Estates managers. Service managers seemed to carry much of the responsibility for getting things done whilst HR, Finance and Estates managers offered a supporting role. This excerpt from one of the meetings dealing with an immediate need to reduce Estates costs shows how the managers switched rapidly between short-term goals and long-term potential for change in quick-fire exchanges:

PETER INTRODUCES AN AGENDA ITEM ABOUT ESTATES COSTS: *This is so fundamental; this is bread and butter stuff and it can't wait. I want an action plan from Tanya, Carole and Anthony* [service managers] *in two weeks time. We need to reduce the number of buildings because it is costing too much ... move to purpose-built buildings ... use hot desking ... more efficient use of resources ... sell* [name] *house to generate funds for capital development.*

ANTHONY: *If we reduce buildings, can we maintain staffing? … We need culture change as well; when you move people to a new building, they are more amenable to changing the way they work. … IT systems are key to using Estates effectively.*

[There seems to be a consensus that IT systems could work better.]

PETER: *[Jokes] It's my aim to eliminate Estates.*
CAROLE: *We need to get a group together and scope – we need to talk to Robert* [director of Operations]; *we need to get a vision and push the initiative and get some early wins to take to the board.*
ANTHONY: *There's got to be something positive for staff with new buildings, decent drinks machines, breakout spaces.*
ELLA: *The biggest problem is clinicians; they want their own rooms.*
BRIAN: *Where your paper bin stands, that's probably costing nearly £200 a year for that bit of space; so if you use that space more effectively then that all starts racking up.*
CAROLE: *We are looking at new ways of working. Now back to the agenda.*

By this stage, a date has been set for the service managers to develop a plan. The meeting moved rapidly on to the next item. The short meeting dealt with many agenda items including the development of new IT systems, new senior appointments, estates planning and Lean recruitment processes. Whilst the service managers had to devise and implement service changes, the supporting managers were taken to task, for example, over why it takes so long to recruit new staff. In spite of the temporal and financial pressures, there was much good humour between managers:

TANYA: *The recruitment system is so un-Lean.*
ELLA: *We'll put it on a diet.*

All the managers had to report at these monthly meetings against dashboard targets for sickness absence, staff appraisal rates, and other organizational and national measures. The focus of the agenda items was to keep dashboard items at green. In a separate interview, Anthony (a service director) related these pressures to the need to maintain foundation trust status:

> *The level of scrutiny has gone through the roof since becoming an FT. When I first started, for example, our budgets were pretty vague and not very accurate, whereas now 80 per cent of it is year-end forecast and stuff.*

Mental health work could be unpredictable in affecting all groups of managers; for example, when patients caused damage to property or a risk to patients was identified. If one patient could harm themselves on the property then all properties had to be adapted urgently. More often, work could be scheduled and was co-ordinated via timetabled meetings. Observations of managers' meetings showed that they dealt with many issues in rapid succession and were, as Peter said, focused on '*business, business, business*'.

Because of the spread of sites and number of subcontracted and jointly provided services, both junior and middle managers spent substantial amounts of time on the phone or in meetings sharing information and trying to get things done. For example, Estates managers like William had to deal with in-house and contract staff:

> *For most of our headings, we have multiple providers, whether that's on the maintenance side or facilities – catering and laundry. We have multiple [outsourced] providers, so managing them can be time consuming. … Where it's in-house [staff], generally I can get things sorted out pretty quickly if there's a problem. If it's a contractual arrangement, sometimes we're one step removed from the contract where we might have a service level agreement with a partner NHS organization who then subcontract to a company like Isis, Mediclean or Initial; and we then have to raise it with the partner trust, who then raise it with Isis, and it just feels like you are too far away from the staff.*

Service directors were responsible for specific income targets related to new services under rapidly expanding spans of control. Their performance was measured in terms of how well they were able to achieve these targets. Poorly made plans were rapidly dispersed to middle managers for them to realize. They first had to discover what was wrong with these sketchy plans. As Tanya explained:

> *Another unit I inherited … the tariff was wrong, the commissioning arrangements were wrong, staffing, not enough demand. Everything was wrong.*

Then they had to find solutions to these problems as the service and responsibility for realizing income was the service managers' responsibility. They were concerned to negotiate down unrealistic objectives and were reluctantly entrepreneurial. This placed them under considerable pressure as the targets, as Tanya suggested, appeared at times to have been plucked out of thin air:

> *Sometimes the execs have a habit of just drawing up plans, then we have to deliver the plans, then the plans become my problem if they don't get delivered. … Once we had an idea about extending [name of building] and having maybe four or five beds for older people. I went to New York and came back and I was told we were doing a 15-bedded unit and I had an income target for that 15-bedded unit being full for 90 per cent of the time. It wasn't based on any market analysis or our recommendations, but I had to make it work. … That happens quite a lot. If it didn't work, it would totally become my problem and I would be performance managed and judged by that. … They say: 'Well let's put in that; we'll do four new units and make a million or two and we'll worry about it later.' … But what happens is [that] we don't worry about it later. It becomes my problem.*

Within this trust, two types of manager were described: first, the home-grown NHS worker who progressed into management; and second, the business manager brought in for their specialist corporate skills. At times, it seemed surprising that there was little antagonism from those who were being replaced. In concert with Peter's view (which follows), there was a tacit acceptance that this was necessary:

> *I think they are both valid. Looking at our directors here, for example – our chief exec, our director of ops, our director of nursing have come up from being basic grade nurses at one point. They were all mental health nurses who've worked their way up. But we have other people on the director's team and the management team who've entered as graduates – entered through the management training programme –, and they bring a good set of abilities and they contribute a lot as well. I think it's probably best to have a mix of different talents and different skills.*

This was something of a one-way street as business managers were more derisory of the NHS home-grown managers. The new director of Estates saw the old-style manager as outdated and harmful for the organization. They were criticized for having a '*relaxed*', '*that will do*' attitude. He outlined how managers who could not keep up were moved into '*a siding*' to allow '*the express train to come through*':

> *There is a point in time when you have got to say 'well okay, what we need to do is move them into a siding for a period of time'; because we can't afford the organization to slow down; because their speed of development is slower that the organization's requirement for speed. So we can actually, not necessarily get rid of them, but put them into a siding in order that we can allow the express train to come through.*

In reality, Brian warned of a change in approach towards managers who were not keeping up. He described how managers outside of head office were thought to be unaware of the extent of the cuts required whereas there was a '*war mentality*' at head office that was forcing through previously unthinkable changes:

> *I use the [term] war mentality. [Given] the amount of money that we are going to be forced to have to save, there isn't going to be any opportunity to say, 'oh I don't like playing with you because I don't think I can trust you'. It will be, 'well we've got no choice so let's agree, you know; whatever the Geneva Convention or the equivalent is, let us agree the rules of engagement and actually put them into place'. … And it might mean a new building somewhere if it means that we can get rid of three or four old and inefficient buildings.*

The war metaphor continued in a discussion of a changed attitude to managers who could not adapt quickly enough:

> *We haven't got time to spend on nurturing them. There are times when you will pick somebody up and carry them on your shoulder, you know, pick the wounded up; but there are times when you've just got to shoot them in the trenches. I think we are getting into that position where we might have to be shooting more, you know; 'there*

are no wounded soldiers here'. ... You've got to [have] *100 per cent performance here. So if you can't run then you will be shot; there is no carrying people.*

Accordingly, Brian described the purpose of his two-year secondment to the organization as being to put '*systems and structures in place to move forward'*. He described how management capability had not been able to keep pace with the rapid growth of the organization and argued that this created stressors for established managers:

> *A lot of organizations have grown quite significantly over the last five, six years and some of them have grown their management structures, but possibly some of the management capabilities have not grown to cope with the growth of responsibility. The sort of effects where businesses suddenly grow ... they might have been superb at managing the small business, but when it becomes a bigger business, it's a different challenge. As a director, it's very easy to go back to the comfort zone, doing what you originally trained to do, your original profession; and you start reverting back to that. But you should be saying, 'hang on a minute, my job is to direct so I've got to let other people ...'. When it becomes a certain size, actually there is a different style of management and different skills that you probably need to do that ... and I think some of the stresses that you see around people in this building are probably because they are trying to actually run a small business even though it's a lot bigger than that.*

For some managers, like Peter, the new system of dashboard reporting (red, amber, green) was a great improvement on previous information systems:

> *You can scan through quickly and pick out where your problems are. ... I was sat in meetings a number of years ago where there were reams and reams and reams of written reports, which are hard to scan through. So yeah, the idea of the dashboard is it, kind of, picks out the key things for you.*

For others, however, this quick reference system was another example of the workarounds that clinical staff found to prioritize repairs. If they were able to prioritize their maintenance jobs and perhaps game the system by rating it a high risk (scoring 15+ out of 25) then it would go straight to the board for action. There was a suspicion therefore that staff used the numerical system to overrate risks and bring their jobs to the top of the list. Estates managers were engaged in trying to assess the *real* level of risk and negotiate these ratings down. '*You sometimes wonder ... is this really a 16? ... Have they given it that just to make sure that it goes in front of the board, and then it'll get some attention – it'll get some resource?'*

This sort of gaming applied across the board as cross-charging departments and services helped in achieving income targets or cost savings. Further and more severe cuts were imminent, and the Estates managers were going to have to halve the number of properties in conjunction with a further service reorganization. They understood as well as any of the managers that these cuts would only be achieved by redefining eligibility for services. As Peter implies:

At the moment, we have 500 inpatient beds across eight locations and we have community staff at 60 community locations; and to achieve the savings they are talking about, we can change that configuration so that perhaps we go down to four sites and instead of having staff at 60 community sites we go down to 30 or 40. You have to just keep reprioritizing your services so that everything's targeted at the most acutely ill. Perhaps some patients that aren't as ill don't meet that threshold anymore. So we would just realign our ... Estates and Facilities services to match that service reorganization.

In common with the previous cases, and as is common in these types of rapidly changing work environments, the trust working environment was high pressure and reports of bullying were widespread. Several managers reported hard-line managerial tactics. Paul, a team leader, received the following reprimand: '*I'm the manager, don't forget that ... don't argue with me. I'm the boss. Just remember that I'm in charge.*' Josie, another team leader, said: '*I had a manager who had a picture of a boot squashing a fly on her office door*'. And Susie, an information manager, told us:

I had a manager who bullied me until I went off sick. I went back and she did it again. I had the strength to take her to a grievance. Seeing her name on a letter made me physically heave ... she was dealt with and my complaint was upheld. She was demoted and went off sick.

The junior and middle managers faced seemingly unmanageable workloads. They appeared to us to be working themselves into the ground by trying to succeed in completing the work of two or more people – a job made all the more difficult by the geographical spread, the diversity of services and the number of different units to cover. The levels of stress and burnout were entirely consistent with the seemingly unrealistic demands being made of them. Nevertheless, they continued to work to provide the best services they could under the circumstances.

Conclusions

At the time of our study, MCFT was unusual among UK mental health trusts: first, because it had achieved foundation trust status at all; and second, because it had managed to maintain and to grow its income stream. We see in this chapter the cost of this rapid expansion and concurrent restructuring on a wide group of junior and middle managers.

Nationally, there had been a drive to reduce the number of inpatient beds and to provide community services instead. Beyond this, commissioners of health services had continued to require year-on-year cost savings even prior to the national austerity measures. As mental health services generally did not benefit significantly from increases in health spending, they were now suffering severe resource shortages. The situation for their junior and middle managers was bleak. Brian described how the balance of managers would shift as new managers – able to manage a large business – were grown or recruited and those who could not grow would be '*restructured*' or '*retired*':

We recognize that you are not going to grow the skills in everybody in the timescale, and we are recruiting people with those skills and that broader aspect to actually help fill that gap. But eventually, through succession planning, we'll probably increase some of the staffing but eventually flatten that off again once we've dealt with the restructuring and take into account succession of those people as they retire ... because we've got two or three people that are coming to the end of their working life.

All managerial roles at MCFT were changing significantly. This was partly because of the management requirements of an organization that had expanded significantly and reduced management costs by more than 30 per cent. Managers were experiencing increasing pressures of work through expanded responsibilities and increased demands in terms of workload as management tasks were passed down the ladder. There were particular pressure points where work demands were almost limitless and areas where work demands could be controlled. Unit managers and ward managers experienced very high work demands whereas the demands on community services were slightly more limited. Most managers were working extremely long hours, although many believed that they had a choice about whether or not to. Opportunities for remote access went beyond on-call arrangements and meant that managers of high-pressure areas were available for work at all hours. All management roles involved increased requirements for business skills, such as understanding budgets, the basics of competitive strategy, the preparation of bids for new contracts (regardless of service speciality), and how to meet targets, etc.; yet there did remain some considerable perceived conflict between business and clinical values.

A further pressure facing MCFT managers was the dual structure. As a result of ongoing restructuring, many managers occupied a position in effectively parallel hierarchies. The first, a historical system, organized services by geographical area and the second, a new system, was organized by service type. The new system anticipated changes to payments for mental health services that had yet to be announced at a national level.

MCFT offers an instructive case study, having undergone both significant changes to organizational form and extensive reductions in management costs in advance of management cuts being faced by other NHS organizations. The effects of this restructuring were evident within the case as the varying challenges facing managers played out in changing management roles and behaviours. It remains difficult to attract funding to mental health services and there is, perhaps, no little irony in the fact that the trust was no longer, predominantly, a provider of mental health services by the end of the study. The middle managers we studied were somewhat reluctant entrepreneurs as they diversified services and created new business to sustain traditional service provision.

The question we were left asking was: What will happen to mental health services now the trust's main streams of income are non-mental-health services? As detailed in the early sections of this chapter, mental health services have always struggled to retain public funding, and various reorganizations over the decades have sought to resolve the problem. However, we found a specialist mental health trust staying in business by transferring its efforts into non–mental-health provision. What we concluded was that this business strategy may be unsustainable. These short-term community contracts were ripe for picking by nationally (or internationally) co-ordinated, large-scale operations in just the way Initial and other companies have come to provide hotel services. In the meantime, mental health services were being reduced and their efforts redirected into profitable areas; for example, secure inpatient services and specialist services that attract higher-level payments. Mental health services are unlikely to attract significant private investment. However, associated services, such as HR, catering and accommodation, offer business opportunities to large-scale commercial providers.

Note

1   These newly acquired community services were not specifically included in the study. The term 'community services', on the whole, in this chapter refers to community mental health services specifically. The term 'non–mental-health community services' indicates the newly acquired services.

7

WHEN ORGANIZATIONS DISAPPEAR

Deconstructing management at a primary care trust

It must be absolutely awful to be a manager in the PCT.

(Senior manager, Millford Acute Trust)

This chapter analyses, principally, the changing work roles, behaviour and experiences of managers in a primary care trust (PCT). The trust was based at Millford, an industrial town in the north of England (and location of the acute trust case discussed in Chapter 4). The PCT managers who participated in the research tended to fall into two categories: on the one hand were what we might call 'specialist' managers with dedicated administrative and leadership responsibilities allied, for example, to commissioning, providing or human resources functions; on the other were those from various clinical specialisms who had management tasks attached to their medical roles – or what we refer to as 'hybrid' or clinician-managers.

Our PCT study, however, also includes a second level of analysis – examination of the organizational environment in which our research on healthcare management was conducted. Initially planned as a study of managerial work in changing (post-global financial crisis) times, we found not long into the investigation that we were also analysing an organization under significant existential threat. Specifically, this was an organization likely to be delayered out of existence in the near future due to major structural reforms proposed by central government. This made the case study of Millford PCT a rather unusual one for research on organizational change and managerial work.

Of the four healthcare organizations studied for this book, it was indeed the PCT that was to be the most drastically affected by the Health and Social Care Act 2012. As we noted earlier, such policies would make significant structural and procedural changes to the NHS, under which PCTs and strategic health authorities (SHAs) were to be abolished. For PCTs, this was to be effected by April 2013, with GP-led consortia assuming most of the commissioning responsibilities formerly held by the PCTs. In addition, public health aspects of PCT business were to be taken on by local councils.

The Millford PCT case, therefore, concerns how healthcare managers attempt to make sense of their organizational roles and work behaviour in times of unprecedented uncertainty, insecurity and transformation. On the one hand, the PCT story reflects the influence of political imperatives on NHS organization with ideological forces paving the way for private commissioning and franchising in what are traditionally public sector domains. On the other, the case reflects issues of personal anxiety, pressure and stress as Millford – a pathfinder organization in the government healthcare restructuring programme – struggles to make sense of what the future holds for its staff as the organization finds itself on the verge of closure.

Managing primary care

In Chapter 2, we discussed how the pace of change in UK healthcare has increased rapidly over the past three decades. Within an era of high-profile reforms, primary care has received some of the most extensive restructuring attention from successive governments. In addition, the character of government healthcare policy has varied significantly during this period (see Baggott, 2004). Links to other public sector bodies (e.g. education and social services) have regularly highlighted the importance of primary care and its central place in the transformation of health services and welfare (Exworthy, 2001). Indeed, there has been a range of structural reforms of primary care in a broad drive to improve the quality of service provided while at the same time enhancing various aspects of cost efficiency (see Ham, 2009). With the announcement of the 2010 healthcare White Paper (*Equity and Excellence: Liberating the NHS*), however, primary care in the UK was about to witness a particularly dramatic series of strategic and organizational changes. To establish a context for our case account of managerial behaviour and organizational change at Millford PCT, we discuss the structure and management of PCTs prior to the passing of the White Paper into law as the Health and Social Care Act 2012. Reactions to these changes ultimately underpin both our ethnography of the roles and behaviours of PCT managers in Millford and analysis of the political changes that brought about the demise of the organization as entity in itself.

PCTs were themselves relatively new organizations, having been brought into being around the turn of the twenty-first century (see Chapter 2). They were multifaceted organizations comprising a myriad of roles, responsibilities and duties (Primary Care Trust Network NHS Confederation, 2010). At the time of commencing our research, the NHS website defined primary care trusts as being charged with

> the care provided by people you normally see when you first have a health problem. It might be a visit to a doctor or a dentist, an optician for an eye test or a trip to a pharmacist to buy cough mixture.

This definition reflected the diverse roles PCTs played in the daily lives of patients. It also mirrored their importance in UK healthcare and why they received such significant attention from central government in recent reforms. In terms of an organizational and managerial perspective, PCTs historically intervened in a threefold process which consisted of the planning, commissioning, and delivering of health services to local communities (see McMurray and Cheater, 2003). PCTs have been charged variously with providing primary care services and commissioning secondary and tertiary care. Crucially, the 'shifting [of] the balance of power within the NHS' (Department of Health, 2001, 2002) more than a decade and a half ago led to a relocation of the public health function and infrastructure from health authorities to PCTs (see Heller *et al.*, 2003).

With the 2010 White Paper, however, a plan emerged to put an end to PCTs by 1 April, 2013, with much of their management and procedural responsibilities being transferred to GP consortia. From then on, GP consortia would be conferred around £80 billion and be the main referents in terms of the commissioning of care. Much of the philosophy behind the 2010 White Paper was that significant efficiencies should be gained from implementing the new management system as it would reduce the level of administrative bureaucracy, which it was argued, served to slow down the care process. The proposals outlined in the White Paper would increase the quality of care provided while at the same time reducing the overall operational costs involved.

The dismantling of PCTs would therefore represent an attempt to foster a more competitive and economical system for UK healthcare. It was argued in the White Paper that the dismantling of PCTs would represent a positive organizational change for the NHS in that GPs would be more effective at setting priorities and making informed choices. Although the changes suggested would undoubtedly lead to regrading, demotion and redundancy among NHS staff – as the Chief Executive of NHS Suffolk, Carole Taylor-Brown, argued – they would also create new opportunities, fostering the development of skills that would promote efficiencies on a larger scale (Parry, 2010).

However, reactions towards the dismantling of PCTs were mixed. There was a dearth of consensus on the utility of reform measures and particularly as to whether the planned changes would significantly contribute to the de-bureaucratization of the NHS and to reducing management costs. There was doubt, in particular, as to whether the reforms would improve the quality of health and care services delivered while saving resources (Ham, 2010). In addition, there was concern over the ability of GP consortia to manage a PCT budget without significant help from wider healthcare management agencies. The Nuffield Trust, for example, suggested a longer stay of execution for PCTs in order to guarantee a smoother administrative transition (see O'Dowd, 2011). Likewise, some senior NHS managers suggested retaining PCTs – as a sort of 'plan B' – in the event of things not turning out as planned or simply in order to pass on operational knowledge to GP consortia, whose potential weaknesses may be a lack of managers, generic managerial experience and lack of commissioning skills (McLellan, 2012).

Given the nature of this context, with political proposals targeting PCTs for closure, the main managerial challenge for our current case study appeared clear – how do you maintain morale and keep operationally focused amidst a climate of incipient organizational decline. Framed by the impact of a changing political ideology and reflecting acute managerial experience amidst imminent institutional demise, this is the situation within which our study of PCT managers' roles and behaviours was set.

Managing Millford PCT

We're half way through a reorganization when nobody seems to know what the outcome of the reorganization will be.

(Sir Gerry Robinson, 2011)[1]

As an organization, Millford PCT was responsible for contracting local health services for the metropolitan borough. Prior to the Health and Social Care Act 2012, PCTs were central to the NHS and controlled 80 per cent of the NHS budget to commission secondary care and provide community care services. As noted, primary care is the first point of healthcare contact for most people. Secondary care covers the services you are referred to by a clinician for further investigation or treatment. Thus Millford PCT worked with the local community and health partners to deliver services that were responsive to the needs of local people. These partners included, for example, general practitioners, dentists, optometrists, pharmacists and local hospitals as well as Millford Council. Millford PCT was established in 2001 and, at the time of our research, had funding and spend of just over under £450 million. It served a population of just under 300,000, which was an ageing one with 18 per cent being 65 years or older (the projection was that this would rise by a further 10,000 people in the next decade). The trust covered one of the most polarized areas of wealth and deprivation in the UK, with those in the most deprived areas having, on average, 12 years of ill health whereas those in the wealthiest had only six. However, Millford was one of the healthier places to live in its geographical region with life expectancy for both men and women being above the national average. In recent years, it has also ranked above the mean in the UK GP Patient Survey.

In terms of organization structure, the trust was based on six main departments: Corporate Services; Finance & Estates; Commissioning; Public Health; Human Resources; and Provider Services. (At the start of our research, Millford PCT operated a *shared* HR service with another local NHS authority, Riverside.) Subsequently, the structure expanded to include functions for Information Management & Technology and Community Health. Allied to this structure was a 'comments, concerns, and complaints' service provided by the Patient Advice & Liaison Service (or PALS), which was housed in the same building as the management functions of Millford PCT – an 11-storey 1970s tower block, Royal

House, the space in which was mostly rented from a local property developer. Ultimately, these main functions were joined by Millford Managed Care, the GP commissioning consortium (Clinical Commissioning Group or CCG) set up in 2007 by over 50 local GP practices. As noted, Millford was chosen as one of the first national Pathfinders in order to spearhead the reform of PCTs. It was, therefore, within the first phase of GP commissioning, placing its GPs at the forefront of local health services development.

In terms of the PCT workforce, the complement was around 1,200, of which 900 represented full-time employees. The vast majority were women – in fact, making up around 90 per cent; this was a common pattern for this healthcare sector. At the time, 56 staff were defined as senior managers; that is, Band 8A and above (or 4.7 per cent of the workforce). Just over 30 per cent of senior managers were men as compared to 10 per cent of the entire workforce; the vast majority (97 per cent) worked on a full-time basis. In terms of the management structure, the highest-level decisions were taken by the PCT's board, which was made up of seven executive and six non-executive directors who were recruited from the local community. This board was advised by the Professional Executive Committee (which brought together representatives of different clinical backgrounds to offer medical advice) and the Management Team, which comprised the PCT's directors.

The Millford PCT study primarily involved semi-structured interviews with senior, junior and middle managers from both the provider and commissioning wings of the organization as well as with managers from the HR function. Given the atypical nature of this study – a climate of organizational closure, workforce dispersal and staff demotions/redundancies – the PCT research differed from previous cases in that we made a request to extend it beyond the period originally agreed. This was done to trace the employment fortunes of certain interviewees as the restructuring process began to take hold. The research was, therefore, conducted in two main phases. The early period mainly reflected the original aims of analysing the changing roles and behaviour of PCT managers. Later data collection, however – in the midst of slated PCT closure – concentrated more on managerial attitudes and workplace culture. Here, the investigations were of a more *emergent* nature with topics being agreed upon as and when changes in the political/organizational climate dictated. Nevertheless, both phases of research reflected our preferred perspective of a Critical-Action approach.

A final idiosyncrasy of the PCT case was that the data was virtually all collected through interview-based research (see Chapter 3). Although our original plan was to base the case on a mixture of interview and observational data, early in the process of research it was agreed that formal observational work (of team meetings, board discussions and other managerial work) would be inappropriate given the increasingly sensitive nature of political decisions and their impact on the organization. However, in the course of the research, we were able to make a number of informal observations and interpretations relating mainly to the changing culture of the organization.

Changing work roles and demands for organizational efficiency

Much of the initial data collected on managerial behaviour at the PCT, therefore, focused on issues of managerial roles and behaviour. Discussion of these issues was frequently framed in relation to the history of large-scale organizational change in the NHS and, in recent times, the adoption of specific management techniques. Signal amongst the latter were philosophies of operational efficiency and systems of task accounting.

Given the nature of this healthcare sector, many of the managers interviewed were what we came to term 'hybrid' managers in that part of their work now involved a management element on top of a dedicated clinical role. This was frequently the case for those we interviewed on the *provider* side where, given a range of inherent and sometimes conflicting pressures, the integration of managerial and clinical roles could sometimes itself require *managing*. As one of our informants explained in the following exchange:

INFORMANT: *So I manage the team, co-ordinate the sort of service that we're going to give. So some of it is in groups; well, a lot of it is groups. Then there's some that's one-to-one. So I split the team up and tell them what they're doing from term to term, look at the* [patients] *who are waiting, split the* [patients] *up. So I do all the day-to-day management of that. But I've still got a clinical role as well. So I assess most of the new* [patients] *that come in.*

RESEARCHER: *Right, so the role is how much clinical and how much management?*

INFORMANT: *Well, my boss has just come back from maternity leave,* [so] *it was very much half and half* [until then]. [But] *it's now gone to point 3 management, officially. ... But we're sort of getting dragged and sucked in to kind of justify our grades. You know, dragged into a lot of the strategic stuff over there* [Royal House]. *So we're having to be quite protective of our clinical roles at the moment.*

In explaining their changing roles, many of our clinician-managers emphasized the increasing level of accountability they encountered in carrying out their daily work. One of our respondents suggested that training in management efficiency techniques, originally derived from industry or commerce, was increasingly important in order to '*justify all the higher grades*' within the NHS. However, our interviews also suggested contradictory pressures being placed on junior and middle managers in this respect.

On the one hand, managers had to be '*more businesslike*' and '*streamline* [their] *services*' amidst a climate of increased efficiency and heightened economy. This was to be accomplished, for example, by adopting Lean efficiency philosophies and systems, such as those based on the Toyota Production System and in particular as explained in the book by Womack *et al.* (1990, 2007), *The Machine that Changed the World*. Many NHS managers and staff had recently been trained in such Lean organizational philosophies. Indeed, we also attended Lean training courses at the acute trust (see Chapter 4).

On the other hand, however, and as a result of an emerging '*blame culture*' within the NHS in which '*everything has got to be justified*', there were simultaneous pressures for increased role accountability. This saw other management technologies, again directed at creating efficiencies in performance, serving in practice to bring about perceived *inefficiencies*. As one manager remarked about this increased accountability, '*there's just so much extra paperwork over the last five, ten years*'. Or as another suggested, '*the amount of paperwork and documentation has just got ridiculous*'.

Modernizing information management: the Lorenzo system (and other role changes)

One of the most controversial techniques discussed in this respect was the introduction of the Lorenzo system of task and event recording. This system – the Lorenzo Electronic Patient Record – is a type of health documentation tool devised by the giant Computer Sciences Corporation (CSC), an American multinational (in the Fortune 500 and Forbes Global lists) that provides information technology hardware as well as professional services to public and private sector organizations, including the US government. Lorenzo was commissioned as part of the UK government's national NHS Connecting for Health programme for improving the service's IT systems.

However, the technology and the corporation that designed and markets it have been mired in controversy. In respect of the multi-billion-pound contract to deliver the national programme for the Lorenzo contract, in June 2013, Margaret Hodge – chair of the Public Accounts Committee (a Select Committee of the House of Commons) – described CSC as a '*rotten company providing a hopeless system*'.[2] In addition, in December 2011, the non-partisan US organization Public Campaign criticized CSC for spending $4.39 million on lobbying while, during 2008–10, not paying any taxes and getting $305 million in tax rebates despite making a profit of $1.67 billion. And in February 2011, the US Securities and Exchange Commission launched a fraud investigation into CSC's accounting practices in Denmark and Australia. CSC subsequently confirmed that the alleged misconduct included $19 million in both intentional accounting irregularities and unintentional accounting errors. The company has also been accused of breaching human rights by arranging illegal rendition flights for the CIA between 2003 and 2006, which led to criticism of shareholders of the company by several governments in Europe. NHS Connecting for Health itself ceased to exist on 31 March, 2013, and some projects and responsibilities were taken over by the Health and Social Care Information Centre.

During our research, Lorenzo was frequently a topic for critical discussion in relation to managerial roles and behaviour. As one of our clinician-managers explained wryly, in practice, the system is aimed at justifying literally every minute of every day:

> So we're spending a good proportion of our time typing in that we're on the phone. And it's got to that ridiculous situation where we're losing so much face-to-face clinical

time. Because everything has to be documented, down to what sort of phone call it was. So they can actually break down now every minute of every working day.

Clinician-managers felt, in general, that underpinning the system was a theory of economic efficiency and, notably, one that determined the optimal type of work to be undertaken by the optimal level of employee. In this sense, the system appeared reminiscent of the early role and task efficiency proposals of Scientific Management (Taylor, 1911), such as the principle of achieving the *one best way* through the *separation of planning from execution* (see Braverman, 1974; Rose, 1985). The specific advantages of the Lorenzo system, however, appeared less clear to our managers – even those who were fairly senior or experienced. A respondent with over 30 years in the NHS suggested, for example, that *'we assume it's* [the data] *just being stored by the PCT to* [confirm] *... that managers aren't doing stuff that could be done by somebody a lot lower'*. This manager offered as an example the sending out of appointments:

> [W]*hy do I have to send my own appointments out? Not that I object to sending my own appointments out, but actually it's an awfully expensive use of my time that could be done by a Band 3 in the office. So that's one of the reasons they're doing it and they're trying to justify it. Well if we looked at Grades 4 to 9, what's the pattern that's emerging when they're putting all this information on Lorenzo? And obviously the lower grades should be doing more of the administrative, routine-type preparation of equipment that they're not doing because they're being sucked into it all. They're actually doing a lot more clinical-type work.*

However, rather than such information gathering being a single event, managers felt it was instead becoming a *'rolling programme'* that was ultimately *'going to take over'*. One manager suggested there was potentially a *'huge mismatch'* between the time taken in collecting data under Lorenzo and the future efficiency savings to be accrued.

Other elements of the system concerned record-keeping and target setting with, again, responses being mixed in terms of the perceived value of the system. While on the positive side, the system was potentially useful in allowing staff to *'type in a* [patient's] *name and see who the last* [clinician] *that ever saw them was and what other professionals are involved'*, with the result that *'it's actually a really good tracking mechanism'*; on the negative side, *'a lot of the information that we have to put in is just ridiculous, and it's having a huge effect on morale across all grades'*. In relation to a perceived climate of poor and decreasing morale at Millford PCT (see later), one clinician-manager suggested that *'over the last few years it is probably "Lorenzo control" that has affected people most'*. Another manager noted similarly that Lorenzo was reflective of *'a culture in which you can be blamed'* or one where *'you're in a no-win situation, almost as if you're guilty until found innocent'*. This same informant linked the new role demands associated with Lorenzo to wider issues of role expansion and, notably, in (dysfunctional) connection to the philosophy of Lean management, which for a while was promoted nationally in the NHS (see McCann *et al.*, 2015b). She also noted increasing moves to devolve the work and responsibilities of wider functions to the level of the clinical-manager with this again expanding and potentially intensifying the work role:

> [W]hen I first became a team lead, it was very much just: 'Right, this is the number of [patients] you've got ... [and] this is the number of [clinicians] you've got, this is the number of sessions you've got. Just work out who's going where and when.' So it was very pertinent to the job that I did. Whereas the role has now expanded phenomenally. And we have to look more strategically at 'Leaning' services and attending meetings that you think, 'actually, this has got nothing to do with the department that I'm working in', which again affects morale because you think, 'this isn't what I trained to do'. I don't mind managing a service that's pertinent to my training, but the role has broadened and all the HR-type issues that in the past we wouldn't have had to deal with, they've been now put down into our layer.

Another clinical department we researched had experienced a similar decentralization of management tasks. A clinician-manager suggested this had served to create greater '*distance*' between organizational layers. The impression was that this had forced her manager to take on ever-greater role responsibilities but for no additional monetary reward. She noted, for example, how:

> Our manager has moved up, so she's now much more distant. She used to do all the human resources stuff, all the annual PDRs, performance reviews. They were all done by her. Annual leave cards, those sorts of day-to-day things. She approved the annual leave and the in lieu time. Whereas she has now totally distanced herself from that and that is very much down to us. You know, we are doing much more of the day-to-day management of the whole department now, and our manager's definitely moved a step higher in terms of – not in terms of salary – but in terms of the sort of job she has to do.

Managers suggested to us that implementation of the Lorenzo system also had implications for working hours. We were told that it served to clarify in particular the difference between '*official hours and non-official hours*' in carrying out the managerial work role. As one interviewee put it, under Lorenzo, '*you should be able to see how many hours people are doing, which you can do*'. She continued that this was '*the interesting thing*', for '*you log in everything you've done for the day*' in a system where, in her specialism, to bring it in line with normative official hours in other areas of the NHS, '*we're supposed to be* [on] *a 36-hour week, slowly building up to 37.5 through the Agenda for Change*'. However, this is the *official* working period for the same clinician-manager who noted how, under Lorenzo, '*you can look at your hours and think, "Oh! I did 54 hours last week"*.' Although in terms of additional hours, this manager suggested that '*there isn't an expectation that you do them*', she also admitted, '*but you've got to get your job done*', with the result that she reported doing '*at least two hours a day over and above what I get paid, easily*'.

Another clinician-manager went on to explain how most of her '*unofficial hours*' were completed in her PCT office rather than at home: '*I only log on Lorenzo the hours I do here and I don't put them on in lieu cards or anything*'. However, she admitted that she was known, on occasions, to '*come in on the holidays*', and at these times she would '*put that on my in lieu card*'. She admitted further that: '*In reality, I very rarely take that time back. It's only if I have to, for funerals or whatever, then I would take that back. But I have got a remote laptop. Most of us have got remote laptops.*' Indeed it was common for many of our managers to regularly work '*unofficial*' hours over the weekend. Another of our respondents suggested how she tended to '*clear emails at weekends*' and said that '*if I've got a report to do at home then rather than staying here until half six at night, I'll take it home*'. As she no longer had as many domestic commitments (her children were grown up), to fulfil her role she tended to do '*a lot more work at home*' and assumed that '*even* [staff at] *lower levels are doing the same*'.

Over two separate interviews, an informant from the Patient & Liaison Service suggested similar issues of increasingly extensive working hours in the PCT. She widened this discussion to issues of work–life balance and, in particular, the need to reinforce this with members of her team. She admitted, however, that as much as she attempted to keep '*work and life in balance*', if someone forwarded an email message to her late in the evening, she still '*felt bad*' if she didn't answer it:

> *It's one of the things we get schizophrenic about, don't we? You know we have a policy called Work-life Balance. It's all about, you know, what it says – work, life and balance. But increasingly it's not uncommon for our managers to work 50-hour weeks just to keep on top of the job. The role expands; the job expands. It's still only one person doing it – there's no extra resources. … But I've had to make a conscious effort to be in control of my work-life balance, and it's the one thing that I nag my staff to do. It's, you know, you've got to look after yourself and, you know, why are you here at this time and what do you need to do? Look at your working week so that that doesn't continue – because it's a priority for me so I see that as a priority for them. However, the culture of working in the NHS is, at the minute, that you've got to be doing things all the time. So people send me emails and it will be, like, quarter to eleven at night when they've sent the email. And then you feel a bit bad sometimes because you're not doing that.*

Downgrading and upgrading: Agenda for Change (and its effects)

Many of those we interviewed at the PCT cited the impact on clinical and managerial roles of the NHS Agenda for Change. This policy represented the grading and pay system for NHS staff (with the exception of doctors, dentists and some senior managers). As such, it applied to more than a million employees and served to harmonize pay scales and career progression arrangements across traditionally disparate groups. The Agenda came into operation on 1 December, 2004, following agreement between the unions, employers and government. In 2013, however, some amendments to the Agenda for Change were agreed: incremental pay rises for staff would be conditional on individuals meeting locally set performance requirements; for the top three bands – 8c, 8d and 9 – increments would be earned annually (and might not be retained where the appropriate local level of performance was not reached); also for the top three bands, employers may introduce alternative local pay arrangements; and finally, there would be overall protection for staff moved to lower-grade posts.

Part of the Agenda, therefore, saw a set of national job profiles agreed to assist in the process of matching posts to pay bands. On the '*positive side*', one of our managers described a process by which '*the NHS looked at everybody's job and everybody had to rewrite their job description*', with the result that '*it supposedly brought everybody's terms and conditions in line*'. So instead of her own clinical specialism '*being on Whitley council*[3] *pay and dentists being on whatever*', those who worked for the NHS '*were put on the same pay scales, from cleaners up*'. Subsequently, each job description was put to an Agenda for Change board and evaluated on a particular scale. Although managers responsible for writing these role descriptions suggested it '*took a phenomenal amount of time*' because '*we had to make sure we got everybody's job descriptions correct*', they suggested also that it had the effect of '*address*[ing] *all those anomalies of people who didn't have a specialist role but were actually doing one*'. Therefore, in an equitable way, the Agenda was said to give '*them credit for what they did*'. Some informants suggested further that Agenda for Change had a positive effect in terms of role development and career progression. One of our respondents noted, for example, how:

> *Whereas* [her clinical role], *traditionally, used to be on something called Senior 1, Senior 2 and Basic Grade, and they only had three incremental points so once you got to the top of your three, you had no career progression; you were stuck there. So I'd been stuck on the Senior 1, which was the top one, for eight, nine years, knowing that unless I became a full-time manager there was nothing to do; whereas with Agenda for Change, it gave you a much broader band of increments. You couldn't move right to the top, but it gave you a broader band and it made career progression a lot better.*

Another interviewee remarked, however, that the exercise had also cost the NHS a '*phenomenal amount of money*'. In particular, it was felt that the HR planners and advisors to the exercise had been frequently overgenerous in terms of the positioning of role descriptions in relation to the remaining increment levels available in salary bands. As a result, '*what the NHS didn't realize was actually how much it was going to cost them*' because '*even though we were assimilated across on what we already got paid, they didn't realize that most people then had another four or five increments to go*'. This clinician-manager went on to suggest a particular problem was where HR had been forced to '*backtrack*' and suggest that job descriptions be rewritten and roles downgraded. A similar experience was described at all of our case sites; of roles, especially clinical roles, ultimately being downgraded.

However, in a process that involved input from both a clinical department and the HR function, there remained the potential under Agenda for Change for influence from both directions. Indeed the system seemingly allows for a situation where '*the odd member of staff says that they now want their job description rewritten because they feel now they're doing a much more defined role*. The problem here, however, lies in the current economic climate for '*if they do get* [their] *jobs upgraded*', the situation can arise whereby '*there's no money to pay them*' since NHS funding is '*currently dire*'. This informant added that currently '*restraints are very, very frightening*', and a general policy of job freezes had existed for a while with this causing particular problems for some departments. Given the high percentage of women employees, such issues could be acute as, for example, '*anybody who goes off on maternity leave*, [their] *jobs aren't being covered, and in a small department like we have, that has huge repercussions*'.

'*Points make prizes*': demands, targets and conflict

> *Erm, it's gruesome, honestly. They set targets and every month you get how many patients you've seen in that month. And that is online for you to reach your target at the end of the year because it's that 'points make prizes'. So the PCT gets paid depending on activity.*
>
> (Clinician-manager)

Amidst discussions of changing roles, we also enquired about the ways in which managers routinely meet increasing work demands in terms of changes to their everyday work behaviour. When asked about the structure of their 'normal working day', dialogue with junior and middle managers often turned to examples of increased work intensity. Expanding on the earlier theme of role expansion, we were surprised by the regularity with which our managers reported they were '*in the office about a half an hour or an hour before the official start of the working day*', reportedly to '*clear the decks*' so that they could then '*begin proper work*'. This frequently meant doing administrative work prior to starting a round of meetings, telephone discussions or direct clinical tasks. As one informant suggested, she was regularly '*in about half past seven in the morning clear*[ing] *emails if I haven't cleared them at the weekend or the night before*'. Another reported similarly, '*I tend to get here about half seven, quarter to eight in the morning and will try and deal with any emails that have come through*', this being useful because '*at least I've got an hour of quietness*'. Doing administrative work outside of official office hours seemed totally natural to our managers and was considered '*just part of the job*' in a situation where it was often difficult to manage the round of daily activities given current resource constraints.

Managers frequently raised issues related to resource constraints and how this could affect their work roles and behaviour. Notable here were the additional demands that could be placed on workloads because of labour supply shortages. Clinician-managers reported how a portion of their work could be devoted to '*troubleshooting*' as, for example, in resolving issues of confrontation with clients. One respondent, for example, described how a percentage of her work was devoted to resolving: '*front-line confrontation*' and typically to '*pacify*[ing relatives] *who want extra* [treatment] *for their* [relations], *and we can't provide it because we haven't got the staff. So we get a lot of that.*'. This was considered a normal aspect of everyday work, yet something largely brought about by the '*squeeze on NHS spend*'. It was also something that served to bring about internal conflict or tension in the PCT:

> *It's all right saying, 'oh yes, but refer that over there because they're* [Millford PCT management] *the ones who've caused the cuts'. It doesn't make any difference because I'm the one that gets that awful phone call from* [a relative]. *You know, 'I want more* [treatment for the patient]. *But, yeah, actually* I *want more* [treatment for the patient] *as well, but this is the situation we're in. So* [we have] *a fair few of those in a day.*

The same informant reflected further on how, in the current economic climate, '*trying to keep on top of* [work demands] *with decreasing staff is very difficult*'. She noted, for example, how:

> *You get in a quandary. So, what do I do? Do I really bust a gut and work every hour I can and keep on top of this 18-week waiting list, which then actually doesn't tell the powers that be over there* [in the PCT management building] *that we've got a problem. Well actually if we see those* [patients] *within the 18-week time frame, what do we do with them after that? We haven't got the staff to see them. But which is best? Do we see them and then know the problems we've got on a waiting for* [treatment] *list. Or do we not see them and we let our waiting list grow?*

This clinician-manager, like others we interviewed, frequently discussed the structural tensions that could arise between medical specialisms and management functions in the PCT. Such tensions were often related to conflicts between task expectations and the level of work intensification in relation to waiting lists. These pressures appeared to amplify as the future for the PCT became increasingly uncertain under ongoing government reforms. She continued accordingly:

> *And then they'll complain over there at Royal House and then we say, 'yes but you've cut our staff' – you know: 'you've taken two full-time equivalents out of my team in the last three months, who've gone on maternity leave and aren't being replaced. So you've got to expect that my waiting list's going to increase.' But then you get more complaints. You're in a no-win situation really. And what I think we're going to do at the moment is, you know, I'm going to see as many* [patients] *as I can see, but that waiting list is going to rise over 18 weeks.*

A related theme that emerged within our discussions of work behaviour was how to deal with task '*monitoring*' and, specifically, the nature of '*targets*'. Here, discussion was often linked to the heated topic of the Lorenzo system, which was seemingly having an increasing impact on work behaviour. Problems could arise, for example, if there was a mismatch of expectations between clinical and managerial functions, as one clinician-manager explained in connection to work being monitored through Lorenzo:

We have annual targets that we have to meet and that in itself poses a massive problem because the person who sort of devises our quota for the year actually doesn't know what we do. So they can say, 'right well you know if you look at [another clinical specialism], they can see … [so] many thousand people in a year'. And they can say, you know, 'their appointments are five, ten minutes each: in, out; in, out. How come [my clinical staff] are only seeing six [patients] in a day?'

Again, respondents in some clinical areas remarked that such monitoring problems could arise in situations in which there was a lack of sensitivity on the part of senior management to key differences between the nature of, and demands on, clinical areas. Clinician-managers felt this was not always appreciated by those who actually managed the monitoring systems. As one clinical manager commented:

Well we're a bit different to somebody with a [minor medical problem]. You know, and every patient of ours is very different. … So I've had arguments with the guy over there [in senior management] … who said, 'So, looking at your diary on Lorenzo, you see one [patient] for half an hour but your next [patient] you see for an hour?' Well yes, the half an hour is a review of a [patient] that I gave a home programme to, so I'm just checking him. Actually a new one is a lot more complex and needs an hour. And [senior manager] says: 'how come with some [patients], you can see them in a group? So why don't you see all [patients] in groups because that way you can see six in an hour?' But not every [patient] fits in a group. So you're working with mathematicians and we're working with real people here.

Another clinical manager suggested that such processes could result in the setting of '*sometimes very bizarre targets*'. Reminiscent of well-known target-setting practices at General Electric (see Hassard *et al.*, 2009) and reflecting, seemingly, an incipient neo-liberal agenda in healthcare provision, she described how '*every year we've got to increase our productivity by ten per cent*'. Commenting critically on this system, she queried, '*how can we increase our productivity with (a) increasing numbers of* [patients] *and (b) less staff?*', and suggested such targets '*are very unrealistic*'. This manager explained in detail how:

Because we're a commissioned service … we have to achieve that [target] otherwise they won't give us the money next year. It's one of the few things they actually look at is how many contacts we've had. And it doesn't matter what quality that contact is. If you can just tick the box that you've seen ten [patients] in a day, that's fine. … And they can't, they just cannot see how we work and [so] they're very unrealistic. The target for this year is something like 12,500 contacts. Now, you just need to get some extremely complex [patients] who take, you know, one [patient] could take a whole morning.

Several clinical managers felt there was often a lack of sensitivity towards the demands on different clinical areas and that this could potentially be dysfunctional for the service as a whole. For example, one manager commented how, due to the complex nature of its patients, a particular clinical service (linked to her own) was working on only '*one and a half contacts a day*'. In concert with the clinical managers at the mental health trust (Chapter 6), this was due to the fact that for each case, '*you're not just offering treatment*' but instead '*you're liaising, you're assessing, discussing the case history, putting programmes into place, etc.*'. This interviewee remarked that in comparison to areas such as this one, '*my team looks super efficient because we're working on six or seven a day*'. She suggested, however, that when confronting such averages, the response from some management functions tended to be, '*Oh we'll have more of you, but we don't want any more of that one because that's a really expensive service*'. Yet the reality was that, in being linked services, '*we couldn't do without them because they're working with very complex* [patients] – *but they can't see that over there*'. As an example, she explained how:

> One of the questions [to our department] *was,* '*how many times do you need to see a* [patient] *before you cure them?*' *You know, I saw a* [patient] *last week who I cured there and then, on the spot, finished.* [But] *another* [patient] *you think,* '*I'll have him until he's 16*'.

Like others we spoke to, this informant elaborated upon a frequent lack of sensitivity to clinical complexity and demands on the ground in suggesting: '*But that's what the management don't realize. … And that is what is so frustrating in our role – that we want to deliver a service but actually we're having this made more and more difficult.*'

Learning the logic of the market

A related theme to that of increased work and target demands emerged in discussions of healthcare practices, in general, being affected by an increasingly market-oriented climate and culture. This was apparent in a comment by one of our clinician-managers, who suggested of recent policy changes that, '*we're now expected to adhere to this "how much an episode of care" logic*' or, in other words, to adopt a more calculative reasoning when considering methods for meeting various healthcare requirements. Once again, this reasoning, when put into practice, could bring clinical employees into potential conflict with other NHS colleagues who were perhaps seen as the messengers of such logics; notably, specialist managers. Clinician-managers often pointed to contradictions (and also a degree of naivety) in the effectiveness messages and efficiency methods being promoted and disseminated in the PCT.

Technologies such as Lorenzo, for example, appeared to make available information regarding, as one informant suggested, '*how many contacts do you see a year and so on?*' As such, the mindset of the clinician-manager was increasingly influenced by sensitivity to the efficiency and '*marketability*' of the healthcare services a department provided. The application of a quantitative logic to healthcare, therefore, could lead to situations where, as another clinician-manager suggested:

> *They could actually say, 'Right well, we've looked at how much you provide for 15.5 full-time equivalent* [clinicians], *but actually* [name of PCT in adjacent authority] *have 15.3* [clinicians] *and they're providing an extra 2,000 contacts a year'.* [And they could argue on that basis] *'Well we're going to buy* [treatment] *from* [the adjacent authority]', *in which case we'd be out of a job. So we've got to make ourselves marketable. Which is why we've got to keep a check on how many* [patients] *we can see, what sort of packages of care* [we provide].

To make their services look economically attractive, we were informed that some clinical areas in the PCT had adopted a practice of not listing certain tasks as part of their '*packages of care*'. In one instance, however, reports from one department noted a feeling of being disadvantaged because a comparative function had '*not includ*[ed] *things like report writing and programme writing*' in its costs. When confronted with such data, the response from the former department was to say: '*Well that's not fair because, yeah, you can do five packages of care if you're not including that in your bit. But actually if you're going to do a real package of care, it costs x amount.*'

Managers suggested to us that the logic of the market was increasingly present in their internal discussions and communications. The backcloth to this increasingly competitive culture was, as one manager suggested, '*the danger that they could go to* [nearby city] *or* [nearby town] *or buy in private* [clinicians]' for the services currently provided by Millford. Our informant concluded, however, by pointing to potential contradictions between issues of quality and quantity in healthcare provision under such systems of management:

> *That's what these Lorenzo contacts are all about, right. You've got to provide us with 11,000, 12,000 contacts a year. And they don't really care what quality it is. That doesn't sit well with a* [clinician] *who wants to do their best for the* [patients]. ... *I was talking to a colleague at lunchtime and she said, you know, we're churning that many* [patients] *through that there becomes a fine line to where you make a difference. And if we see too many* [patients], *we're not making a difference.*

In order to achieve a greater measure of resource flexibility, while also balancing the budget, some clinical departments suggested they had started to become '*somewhat entrepreneurial*' in considering new or available options for '*income generation*'. They remarked to us that some areas of Millford PCT were now in fact '*very, very good at income generating*', with one of our clinician-managers offering a personal example of such activity and how it related to current resource management:

> *For example, I produced a couple of intervention tools which we got published and are now used nationally. So we get royalties from those and I go round the country delivering instruction on that. So obviously we income generate my time; we charge for my time. So all that money we income generate, we put into staffing. So we pay for fixed-term staff who help support the waiting list and what have you.*

For this manager, however, a potential problem with such revenue generation was that in the longer term, it can become incorporated within target estimates. She explained how '*unfortunately those figures get absorbed, so Royal House think, oh we're doing really well because we've got 25 members of staff here; but actually they're only paying for 20 of them and the other five* [are because], *myself or another couple of* [clinicians] *are income generating*'. She continued by suggesting, '*so basically what they're saying is all my income generation is going over there now as* [part of] *our target*'. With the tightening of targets, and especially demands that '*we've got to make ten per cent savings financially*', this manager described a knock-on effect whereby:

> *We're having to lay staff off. Fixed-term staff, we're not able to keep. So those targets they gave us become unsustainable. Fixed-term staff tend to be cheaper because we tend to take on assistants who can work with a therapist by pooling the numbers of* [patients] *we see, or they can work with individual* [patients] *with a very definite programme that we give them. So actually they are very, very cost effective because they're cheaper and they can get through a lot of* [patients]. *But we're not giving them the complex* [cases]. *So we're in this awful situation that, you know, I'm going off to do training, but actually the money I'm producing is going over there to plug some deficit. So again, that affects morale because there are fixed-term staff holding up a core service.*

Other clinician-managers reported examples of incipient entrepreneurial activity and the development of a business-oriented institutional narrative. One outlined how her boss had become '*very good at income generating and seeing gaps in the market*'. In fact, she suggested this colleague was so adept in this respect that '*you can see her ending up in business*'. This example of a business-oriented culture emerging on the ground was often reflected in descriptions of PCT staff generating income for the purpose of underwriting staffing or associated costs. In describing the entrepreneurial activities of a colleague, this quote from one of the respondents appears ingrained with business logic:

> *She's a national* [corporate brand name of clinical technology] *trainer, and she does training that brings in the money. … And you know, as a manager, we're constantly now looking for gaps in the market. You know, what can we provide? What could we actually sell?*

Another of our respondents, however, suggested this represented something of a culture change in healthcare provision historically. She explained that while earlier in her NHS career, external offerings would most likely be provided on a *pro bono* or *gratis* basis, the contemporary climate in Millford PCT had seen the emphasis change from a '*public*' to a '*business*' service. As an example, she described the adoption of a more commercial orientation when working with groups in the local community:

> *So I had a phone call from somebody last week* [saying] '*could you do some evening, twilight sessions to* [groups in the local community]*?' And whereas in the past,*

I'd go 'yeah just let me get my diary – yes, when do you want me?' It's now a case of, 'right, well, we'll have to charge you'. And even now I'm in that mindset. … So we charge. And obviously that money comes back into the department. So there's a huge need to do that.

Other PCT services provided outside of the clinical setting could be arranged on a habitual contractual basis. In regard to Millford public services, for example, such agreements were increasingly underpinned by market logic. In this respect, a clinician-manager noted how: '*We've got three or four what we call service level agreements with outside agencies. … So they're buying in a contract with us for so many sessions.*' She commented further on how custom and practice for such arrangements had changed significantly, as had the outlook of those within Millford PCT:

A few years ago, if you'd have said to me that all that training you do in [Millford public health services] *and things, you're going to have be paid for it, it would have sat very uncomfortably because, as a* [clinician], *you're there to provide a service. But the culture is* [now] *that the ones who want the training haven't got a problem. They know that they're going to have to pay for services because, well, we are still super caring but it's not this, you know, we can open our arms and take anybody on board anymore.*

As we saw in previous chapters, discussions of the onset of a more business-oriented culture within Millford PCT could regularly see respondents reflect on an initiative mentioned earlier – Lean management. So prevalent was this emphasis on Lean in internal staff development that, as one respondent remarked, '*in any training you go on, they start to talk about Toyota*'. Another manager suggested that although the '*Lean logic*' had not yet been '*fully cascaded down*', it was beginning to happen on the ground. She suggested further that this was not just about '*tidying your desk*' but the wider re-evaluation of roles with a view to placing some duties within lower skill bands. In this respect, her department had been an early adopter of such efficiency proposals:

When anybody leaves or goes on leave and comes back part-time, we actually relook at their job and think, right, well we're saving three days' worth of a Band 6. Do we really need a Band 6 or could we use a Band 4? So we've done that constantly. So we're totally skill-mixed now. … So I think we have been, as a department, very, very good at 'Leaning' wherever we can.

We discuss the impact of Lean-related philosophies, initiatives and practices at Millford NHS in connection with the acute trust (see Chapter 4). As such, we do not rehearse them again in respect of the PCT for ostensibly similar themes were found to emerge (see McCann *et al.*, 2015b). Instead, we move from our analysis of changing managerial roles and behaviour to the second phase of our case study: research into the wider political environment in which these and other changes took place. Specifically, we focus on the various reactions of our PCT managers to the realization that their organization was slated for closure in the not too distant future.

Dismantling the organization

So that's when the restructuring came about. And they said to me, 'half of what you do is going over there and half of what you do is going over there'. So I said, 'so where do I go? Am I with that way or am I that way?' [And they replied] '*Um, well, we don't know'. … So for the last year, I've been floating.*

(Clinician-manager)

We explained earlier how, in contrast to previous case accounts, the PCT includes a second, more contextual, line of analysis in addition to that of studying managerial roles and behaviour. This represents analysis of the remarkable political climate in which the research was conducted. Not long into our study, we became all too aware that Millford PCT was an organization under the threat of imminent closure. Expressly, this was an organization that was likely to be delayered out of existence given structural reforms soon to be implemented by central government under the Health and Social Care Act 2012.

With this always in mind, we focused on the politics of organizational change as much as the roles and behaviour of healthcare managers. Discussions with managers became methodologically double-edged as early interviews on managerial work became overlain with probes for information regarding the changing culture and climate of the PCT in the last months of its existence. This strand of research began to assume a central role in our investigations at the PCT so that when the formal end point of the research was reached, we made arrangements with a subset of managers to continue our discussions. This saw informants keep us abreast of the latest restructuring events and issues affecting the PCT, its managers and staff.

In this section, therefore, we present data from this aspect of the research. In line with our Critical-Action approach, the aim has been (as far as possible) to let the managers set the agenda and tell their own story of the last days of Millford PCT. In the process, our role has been to compare and contrast those views and put them into logical, largely chronological order. In so doing, we sought to explain three main issues in the period leading up to the organization's closure: i) the organizational context, by explaining key issues of the political climate of the period; ii) the restructuring options available to the PCT as it sought the best outcomes for its departments; and iii) the way in which closure affected staff personally in terms of their careers, relations and livelihoods.

Context of change

As we see in Chapter 2, although healthcare is usually at the forefront of political debate in the run-up to a general election, there had been little hint in the election year of 2010 that major healthcare reforms were in the offing. Indeed, the proposals that were to frame the subsequent Health and Social Care Act 2012 were not discussed at all during the election campaign, nor were they contained within the Conservative–Liberal Democrat coalition agreement (Delamothe and Godlee, 2011: 237).

Within two months of the coalition government's formation, however, a White Paper outlined what the *Daily Telegraph* suggested was 'the biggest revolution in the NHS since its foundation' (Porter, 2010). Some months later, in December 2010, this policy document – *Equity and Excellence: Liberating the NHS* – was followed by an operational plan, in the shape of *Liberating the NHS: Legislative Framework and Next Steps*, which the American consultancy corporation McKinsey & Co. had been heavily involved in drafting (McKay, 2012). McKinsey was also involved in discussions around what would subsequently be the Health and Social Care Bill 2012.

This Bill had implications for the whole of the NHS. In particular, both primary care trusts and strategic health authorities were slated to be abolished, with projected redundancy costs of around £1 billion for around 21,000 staff. In addition, around £60 billion to £80 billion worth of commissioning would be transferred from PCTs to several hundred clinical commissioning groups, mainly run by GPs. Also around 3,600 facilities formerly owned by PCTs and SHAs would be transferred to NHS Property Services, a limited company owned by the Department of Health. The Bill would abolish the existing cap on healthcare trusts' income from non-NHS sources, which in most cases was previously set at a relatively low, single-digit percentage.

However, after opposition to the Bill from a range of bodies and institutions, including pressure from the British Medical Association, the coalition government instigated a listening exercise to countenance views on the proposals. Thus on 4 April, 2011, the government announced an official 'pause' in the progress of the Bill – to allow the government to 'listen, reflect and improve' the measures. In so doing, Prime Minister Cameron stated that 'the status quo is not an option', and in particular the formation of clinical commissioning groups was not open to discussion as they were too far along the path to completion to be blocked. A key component of this listening exercise was the creation of the NHS Future Forum as a kind of advisory council. However, as the magazine *Private Eye* (2011) pointed out, many of the 43 'experts' appointed to the Forum appeared to be 'hand-picked' supporters of Health Secretary Andrew Lansley's proposals. Despite this, Professor Steve Field, a GP who chaired the Forum, suggested many of the doubts the public and medical profession had about the Health and Social Care Bill had actually been 'justified' as it contained 'insufficient safeguards' against private companies exploiting the NHS (NHS Future Forum, 2011).

Around this time, David Cameron established a separate panel to advise him on the reforms, this including Bill Moyes, head of global health systems at McKinsey, as well as Mark Britnell, head of health policy at KPMG. Apparently, some months earlier, Britnell had informed a conference of private healthcare executives that: 'In future, the NHS will be a state insurance provider not a state deliverer'. He had also, according to Boffey and Helm (2011), stressed the role of Lansley's reforms in making this possible, suggesting: 'The NHS will be shown no mercy and the best time to take advantage of this will be in the next couple of years'. Although, in defence of Britnell, KPMG issued a formal press release response, several years later the full report of the conference remained online and unaltered.

Despite all the objections raised about the nature of the legislation and criticisms made of those involved as policymakers or advisors, following the completion of the listening exercise, the Bill was recommitted to the House of Commons on 21 June, 2011, completed its committee stage on 21 December, 2011, passed through the Lords on 19 March, 2012, and became the Health and Social Care Act 2012 on 27 March, 2012 – an Act that David Cameron insisted would form a central plank of his agenda for the Big Society. The Act, however, continues to have its critics, notably over the level of *creeping* privatization it has engendered. For many, it is widely regarded an unnecessary and expensive exercise in reorganization; one that has failed to result in genuine improvements in terms of healthcare provision. Critics argue that it has even resulted in a recent deterioration in service levels, notably in terms of increased waiting times for patients.

Managers, politics and change

> *And people still don't realize, they're asking us to build our own gallows!*
> *(Human Resources manager, Millford PCT)*

Our discussions with PCT managers therefore took place amidst the onset of these rapid and complex changes in healthcare policy and practice. In our early discussions, the thing that struck us most was the bewildering sense of uncertainly over what the future held for the organization and its staff. Manager after manager, from a range of seniority levels and functional areas, appeared unsure as to what the future would look like when the new legislation took hold. All that managers and staff seemed to know for certain was that government planning for this reorganization was well advanced – due possibly (as one of our informants suggested) to '*years of planning*' by Andrew Lansley when he was Shadow Health Secretary – and that PCTs and strategic health authorities would bear the brunt of it.

An early discussion with a senior manager in the HR department – a key department in terms of handling people issues related to the planned changes – soon led to expressions of '*battle weariness*' when the subject of reorganization of the NHS was raised. His view was that such campaigns were, above all, '*political*' phenomena and exercises that were frequently counterproductive in respect of improving effectiveness. Reflecting on his own career in the NHS, he argued that national politics was in fact a major part of the problem:

> *We all know it's highly politicized … I've spent 25 years in* [the NHS] *and it's certainly not the NHS that I came into. I've probably been through five or six different reforms, you know, Griffiths and all that sort of stuff. I've been through all of that. And you come to a point where you're sort of battle weary really. It is a total mess. It really is.*

For this manager, one of the main problems caused by this politically inspired reorganization was the degree of uncertainly it engendered in the workforce, which was a particular problem for commissioning functions. Of all the healthcare reorganizations he had experienced, this had been the most damaging for, as things stood, the PCT '*ship was sinking*' with only the resilience of the staff keeping the organization afloat:

> *Well* [Millford PCT chief executive] *was here this morning and I used the term that, you know, 'we're taking in water now and it won't be long until we're holed below the water line'. Because it feels like that. We've always been, through all these changes, reasonably resilient. But we always knew it was going to be resilience, resilience, resilience until we're off the cliff. And that's coming soon. And this is a sort of small, what's the word, microcosm. We're an example of what's going on in the bigger picture. Do you know what I mean? Whereas if you put the context around it, suddenly you think, whoa, you know. But what staff have been asked to do at this time is nothing short of remarkable to be quite honest.*

Nevertheless, despite such staff resilience, the severity of the reorganization had begun to affect staff morale. The senior human resources manager, himself a PCT board member, described how a recent attitude survey had yielded '*very disappointing results*' in terms of staff satisfaction and motivation. As head of HR, he had to report to the board on such matters and advised us that a paper on the issue had been submitted that day. He also noted that if the board had been presented with the staff survey results '*cold*', there could have been an outcry. As such, he had been forced to put the results '*into context*':

> *It's* [the paper for the board] *gone up this morning about the staff survey, which is significantly worse than last year. It might as well have said, 'your staff are pissed off'. It's the only restructuring I've experienced where staff are going to be worse off. So I've had to put something in there. I've put a little heading that says 'Putting the results into context'. Because if all this wasn't going on around us, it would be absolutely dreadful. You know, all of the execs would come back and say: 'what the bloody hell's happened here?'*

For many of the managers we interviewed at Millford, there were two main problems with this reorganization: i) the degree of structural complexity involved; and ii) the speed of policy implementation suggested (despite the government's pause for reflection after widespread complaints). Another Human Resources manager, who had previously worked for a multinational, reflected on whether such a colossal change programme, with all its convolution, could be attempted so quickly in a large corporation, especially when she felt there was actually little wrong with the current organizational architecture:

> *If we were sitting here* [in a] *global company, Shell or whatever, we wouldn't be saying: 'Let's have a big national reform going on. Let's reduce management costs. Let's get rid of a lot of people. Let's bring in clusters. We'll bring in the GP consortia*

as well. And that's on the back of TCS as well; there's TCS going on. What else are we doing? We'll change all the MP stuff, all the IT stuff. We'll stop all that and we'll start something else.' You just wouldn't do it. [Instead] we'd be sitting here thinking, 'what the bloody hell are we doing here?' They are trying to fix something that largely isn't broken.

Amidst the throes of the proposed reorganizations, PCT managers appeared increasingly sensitive to criticisms that they, personally, were receiving at this time, often from politicians and the media. These criticisms were frequently along the lines of managers being expensive impediments to NHS efficiency and effectiveness. A common narrative, frequently rehearsed in the media, was of management strata equating to 'wasteful bureaucracy' – absorbing resources that could be better spent on clinical services. A manager from the Patient Advice and Liaison Service responded bluntly to such suggestions: *'the idea that you don't need management, I mean, for goodness sake; it's the lifeblood of an organization'*. Or as another PCT manager suggested, *'in order for the clinicians to keep doing what they're doing, there's got to be somebody organizing, planning and developing'*. As we see in Chapter 2, the NHS is relatively undermanaged; however, as a senior human resources manager suggested, such figures rarely get in the way of the predisposition among politicians, the media, and also the public generally for *'bashing'* NHS managers:

> *Let's stop bashing managers. You know, despite its faults, the NHS has got many a vote. It's still seen as world class or the envy of the world. Do you think this happens just by clinicians do you? I think it's, what, three and a half, four per cent of staff and managers in an organization that's got 1.4 million staff. … I am bloody qualified at this [i.e. management]. They're all clinically qualified. But you know I've done management courses. And you've spent most of your career with large teams, you know, dealing with people and all the rest of it. But what [they] see is 'bureaucrats'. [So you think] Thanks, thanks a lot. Thanks.*

This sense of disappointment with the treatment of managers was compounded by a general sense of frustration over the lack of appreciation for NHS staff during what had appeared to be a recent period of relative success for the Service. In the years running up to the reorganization, measures of patient and staff satisfaction, as well as indices for clinical success, often pointed in a positive direction:

> *And by the way, staff satisfaction, patient satisfaction, the outcomes for cancers, all the way, yeah, all getting better. And then you're thinking [the politicians are saying] 'Well, thanks guys but we'll have none of that'. You know, that's what it feels like. That's what it feels like. And I think that what annoys me most about that thinking, it's that, I mean, a politician knows better about health than we do? So there's something about why do we allow that? And the mandarins around them should be setting them straight.*

Such measures, therefore, seemed to be regularly overlooked in the politicians' drive for what, in reality, was ideologically driven change, and especially changes designed to achieve a more market-oriented or privatized approach to healthcare commissioning.

'Leaving the sinking ship': managing change on the ground

This sense of frustration among managerial personnel regarding a lack of appreciation for their expertise was perhaps incidental when compared to the problems many of them faced on a daily basis in managing on the ground. Millford was one of only two PCTs in the UK without a home to go to, and discussions with the SHA had yielded little in terms of substantive suggestions. In the early phases of our research, the situation was that 950 of the 1,200 PCT staff faced uncertainly as to where they would be located in the new system. There were also issues of redundancy, demotion and relocation to consider as well as pension arrangements for staff potentially moving, for example, from the NHS to the local authority (staff who may thus face harmonization problems). Redundancy-related schemes such as MARS (Mutually Agreed Resignation Scheme) and RETS (Retention and Exit Terms) were mentioned increasingly in our interviews at PCT headquarters, Royal House. In addition, black humour seemed increasingly prevalent – as reflected, for example, in jokes about '*RETS leaving the sinking ship*'. Other discussions concerned options for staff through TUPE (Transfer of Undertakings – Protection of Employment – Regulations), with staff frequently discussing the merits and shortcomings of '*being TUPE'd*'.

To handle the significant HR problems emerging at Millford, an interim head of Human Resources and Organizational Development was brought in from the SHA. At our first meeting, he suggested to us jokingly that, '*I've come from an organization that's going to be abolished to an organization that going to be abolished. I introduced myself as the Director of Workforce Reduction and Organizational Demise.*' He went on to explain how:

> We've lost 160 staff in the last 12 months. We've participated in the last two rounds of MARS. There's a third one coming. We've got people [who have] left on voluntary redundancy. We've made probably about 40 compulsory redundancies – and these are clinicians, GPs, nurses, speech therapists, which never happened before – and there's more to come. You've had, what else? People have left – we don't fill the vacancy, so people left behind are actually working harder. … If you take HR, I've got seven staff left – when I came here, it was 44.

During our early interviews, we had indeed been informed that around 50 PCT staff had already been laid off and there may be another 100 or 150 to go. We had also been advised that the HR department, in particular, had seen a significant reduction in headcount. In what we felt was an astute observation in this respect, the head of HR suggested: '*As soon as you mention the word "abolition", change starts from that point forward. People have only got an eye to their future and trying to keep themselves in a job.*'

Despite ongoing (local-level and national-level) discussions about the form the Lansley reorganizations would take, plus extensive dialogue under the government's eight-week pause, Millford staff indeed made it clear that in people's minds, closure started from the day that abolition was proposed and not from some projected date for PCT termination in years to come. From virtually the day he had arrived, in addition to a vacancy freeze, the head of HR began to lay off fixed-term staff and contract consultants, despite feeling personally that some fixed-term employees were '*vital*'. Various cost-cutting measures were also conjured up with, for example, sandwiches and coffee at board meetings discontinued, the cooling machines for mineral water replaced by (cheaper) water filters, and the services of the company that tended the office plants dispensed with.

The main preoccupation on the ground, however, was with the various options presenting themselves as destinations for the provider and commissioning staff that comprised the vast majority of PCT employees. Uncertainty abounded on both sides. For the 200 staff of the commissioning side, there appeared four logical destinations – GP Commissioning, Transforming Community Services, the National Commissioning Board or Public Health; although the various allocations still had to be calculated and agreed. For the 1,000 or so provider staff, the presumption was that they would transfer to another body almost *en masse*. Nevertheless, a variety of possible destinations began to be considered for their services (despite some appearing – to outside observers at least – counter-intuitive).

We were also made aware of how internal roles had changed significantly in light of the restructuring proposals. An interview with an HR manager revealed how recent events had seen staff from that function aligned to either the provider or commissioning sides of the PCT rather than, as previously, members of a generic HR function. In her case, it meant than instead of covering the whole of the PCT, she and other selected members of her team had been lined up exclusively with the provider side of the organization. As a result, this meant that they would ultimately be '*part of the portfolio of people to be TUPE'd out of the PCT*' to whatever destination was ultimately deemed suitable. The remaining HR employees, however, would stay for the time being within the PCT – under commissioning – to await further information on their fate.

One of the initial options mooted for the provider side was to transform it into a '*social enterprise*'. Although many staff seemed enthusiastic about this, others suggested it was too great a leap to take. In the end, the concept was dropped. Informants suggested the failure to develop plans for a social enterprise mainly resulted from time problems and specifically the short deadlines involved in submitting a '*realistic*' set of proposals. This was apparently compounded by problems with '*getting all the staff on board*', which had not been easy; plus there was resistance from the trade union '*whose default position was "No!"*'. In the end, Millford only had around a month to assemble their main proposal and this was nowhere near enough time, especially as the SHA felt they had failed to indicate realistically their preferred '*direction of travel*'.

As the social enterprise concept came and went, another destination was proposed for elements of the provider side: integration with a healthcare authority based primarily on the other side of the nearby city – a community trust seeking foundation trust status and which covered several geographical regions. Under TUPE arrangements, while some areas of the PCT would now become vertically integrated with the Millford Foundation Trust, the majority of Millford provider-side staff would have a new employer from 1 April, 2013; albeit that these arrangements were to be for two years only in the first instance. As one PCT manager suggested, the logic provided for joining the community trust was that:

> We felt that we wanted to go somewhere where the ethos was around community services, as opposed to community service being one business unit in an acute setting [as at Millford Foundation Trust]. We didn't know whether the acute setting would foster the right level of support and commitment because obviously community and acute are very different pieces of the jigsaw.

To us, however, the merger with the community trust always appeared counter-intuitive, mainly given the considerable geographical distance involved. Badging provider services in Millford under the logo of the community trust – parts of which were almost 40 miles away – appeared anomalous. When questioned on this, one senior manager in the PCT outlined some of the geographical and structural complexities involved. He noted in particular that Millford would not be the only NHS provider potentially transferring services to that community trust. The suggestion was that this was not such an unusual suggestion given an increasingly competitive environment for healthcare services. This was an environment where NHS providers may need to combine in the face of an uncertain future – one where private entities would start to challenge public for the provision of services:

> Yes, I mean we don't share any boundaries with them [community trust]. There are two other providers going, possibly three, who are over more in that area. And they are also taking on quite a number of community dental practices, including our own. And they're all over the patch – [adjacent town – west] is going in, we're going in, and I think [adjacent area – east] is going in. So they're dotted all over the place really. So you know, their empire has, I think it has more than trebled overnight or it will do from 1 April [2013].

However, in the tumult of the period, insufficient consideration had possibly been given to the fact that the proposed community trust itself was to incorporate services from other authorities. It was thus at this stage that an acute sense of realism seemed to emerge in relation to the possible employment outcomes of such arrangements (as we see in Chapter 6). One senior PCT manager seemed only too aware of some of the likely repercussions:

> I think that the back office functions are going to be most heavily hit. And there is no doubt about that because just at a glance you can see that there are three organizations going into [community trust], so they're not going to want three directors, they're

not going to want three deputies, and they're not going to want three separate groups of HR people. We'll have one team that will look after all the three divisions, which makes business sense doesn't it? So there will not be enough jobs for everybody; there is no doubt about that. You know, it could be applied to all the other functions like IT, Finance, any of the support functions.

In our discussions with PCT managers about mergers and acquisitions, there had indeed always seemed a large and rather obvious *elephant in the room* – Millford Foundation Trust. In terms of initial dealings between the PCT and the acute trust, one manager offered the insight that '*I suppose there wasn't a coming together of minds*', which appeared to be an implied understatement. Another PCT manager put it more bluntly: '*the relationship between us and the FT can be abysmal at times*'. Informal discussions of the relationship between the PCT and the acute trust often revolved around issues of '*vision*' or, rather, differences thereof. There were, however, a range of views among PCT managers on what the optimal '*arena for change*' should be.

When we pressed further over reasons for the seeming reluctance of Millford PCT and Millford Acute Trust to be engaging in meaningful discussions, one thing became clear: reference to '*different visions*' was often a euphemism for the fact that the respective chief executives simply did not see eye to eye personally. Managers suggested that this personal antagonism was one of the main stumbling blocks to fruitful negotiation within Millford. As one manager explained:

> *In [Millford] for years there's been a very political divide, that's very well known, between the two chief execs. You would be in a room full of the public and they would start a slanging match; really, this kind of public. ... It's very political and very obvious ... I mean Robert [PCT chief executive] is the statistician guy, you know, by his background. And I'd say that Colin [acute trust chief executive] is very much a businessman. ... They are such different personalities.*

Relationships at the top of these two organizations appeared to trigger effects further down the hierarchy. It was suggested to us that there seemed to be a restriction of information on restructuring options at the PCT around this time as '*we weren't told much about what the FT were going to offer*'. An informant stated a widespread belief among PCT staff – one which fuelled resistance – along the lines of '*the FT will swallow us up*' when it comes to the joining of activities. Another belief expressed to us was that if redundancies do occur then they would be found '*primarily among PCT staff*'. As one respondent suggested, '*this was why people went with* [the community trust]' – because they thought '*great, it gives us a bit more time*'.

In the end, however, informants suggested the '*plug was pulled*' on the community trust proposal because of three main pressures: i) '*the hostility of local GPs*'; ii) '*we weren't financially viable*' (especially when the community trust wished to add a levy); and iii) '[Millford] *Managed Care said if you go with them, we won't commission you*'. Ultimately, the only remaining option on the table was that which had seemed most evident from the start (at least to outside observers): the so-called '*default position*' as one PCT board member called it – that of joining the '*council of last resort*', the local acute trust.

Restructuring, insecurity and stress

We have described the political context surrounding events in the last years and months of Millford PCT's existence and the various structural options available to it as it began to transfer its functions and services to other bodies and institutions. However, at a level deeper than political context and organization structure are the personal reactions and opinions of those experiencing the sharp end of change: PCT managers and staff. Towards the end of our research, having documented how formal roles and structures had been affected by recent changes in healthcare policy, we concentrated increasingly on the more personal experiences, thoughts and feelings of a small number of informants who we interviewed on more than one occasion. In so doing, we were able to gauge not only changing events in the final days of the PCT but also, in some instances, how staff views on restructuring also changed as the organization neared the end of its road.

We have noted how, in the years preceding the 2010 general election, there appeared scant public awareness that a major restructuring exercise was in the offing under a potential change of government. In fact, both parties to the Conservative–Liberal Democrat coalition had denied as much. However, we were still surprised that, with a history of major reorganizations in the NHS, professionals on the ground reported they too had not anticipated the seismic reforms that were to come. As one senior manager suggested:

> No we didn't expect it. I think people felt that if there was a change of government that there would be changes in terms of finances and all the rest of it because that was going to happen whether the same government was in or a new government. But I think the scale of it was very unexpected.

According to respondents, the reforms to UK healthcare were especially startling in that the system appeared to be operating satisfactorily in the years running up to the 2010 election. Radical change was not on the radar, health services were generally concentrating on the '*here and now*', and professionals saw little need for major reorganization. Indeed, when the changes were announced, experienced staff reported they often appeared as much backward-looking as forward-looking. One of our informants suggested that staff were often struggling to find the '*positives*' in the exercise:

> When you're caught up in the middle of it really you can see how much change is involved. And I think people are struggling to find the positives in it all, really struggling to identify the positives. … I think that a lot of people don't really understand the need for the change because everybody is busy working away at making the current system work more effectively. And then all of a sudden that's just gone and

a lot of people are saying it's like going back to the old health boards, you know, with all the budget people or whatever. I mean, I wasn't around then, but lots of people who were have said that it just feels like that.

Many respondents also suggested the scale of spending involved in the reforms seemed capricious given recurrent political drives to reduce NHS expenditure. One informant suggested the costs involved appeared '*colossal*' in the context of recurrent political mantras suggesting there was little in the coffers. Indeed primary care was one area in which the need to make financial improvements was always at the forefront of consideration:

The cost of making these changes is going to be huge. I'm not convinced where the pay-off is because I personally don't know what was so terribly wrong with the current set-up to justify the huge amount of cost in getting this through. So it doesn't all seem to fit together because we're struggling financially anyway and then something else comes along which is just going to make that financial burden apparently worse. And it will *make it worse.*

Nervousness abounded over the future destinations for the PCT's operations and services and the careers and livelihoods of staff and whether or not individuals would secure employment in the post-reform system. A second interview with a senior PCT manager revealed not only the extremely low level of morale among PCT staff, but also that there still remained uncertainty over the future roles that employees would play even relatively late in the reform process. These issues were compounded by the scale of efficiency targets to be met in bringing the restructuring process about.

Moreover, even where the destination of PCT services and functions *had* been established, there were still significant worries about what would happen to staff when they arrived at their new homes:

Well, it's very gloomy really because for people in the provider, you know, the questions on everybody's mind is, 'where am I safest?' and 'where is the safest place to be?' And really there isn't a safe spot for anybody. For the people who are part of the provider transfer, the advantage of being part of that is that you know where the service is going and that you're going with it; but the unknown piece for that is 'what's going to happen when we get there?' Because whilst everybody is going en masse, there have got to be efficiencies once we get there because of all these efficiency targets that we've got to meet. So there is some kind of immediate relief there, but post-April [2013], who knows what's going to happen next? [And] if you're on the commissioning side, all you know at the moment is that you don't know what the new organization is going to look like. But again there are too many people around for the jobs that are going to be there, you know, and that's a certainty. So there isn't a safe hiding place anywhere.

During the last year of the PCT's existence, cost cutting and making efficiency savings had become acute. Indeed it extended far beyond the more peripheral savings made initially by senior management in respect of coffee, sandwiches, and mineral water, etc. Efficiency savings now extended both to front-line services and administrative management:

> *It is very difficult really. We have, for the last 12 months, been going through really, really severe efficiency savings; and you know, that has affected the number of people out there doing front-line jobs. We've got to meet the cost of management efficiency savings as well. And then we've got to save generally on non-pay costs. So from every angle.*

Informants went on to describe various services that had been decommissioned over the year. There was a sense of irony here in that some services were ones later to be encouraged in healthcare policy, such as clinical intervention prior to attending emergency departments. Although the majority of PCT clinical staff would ultimately be redeployed, a sizeable percentage would decide to leave:

> *So we've decommissioned three services. We've decommissioned the early intervention service, which was set up probably 12 months ago. The reason that was set up was to divert people from turning up at A&E at the FT. That's gone. We've decommissioned the community falls service and we've decommissioned another one which is within the children's services, but that's not finishing until February. So for the first time, you know, doctors and nurses and therapists have been made redundant. Oh, and there's another one, which is called active case management as well. And again they were a group of nurses who worked to stop people keep going back into hospital. I think there were about 50 people affected overall, or something like that. Now we did manage to redeploy some of them, but not all of them. I think about a third of people left. We had some GPs with special interest: they've gone. Some nurses have gone, and a therapist.*

Another manager in the PCT expressed views of a more personal nature regarding the effects the restructuring proposals were having on staff. This informant admitted that in being an experienced professional, she was used to taking the '*hard knocks*' and had '*built up a bit of resilience*' over the years. However, despite experiencing previous change exercises, this one was of a different degree of magnitude and, as such, had made her reflect on whether she wanted to remain in the NHS. It was also a programme that was resulting in a marked change of attitude on behalf of many staff she dealt with – mostly in a negative direction. It had seen around 40 per cent of the workforce offer responses on HR measures that reflected significant problems with work and the workplace, especially regarding levels of anxiety and stress. When presented with the data, members of PCT senior management team admitted privately that they had regarded the statistics as '*shocking*':

> *It's not a job at the moment which makes you glad to be alive, because it's dealing with the anxieties of people and the organizational uncertainty. And it brings out the worst behaviours in people; you know, when people are feeling threatened and angry*

and that? So it is hard going because all the niceties of the work – you know the creative, forward planning and all of that – just doesn't happen at the moment. So I do question how long I'll be doing this for.

Another senior manager suggested that the number of problems being signalled had become so great that they had asked the HR function to do '*development work*' with team leaders in order to help them and their staff through the period of change. Staff in the HR function itself, however, felt that the offer of such '*support*' was essentially a '*one-way street*' – one running in the opposite direction to themselves. Indeed, earlier interviews with staff on both the commissioning and provider sides of the organization (as detailed earlier) had often seen the HR department portrayed as being in some ways *responsible* for the restructuring messages they had to deliver:

As an HR team, we do soak up a lot of the anxiety of the organization. You know, because we front a lot of it with managers or whatever. And people just think it's our fault basically [laughs]. So it's about how we manage ourselves as a team as well in terms of making sure that we're clear about where the boundaries are, you know, so that we can be clear with other people. Well [sighs], yeah I mean I think we all have periods of time when we're less able to deal with it. But generally speaking, you know, I think that we are reasonably okay at looking after ourselves, you know. Because it goes with the territory, and I think that you have to develop that skill. If you're practising in HR for any period of time, you have to develop that skill.

Despite the resilience of the HR department – and the ability of its staff to '*look after themselves*' – the last few months had put a heavy strain on a group whose headcount had already been reduced significantly. What remained of the department had, as noted, been split into two groups, which were now operating on separate floors of Royal House. However, the process by which the commissioning side was to *decommission* services, in advance of CCGs, had been rapid, with the result that this impacted significantly on the status of provider services, which, in turn, had put strain on the HR function:

In the summer, it was particularly bad because the commissioning part of the organization had made a decision to decommission the services, but the actual impact was on the provider part of the organization and it was all done very quickly. You know, the NHS has loads of processes and procedures that we have to follow. You know, it's not like a private business where you make a decision and the people are out on the Friday. You know, where you can tell people one day and they're out the next. It doesn't work like that in the NHS. You know, nationally you've got the Department [of Health] saying, 'We want to minimize redundancies and avoid redundancies at all cost'. But then, on the other hand, you've got organizations in turnaround and the only way of bringing them back into financial balance is to get rid of cost. And the only way we can do that in the NHS is through losing people.

Another PCT manager expressed similar views on how restructuring had very much pitted the two sides of the organization against one another. Again the view was that this part of the exercise had been '*very hard*' for all concerned, notably as it was the first time in memory that such a large number of staff were to be lost in various rounds of realignment, relocation and redundancy:

> So you know, you get these odd strands that don't marry up. So yes, that was a very difficult time because you had the two parts of the organization up against each other, and I did feel that we were in the middle trying to make it happen, you know? And everybody naturally involved was very upset that the services were going, and okay, some people were redeployed but some people weren't. And it was just the anxiety of going through all of that for people, and you know it was the first time we'd done it. You know, if you're trying to [lose], I think it was between 40 and 50 people … if you've got a group of 40 or 50 people and you've got to get them all through this process in the space of three months so that everybody feels that they've got an equal chance to be considered for jobs and all the rest of it, it was quite hard.

The stress placed on HR over redundancies and redeployments was exacerbated by the fact that many managers in line positions were not used to having '*difficult conversations*' with staff over such issues. Despite extensive explanations at team briefings, HR personnel suggested line managers were often ineffective at '*getting out the message*', which could see them rely on HR staff to lead such discussions. In the event, the HR department had worked closely with the trade unions to make sure they were '*in the picture and to bring them on board*' regarding the types of decisions that had to be made. Also HR had developed a dedicated email account for people to put questions on restructuring issues. As a result, those affected by the changes often seemed to perceive HR as the ones making the decisions, despite the fact that their staff were going through the same painful process:

> I suppose this could have a historical element to it, but I think one of the line managers – I'm talking generally here – but line managers generally are not great at having those difficult conversations, so they relied very heavily on HR. And then of course if you're the one doing all the talking, the person thinks that it's your role to make all the decisions and that but, you know, it isn't really. … But you know, there is only so much [you can do]. At the end of the day, the decision has been made, and I suppose what we have to do is to implement it in as reasonable a way as we possibly can. But it didn't suit everybody. … We support people who are going through organizational change or whatever and soak up a lot of their angst around that. You know, and as an HR professional you learn to deal with that. But it is more difficult when you are also going through the same thing.

The Millford HR function had of course already been hit hard by the restructuring. A senior HR manager outlined the degree of fragmentation that had occurred, noting how staff aligned to the provider side had possibly been affected less than those on the commissioning side. Again the decisive factor when it came to levels of morale was whether or not staff perceived they had a positive future – something that for both sides of HR was yet to be established. For many staff, there was indeed a sense of '*creeping death*' about the commissioning side of the function:

> *So some people have gone back to* [Town East]: *so physically upped sticks and gone to another organization. Some have come here* [and moved upstairs] *to the provider bit, and some are still downstairs in the commissioning bit. Now I think the feel of the team up here is more positive than the feel of the team downstairs. And I think it's to do with moving on to something new, which has a more positive connotation than if you feel that you're being left behind downstairs. And it's almost a bit like creeping death because, rightly or wrongly, what we've done is, over a period of time, we've brought more people* [upstairs]. *It started off with myself and I think it was three others, and then we brought somebody else up, and now we're looking to bring another couple up, or three up, or whatever. So I think it must be terrible downstairs; you know, putting myself in their shoes, seeing the team that you've been surrounded by disappear and wondering whether you're going to be part of the new bit or whether you're going to be* [made redundant]. *And I deliberately sort of tried to phrase it very positively in terms of, 'you're allied to providing or commissioning; it's not that you're moving out and you're staying'.*

The sense of impending loss brought about by the restructuring had ultimately led to increased levels of stress on the part of many managers. One informant we spoke to had previously been a manager with a large private sector organization and admitted to being a '*tough cookie*' and having been '*around the block*'. However she also admitted that '*I have increasingly been stressed*' while working at Millford PCT. This manager, who we got to know well over the course of the research, appeared ever more tense, anxious and drained on the various occasions we met. One of her parting shots appeared to summarize the dual sources of much managerial anxiety in the PCT – progressive downsizing on the one hand and work intensification on the other:

> *I have found things are getting more challenging and I am getting a bit more stressed because the resources* [are dwindling]. *We've not been replacing so there's less and less people. And we're having to choose more about what is a must, what's a should, and what's a could. And that's a process that we're working through. It is more stressful.*

Redundancy and demotion

Ultimately, the greatest stress experienced by managers at the waning PCT would probably be among those demoted or made redundant as a result of the restructuring process. Although this happened to several of the specialist and hybrid managers we interviewed, in two cases they were among the small sample we interviewed on more than one occasion and whom we began to know quite well. In these cases

– Clare, a manager made redundant, and Diane, a manager demoted – we only became aware of changes to their circumstances in the process of conducting final interviews. Both interviewees indeed appeared somewhat reluctant to divulge the facts of these changes. In what follows, we let our managers explain their respective situations by way of short, discrete accounts. These offer insight into how organizational politics can be at the heart of restructuring decisions.

Clare's story

In the case of Clare, she disclosed her change in circumstances within a general discussion of the context in which redundancies, demotions and other forms of employment change had arisen in the PCT. Like other managers we talked to, she acknowledged that pressures on staffing levels had actually predated the change in government, as had concerns over budget levels, which had already seen an acrimonious divestment of some services. Her own redundancy had come about as a direct result of the transfer of powers from the PCT to CCGs. It had happened mainly due to Clare being a senior manager, on a higher salary, in a public-facing service: one which would be threatened under restructuring. As such, she knew she was '*at risk*' and, thus, '*with her manager's head on*', had very much seen redundancy coming.

As in many such cases, Clare's situation was a complex one and involved a range of procedures and policies, but ultimately ones that related to reducing costs. In her case, it involved the practice of converting two posts into one. Clare's case, in fact, involved choosing between her and a member of staff in the same function who was also deemed '*at risk*'. However, as the requirements of the new post were presented, it became clear these were at a level significantly below Clare's existing management responsibilities. As she suggested, '*I could have gone for* [it], *but it definitely wasn't me*'. Clare explained the complex situation involved in the restructuring of roles within her function:

> So what they did was, there was another member of staff at risk; although a band lower than me. So instead of having the equality and diversity engagement over here and other things spattered around the organization in different directorates (not even in our directorate), he created a Head of Compliance and she's got five areas where she's responsible, not to do it, but [to be] responsible for ensuring that it's done. And she's got Risk, she's got Engagement, she's got Equality and Diversity, I think she's got Child Protection and another one that I can't remember; and all of those statutory duties to comply are in her job description. And she's a bit like, I suppose, the person in the role needs to be a bit like a prison warden, as I visualize it, who goes round and says, 'right, I'm banging you up and you haven't done that, and you haven't done it by'. You need to be that kind of person. Very policy orientated: writes policies, produces policies, monitors and makes sure people do what they want. And that was a job I could have gone for but it definitely wasn't me. So I didn't; I decided not to. And that person then did get that job and that took her out of the threat of redundancy.

And she's the right person for the job and it wasn't me, and I wouldn't have wanted to have done it. But then that meant that my statutory role around Engagement was transferring to that post and I would be surplus to requirements.

Clare suggested, at that stage of the restructuring process, she was really the '*only big scalp that they got*' as many of the posts to be taken out were from lower in the PCT hierarchy. She also suggested that few staff were keen to accept terms under the MARS voluntary severance scheme for, in comparison to taking voluntary redundancy, these were seen as '*unattractive*' financially. Clare in fact offered insight into the many and varied exit, redeployment or realignment routes that managers were faced with when abolition of the PCT became clear:

> *Nobody took the MARS offer, not surprisingly. A number of people said well I'll go if you want to make me voluntary redundant, thank you very much; and a number of older people did that in secretarial roles and those sorts of things. So they were savings, but they were at the lower end of the scale. I think my post is the only big scalp that they got. Others were in a redundancy situation, but then one of them got another job, one would leave, so that would remove the redundancy situation, and mine was the only one. In Public Health they did a kind of a going round the houses approach to it, where six 8As were told that one of them would have to go. And it wasn't handled particularly well, and in the end they came up with their own solution which was we'll all take a half a day cut, and they did that rather than lose a post. So that would have presumably ring-fenced those monies anyway to transfer into local authority.*

In the event, Clare accepted compulsory redundancy. After an earlier career in management with other public bodies, she had worked for the NHS for 13 years and felt that on balance she would receive a reasonable amount in redundancy settlement. There had, in fact, been major changes to Clare's role and function about a year earlier, and she admitted to not really having '*embedded*' into the new team. Indeed, she felt that she lacked some of the new skills required and that there had been insufficient support in terms of training. Now in her mid to late fifties, Clare found herself increasingly '*a square peg in a round hole*'. There was some light at the end of the tunnel, however, for an agreement was struck that if she agreed to come back to the NHS four weeks after being made redundant, she would be offered a fixed-term role for 15 hours a week for six months to conduct a dedicated project. Whilst not ideal, Clare felt this not only offered an employment '*buffer*' but also allowed her to '*go out on a high*'. As such, when the redundancy axe came down, she did not resist. In fact she appeared resigned to it, chose not to appeal, and admitted to us that she had basically been '*compliant*'.

Diane's story

Compliant, however, is not a word that readily springs to mind to describe the reactions of our second manager to receiving news that she was to be demoted.

Discussion of Diane's new employment circumstances again only emerged at the end of a long and wide-ranging interview on restructuring events at the PCT. After a discussion of about 90 minutes, she made an elliptical remark to the extent that if we had interviewed her the previous week then she may have been '*a lot happier*'. On being asked, '*so what's happened this week?*', she replied bluntly, '*I've been downgraded*'.

Diane then outlined how this had largely been unexpected for, notwithstanding an environment of uncertainty and flux, she personally had felt relatively secure within Millford NHS. Despite advice from her line manager that under current organizational changes (where PCT staff were being integrated with the local acute trust), '*everything's up for grabs*', she was confident of remaining if not in her present post then at least in grade given that she had experienced restructuring affecting her position previously and had '*won each time*'. However, in the context of the current integration of services, the outcome was more complex and resulted ultimately in her and a colleague being placed in direct competition for a post:

> I am normally quite an optimistic person, but I didn't see it coming, I didn't see it coming. And that was when I just thought, gosh, if it's me, I'll be really devastated. … And they need to get rid of the 8Cs and 8Bs, so the associate directors and the 8Bs. So we had two associate directors [that] took voluntary redundancies and three 8Bs took redundancy, just took the money and ran. And that left myself and Kath with District Nursing; and well you don't need two 8Bs. And I'd been saying for a year [that] I hope in this [new] structure you don't have the pair of us managing, because this is just madness. And so it then came up where we had to go into competition.

For Diane, the situation was complicated for a number of reasons. Not least was the fact that she had known and worked with her colleague Kath for many years and, in fact, considered her a '*good friend*'. Several years earlier, Kath had left District Nursing because she '*found the management side quite difficult*'. It therefore came as a surprise to Diane that when Kath returned, five years ago, it was into a management role and on a relatively high grade. A further complication, Diane felt, was that when she discovered there would be competition for the post, she also realized that Kath and the associate director responsible for the reassessment were '*very good friends*':

> We worked together before, but she left – and actually downgraded herself – because she found the management side quite difficult. And she came back, has been back five years, and has been managing District Nursing. And all that time there's, you know, there's very much between her and the associate director … very good friends. So she arrived back on this grade, and I'm going, 'where the hell did that come from?' But it makes no odds to me what anybody else is paid; that's fine. I was still being paid my 8B.

But for Diane, the result of the reassessment exercise was ultimately not the one she had expected:

> *I lost. And I was shocked. I saw it as a stitch up, an absolute stitch up. So I'm now downgraded to an 8A. I've got protected pay for two years, but in two years' time I lose effectively about ten grand. So I'd been at the top of my 8B now – because I've effectively been senior manager for nine, ten years – whereas Kath has only just gone in. And she was saying, 'oh, you know, [I] want to get [my] next increment' and 'if I'm going to be the one they downgrade, I want my next increment'. Whereas I'd been at the top of mine for years because I'd done it for years.*

For Diane, this had been a very frustrating time. She was a highly qualified, relatively highly paid member of the management team with an impressive career profile; someone who had been brought in originally because of a previous incumbent's difficulties in managing a function. However, in the period running up to the reassessment, Diane had made it clear that if she was to manage the service, it would be on her own terms and not on the basis of co-managing with a colleague. She saw herself as very much a line manager and someone who took decisions because '*at that grade, you have to make decisions*'. As Diane suggested: '*Effectively I was the instigator of my own fate – because I don't manage that way. Not that I'm better. I'm just different.*'

To make matters worse, this change of employment circumstances had been compounded by the fact that, for Diane, this was very much her *annus horribilis*:

> *My relationship of 27 years has split up. So I'm now left with the house, [I have] no children, then my dog died, and then I wrote my car off. [Laughter] Oh, I've been diagnosed with rheumatoid arthritis as well.*

Ultimately, this confident and apparently effective manager suggested that her main thoughts were '*just to get out*'. Diane explained her disillusionment with events at Millford and how, as a result: '*I've applied for another job in [Northern City], which they've already integrated. So I'm hoping for an interview.*' However, with a nod towards the current uncertainty regarding NHS management positions, she reflected '*whether I get it is another thing*'. Diane's parting shot was to suggest that, personally, she was '*not looking forward*' to the move to the acute trust. Indeed, if she failed to obtain the post at Northern City or else a comparable post outside Millford in the near future, she would undoubtedly be in a '*Catch 22 situation*' career-wise:

> *When we do integrate, I'll get TUPE'd over onto an 8A job, doing an 8A job. And people don't like paying people in 8B for doing an 8A. And also, unlike someone 'at risk', if you're TUPE'd on an 8A and there's an 8B going, you can't go for it. So I can't even go for what I was. So I keep a job, but in the restructuring is there a job to be kept into? You're formally prevented from going for the job that you'd worked your way up to. It's crazy. We even went to the unions saying, 'well if there's not an 8B, surely I could have been made redundant?' [But] I was 'critical to business' so I wasn't entitled to redundancy, but then [I was] downgraded ... I've*

got two years to find something else otherwise I'm in trouble for I'm now paying a
mortgage by myself. But something will come up. And anyway, I won't have the
stress of managing something.

End of the road

As a consequence of the Health and Social Care Act of 2012, Millford PCT was
scheduled to be dissolved on 1 April, 2013. Its functions and services would be
transferred to various new or existing entities, including: Millford Clinical
Commissioning Group; the Department of Health; NHS England; Millford
Foundation Trust; and NHS Property Services. As obliged, the PCT followed the
official closedown procedures set out by central government. Accountability for
the closedown of the PCT resided with the NHS chief executive of [Northern
city], within which Millford is a region, with the local closedown being discharged
officially through the PCT directors of finance (up to 31 March, 2013) and the
CCG chief finance officers (from 1 April, 2013). The closedown required that all
PCT assets and liabilities, including staff and estates, be formally transferred to these
other organizations. In the process, the PCT carried out a review in line with
national guidelines, and all its assets and liabilities were recorded in a formal
agreement with NHS legal advisors. This facilitated production of the final transfer
document as required by the Department of Health. With this, responsibility for all
the organization's activities was formally transferred and Millford PCT ceased to
exist on 1 April, 2013.

Conclusions

> The current disengagement evident across key groups like healthcare
> professionals and managers represents a serious challenge to the reforms. It
> would be a mistake to assume that these groups will simply come to accept
> the reforms in time.
>
> *(Walshe and Ham, 2011: 3)*

In the early sections of this chapter, we offer examples of data from our ethnographic
study to highlight trends associated with a perceived intensification of managerial
work within PCTs, and focally Millford PCT. Overall, in terms of specialist and
hybrid managerial work, such examples serve to relate the expansion of occupational
roles to an increased intensity of work and a range of techniques for greater role
accountability. They also describe ways in which managers within PCTs reacted
to such changes in a period of heightened organizational uncertainty and
occupational pressure.

In addition, we note how managerial role expansion and work intensification
has also been linked to behaviour consistent with an increasingly business-oriented
or commercial culture in health services. Many of our managers had adopted

behaviour patterns consistent with those traditionally associated with private sector organizations and marketization. Examples included working long hours, developing activities reflective of entrepreneurialism, setting and meeting operational targets, and establishing institutional relations based on a contractual or commodified logic. Although only scratching the surface of the extensive interview data produced in the course of this case research, our analysis demonstrates the changing culture and symbolism of healthcare management in an era defined increasingly by neo-liberal philosophies and private sector business techniques. Such an era, however, is not universally perceived as positive by all professionals exposed to it or commentators trying to make sense of it.

Finally we also note that in addition to our formal research on managerial roles and behaviour, this case study was affected significantly by the announcement that ostensibly heralded the closure of PCTs. Given this situation, our study of PCT managers began to focus increasingly on how such organizations were managing within a context of '*workforce reduction and organizational demise*'. Although supplementary to our original research aims, we felt it important to assess how managers attempted to keep staff motivated and operations stable in a period characterized by demoralization and decline. In many ways, the Millford PCT story became an emotionally charged one as staff began to assume, psychologically, that the organization had closed from the day the White Paper was announced, rather than the date the organization was projected for closure. However, as Walshe and Ham (2011) argued, the inheritance of the new care commissioners and providers may ultimately be far from straightforward. Indeed one of the last comments we received during the PCT research was a cautionary note from a senior manager: '*I don't think GPs have appreciated that not only* [are] *they going to inherit the budget but they* [are also] *going to inherit all the inherent problems with the budget*'. Certainly, in the period since we completed our fieldwork, we have not yet seen resources in NHS organizations become more plentiful or workloads less demanding.

Notes

1   *Newsnight*, BBC, 8 May, 2011.
2   Margaret Hodge, Public Accounts Committee, 12 June, 2013.
3   Whitley Councils for the health service decided pay scales and working conditions for NHS employees. They were replaced by the Staff Council (Agenda for Change).

8

MANAGING THE IMPOSSIBLE

The challenges of organizational change in the NHS

In the preceding chapters, we illustrate differences in the ways and the extent to which middle managers were affected by increasing marketization – from increasing work intensification, including competing demands to meet both commercial and care priorities, through to redundancy and the wholesale abolition of organizations. Yet despite clear differences in purpose, work and effects of rearrangement as well as the varying severity of financial pressure of the four NHS organizations, we were struck by the experiential similarity of so many junior and middle NHS managers as they attempted to fulfil the contradictory role expectations of administrator, bureaucrat, business person, leader and entrepreneur. Our findings resonate strongly with those of several classic studies on the realities of managerial work in that *management* is not some kind of scientific process that can be measured, controlled and influenced by textbook-derived *best practice* systems, but is a complex, messy human endeavour – a 'craft that requires experience, skill, and artistry' (Tengblad, 2012: 5). This kind of work is essential for 'keeping the show on the road' but is routinely undervalued and under-resourced, meaning mid-level managers struggle with a huge volume of duties and operate under much duress (Hassard *et al.*, 2009; Mintzberg, 1973: 29–30; Osterman, 2009).

It would be wrong to say that the changes have been unfavourable to all managers, as a new cadre of managers working to commercial goals are emerging, and managers in NHS departments – such as Marketing, Publicity, Communications and Human Resources, where they aren't already outsourced – are coming to resemble those of other commercial corporations. However, there is strong evidence to suggest that the working lives of most junior and middle managers, particularly those in clinical and operational managerial roles, are considerably more pressured and insecure than they once were. Moreover, the overall demotion of need for care as a determinant of resource allocation was a widespread finding – one that was deeply troubling for NHS managers, who are often clinical professionals with a deep belief in the NHS's *free at the point of need* ethos. Even when they didn't have clinical backgrounds, many were passionate supporters of this ethos.

This chapter draws together analysis across the four preceding chapters to examine the effects of New Public Management on junior and middle management roles and behaviour in UK healthcare. This encompassed an examination of the realities of managerial life for junior and middle managers in healthcare organizations. As we describe experiences common across the board, the following discussion reflects our particular Critical-Action perspective (Chapter 3), which highlights the interaction of interpretive and ideological forces. Within this, we include comparisons of the various roles and behaviours of junior and middle managers in respect of competing organizational governance regimes and an exploration of the interactions between managers and front-line staff and their impact on service delivery.

The constant flux: a system designed to fail

Change as a permanent state appears regularly as an oxymoron in describing working conditions in modern organizations. However, we use the phrase for a specific reason here. Several senior managers offered a cynical assessment of the purpose of structural changes to the NHS. They argued that the latest structural changes, those enshrined in the Health and Social Care Act 2012, were specifically designed to fail, thus clearing the way for private providers to enter. This Act of Parliament also mandated regular recommissioning of services in its controversial competition clause. The suspicion these managers held was that once the management of NHS organizations became truly impossible, the way would be cleared for private providers to enter and correct the problem. The metaphor in use was unpleasant but explanatory: '*they aren't changing the fish in the goldfish bowl; they're making fish soup – something that can't easily be reversed*'. One example given to describe how commissioning of health services might be outsourced was the clause abolishing the commissioning role of primary care trusts. By forming a new group of inexperienced commissioners who had to recommission services regularly, these managers argued, a situation was being created that meant public servants were almost bound to fail and, therefore, to need subsequent rescue by private commissioning services. Such companies already exist, such as those involved in managed care in the US, which have an increasing presence in the UK health market. Leys and Player's (2011) notion of a 'plot' to privatize the NHS seems entirely accurate.

The preceding four chapters demonstrate how the roles and behaviours of junior and middle managers must take place in the context of a more or less constantly shifting policy environment. Junior and middle managers had their own views on government policy with some predicting the privatization of the NHS and others (accurately, as it turned out) predicting job losses, particularly amongst their own ranks. National NHS policy, in a less overtly political sense, exerted a powerful influence on junior and middle managers; this tended to be manifested most significantly in the New Public Managerialism with its implications for monitoring, information collection and management and its 'rituals of verification' (Power, 2000) and 'utopia of rules' (Graeber, 2015). For many managers, complying with governance policies through information management was a significant draw on their time. Aside from the actual burden of data collection, when commenting about the fact that NHS policy seems to operate in something of a state of flux, managers were ambivalent at best. Their attention was diverted onto the short-term survival of their organizations even as commercial concerns were gaining large-scale contracts to provide NHS-badged services covering multiple trusts.

Indeed, at a more micro level, as our fieldwork at the acute trust was coming to a close, the role of matron was eliminated. Similarly, Lois, another nurse manager with whom we spent time at the trust, was *restructured* into a lower-grade project management role whilst being asked to retain her out-of-hours on-call duties. Her subsequent temporary contract expired beyond the end of the project and ultimately she was no longer employed by the acute trust.

The frequency of organizational restructuring at all four cases gave observers, and perhaps managers themselves, an impression of almost constant change. In the acute trust, for example, having moved to a system of managing different areas through business groups, some associate directors had begun to feel that such a system encouraged silo working, limiting collaboration across business groups and potentially impacting on co-ordination more widely. The original intention of the move, to allow managers to focus on their areas of specialism, appeared to have had some negative consequences.

This constantly shifting terrain was perhaps even more apparent at the mental health trust to the extent that mental health services formed but one part of the service provision by the end of the study. The organization had doubled in size by taking on non-mental-health community services from disbanded PCTs, thereby diversifying both the business and the demands upon managers. In addition, new business developments were targeted at high-value services such as providing secure inpatient units that could command higher payments than standard services. Mental health services had struggled to maintain their income, even during the preceding period of increased investment, and, as a result, Millfordshire Care Foundation NHS Trust had recently reduced management costs by 30 per cent. This meant that the responsibilities of the remaining managers were increased considerably, and senior managers worried that many middle managers at the trust were not able to cope with their expanded roles.

As levels of management were eliminated across the NHS, these service vacuums were expected to be filled by other providers, such as private contractors. This issue surfaced readily in the ambulance service, which was only able to contract for a year at a time before entering into a wide array of new contracts with a range of new commissioning groups. This was but one example of the ways in which the scale and implications of NHS legislative change was making it hard for trust managers to plan ahead properly.

Of our four case studies, however, the PCT was obviously hardest hit by the changes. We have described how much of our analysis of roles and behaviour at Millford PCT was conducted against the backcloth of imminent closure. Before that announcement, a middle manager noted how at Millford PCT: '*It's a constant programme of restructuring and service modernization and service redesign*'. A few months later, in the wake of the announcement of the closure of PCTs, the incoming interim head of Human Resources and Organizational Development, in paraphrasing his official position, felt able to introduce himself to PCT staff as '*the Director of Workforce Reduction and Organizational Demise*'. The newly formed clinical CCGs made up of general practitioners, inexperienced in large-scale commissioning, were in a poor position to take up their responsibilities, leaving the door open to 'any qualified provider'.

Across the three remaining trusts, middle managers were rapidly acquiring skills to produce business plans and respond to calls for proposals to provide their own services. Although they may have been in the best position to provide the services, they were not always skilled in this type of business transaction. If this sort of contracting follows the experience of contracting out of NHS cleaning services, then many front-line employees will retain their jobs under worsening terms and conditions of service while large companies acquire sector-wide or large regional contracts and the middle-managerial roles connecting vital but disparate parts of service networks are removed. What we saw was the attention of NHS managers being diverted – them trying to retain their current services while commercial concerns were gaining large-scale contracts to provide manageable segments of the same.

Servicing business needs and patient safety: 'you can't do both – something will give'

The managers we spoke to were acutely aware of the importance of managing their budgets effectively and planning financially for the medium term. They were also very aware that financial resources available to them were under pressure, even as demand for services continued to grow. They were sometimes faced with difficult dilemmas, having always to balance patient safety with limited available resources. They carried responsibility for making cuts and for making sure there was no loss of service; an impossible demand to meet.

The mental health trust had experienced cost pressures for longer than the other three trusts. It maintained its income level by expanding service provision and cutting management costs. The organization was suffering severe resource shortages and focusing developments on areas that attracted better funding. Income targets were being allocated to service managers as a means of managing costs, although these targets were said to be somewhat arbitrary – accused of being '*back of the envelope*' calculations that bore little relation to market prices or demand. However, once targets were itemized at a performance management meeting, it became the managers' responsibility to meet them. Service managers, essentially middle managers with little discretion, had to find the means of achieving the targets. In one case, this meant redesignating a newly built facility to provide services for patients that attracted higher payments. This decision was based on business needs rather than patient care priorities. These conversations extended to clinical care so that nurses were acutely aware of the costs of treatment decisions and that the need to reduce costs was paramount.

Vicky, a middle manager in the ambulance trust, put it well with a very simple phrase: '*you can't do both – something will give*': by '*both*' she was referring to servicing increasing demand for ambulance journeys with no extra staff or vehicles and sustaining levels of patient care. And in the case of Millford PCT, we discussed the impact of targets and target setting at length. One clinical manager described the '*very bizarre targets*' that could be set for her department in a financial climate where '*every year we've got to increase our productivity by ten per cent*'. This manager commented on how increasing '*productivity*' in line with this target was extremely difficult because of '*(a) increasing numbers of* [patients] *and (b) less staff*'. As a result, this could lead to unrealistic targets being set for clinical departments. Other organizational changes at Millford PCT related to the goal of being more cost-effective. This frequently saw departments encouraged to be more *entrepreneurial* and thus to generate income from offering services – such as training – to outside bodies. Informants described how training for local voluntary bodies, previously offered on a *gratis* or *pro bono* basis, was now charged through formal contracting. As such, the contemporary climate had changed from that of a *public* to a *business* service. A potential problem arising from such entrepreneurial activity, however, was that over time the income generated could become incorporated within a department's target estimates. Beyond that, the work of each organization was changing incrementally with an ever-increasing emphasis placed on maximizing business potential and income generation.

Conflicted role identity: public servant or business person?

The tension experienced in trying to resolve conflicting demands for higher-quality care and reduced cost in the face of increasing demand was pervasive. These forces generated a conflicted sense of identity in the workforce as expressed by a number of clinical managers as well as some of the business and senior managers with whom we spoke. Such conflict was also seen in the very roles that NHS junior and middle managers must perform. As we have seen, they were focused on business imperatives yet, at the same time, had to prioritize patient care. Indeed, we saw changing aspects of all their main managerial roles reflected in various stages of NHS deconstruction. We saw the challenges managers faced, for example, as they were told to reimagine themselves as entrepreneurial, transformational leaders and effective business people whilst also administering and monitoring their public services.

Although some managers were '*fairly comfortable*' with having to balance cost concerns with patient care, many often reported a '*constant tension*' in the process. Although delivering '*patient care*' was a rhetorical priority, managers were in no doubt about the simultaneous influence of a '*business ethos*' and the need to manage '*scarce resources*' for their organization, commonly referring to the NHS as a '*market*'. The use of the phrase '*the other side of me*' neatly conveyed the sense of tension within a healthcare manager's identity created by the necessity of fulfilling these two overarching, yet arguably conflicting, roles simultaneously. However, we must stress that the pressure on middle managers to adopt increasingly business-oriented role identities was recounted in all our case study organizations.

Indeed, mental health service middle managers were operating primarily as business managers. In HR, many managers had been recruited from the private sector and were introducing corporate HR practices to manage *business performance*. For junior and middle managers in other areas of the service, areas of work were increasingly divided into projects, and each project could attract a different rate of pay depending on how the work had been graded. Managers in Millford Care Foundation NHS Trust were commonly identified as either '*NHS home-grown managers*' or new '*business managers*'. Although the trust had managers who had worked there a long time, it had moved to bring in business managers at a senior level; for example, in the Estates department. When restructuring the levels below, these senior managers indicated a preference for *business-minded* managers in key roles.

In Combined Counties Ambulance Service NHS Trust, the phrase '*patient care has gone out of the window*' was used by several staff members we had observed and interviewed. On one occasion, a junior manager in Patient Transport Services used this phrase when describing the large number of patients they had to convey with limited resources per patient, making the process increasingly fraught: '*it's like they want them to be treated like we're transporting boxes*'.

At Millford PCT, many managers described a shift towards a more business-oriented culture within PCTs: '*it is a business … our business is delivering healthcare*'. The same manager noted the potential for role conflict inherent in moving towards '*business line management*' and how, for many staff, adopting such a management role '*is a big jump*' as more junior managers were also practising clinicians.

This tension between competing managerial roles was perhaps manifested most concretely within the occupational culture of nursing. This may explain why, increasingly, the more senior roles in middle management were being filled by people with a private sector business background; people who: '*had the business knowledge, but not the nursing knowledge*'. Our experience, however, was that business managers also had a deep sense of the importance of patient care. Indeed, like nurse managers, helping patients was often what motivated both their choice of career and their daily work. Perhaps selecting managers with a business background was primarily a pragmatic strategy for embedding business knowledge and skills into the management framework; skills that would be expensive and time-consuming for trusts to impart to clinical managers to the same extent.

Overall, we traced five eras of management associated with the incremental deconstruction of the NHS and the New Public Management: *manager as administrator* – problem-solving, inward-looking, acting reactively; *manager as bureaucrat* – responsive to government demands, concerned with financial control, closely monitoring; *manager as business person* – competitive orientation, focused on managerial control, promoting business culture; *manager as leader* – leading change, promoting decentralizing control, setting direction; and *manager as entrepreneur* – competing for business, winning contracts, doing what pays. Our study suggests, however, that rather than forming discrete managerial types in distinct time periods, elements of each managerial role coexist over time. The newer roles, such as manager as business person and manager as entrepreneur were, though, undoubtedly gaining prevalence, often in an awkward, uncertain way – jostling uncomfortably with traditional modes of identity associated with carer and clinician.

Unmanageable middle managerial work: a job with limitless demands

The first major shock for clinicians who had moved into managerial jobs was the sudden loss of fixed working hours. While many of the more junior staff had contracts detailing hours of work and arrangements for overtime and on-call payments, the expectation on managers was 'get the job done' and to provide on-call, out-of-hours managerial cover. Across all four trusts, we found managers who were unable to limit the work required of them. Any new demands for immediate information – to deal with a complaint, to find savings or to respond to an emerging or ongoing crisis – landed readily at their feet, and this was on top of an already teeming workload. A common feeling among many managers was that if only they organized their time better then these unexpected demands would be completed within a regular working week. This struck us as a kind of blameworthiness used as a way to try to rationalize the extremely difficult managerial situations in which they found themselves. Our assessment was that most of these jobs were bordering on the impossible. Often, work could only be completed by addressing emails virtually on awakening, then struggling through the demands of the 'day job', and ending the day by continuing with tasks at home and responding to new enquiries by sending out emails before going to bed. This is a generalization, of course; but this kind of working treadmill is reflective of many of the managers' experiences.

Junior and middle managers across the four trusts, therefore, occupied and enacted a challenging and demanding set of work roles. What is more, the same managers had to employ a range of diverse and adroit behaviours in order to properly fulfil them. At the core of their work behaviours, however, were two basic strategies – working more *extensively* and working more *intensively*. For the former strategy – working longer hours and taking work home – this was reported in every case study and by almost all the managers we interviewed. Informants in the Millford PCT case were typical in this respect with managers regularly reporting that they were in the office long before the official start of the working day in order to '*clear the decks*' before they began the '*proper work*', which on the *provider* side, usually referred to carrying out a clinical role during the *normal* day. One manager in a clinical specialism was typical of many when reporting that she was regularly *'in about half past seven in the morning clear*[ing] *emails if I haven't cleared them at the weekend or the night before'*.

For the latter, we have noted how managers were required to work at high levels of intensity. This included meetings where issue followed issue and with (for the observer at least) dizzying rapidity. Not uncommon here was for middle managers, often those with a more senior role, checking their beepers for important messages and then responding if necessary. During on-call night shifts, we observed phone call after phone call, beep after beep and task after task. What was more surprising was the fact that most of this work was done on the move as managers walked or drove between many locations. Even on a standard shift, there seemed little time for breaks. Not every day was manic, we were told, but personally we did not see any quiet on-call shifts.

A tactic sometimes deployed to deal with work intensity was simply that of trying to avoid problems where possible. At the acute trust, for example, junior managers spoke of managing '*monkeys*', as in dealing with *monkeys on my back*. Ward managers and other senior nurses coped with an almost constant stream of demands as they attempted to make their way from one end of the ward to the other. These were the so-called monkeys – issues constantly brought to them by colleagues and that could mount up to virtually unmanageable levels. Senior managers at the trust encouraged junior and middle managers to try and avoid taking on '*other people's monkeys*', but this was often easier said than done.

Also relevant here is that staff shortages were a feature of all four cases. While usually episodic, absences have also become effectively systemic, encouraging managers to 'improvise' and 'firefight' in order to manage day-to-day patient and task demands. Work intensity was notably apparent at Millford Care Foundation NHS Trust among ward managers, for example. As noted, many of these managers described their extended working hours as a choice or the result of their own lack of good time management: '*I probably still spend quite a bit of time with patients, but that's because my time management's really poor'*.

Not only was the workload tough to manage in terms of its intensity, it could also be emotionally draining. Emotional stressors were often the result of the life and death nature of much of the work they were involved with. Other pressures could be caused by unpleasant forms of workplace conflict. In the ambulance trust, for example, several managers recounted stories of resistance and obstruction by front-line road staff – ambulance trusts having a complex and sometimes difficult industrial relations climate. Such stories included road staff resenting managers' visits to their ambulance stations; and dealing with sicknesses, complaints, grievances, and investigations were common and often stressful tasks for Combined Counties Ambulance Service NHS Trust managers. One manager spoke about how the sheer intensity and volume of work was essentially unmanageable, leading to staff burning out and become unable to cope. In order not to compromise patient care, the staff that remained – including junior and middle managers – faced a higher workload and thus intensification of their work. Such a situation was part of the culture of 'normalized intensity' (McCann *et al.*, 2008) that was evident across all the four cases.

But higher workloads had consequences – sometimes resulting in sickness or associated with bullying. The former, of course, could lead to further staff shortages and greater work intensification. So how did managers cope with normalized intensity? We uncovered substantial evidence of managers simply accepting these conditions as part of the job, stating that they '*just have to get on with it*'. Connectedly, they also drew on their own senses of professionalism – they were motivated '*to cope*' by their professed commitment to patient care. This came through strongly in almost all individual cases, whether managers had a clinical or non-clinical background. It led us to conceive of these junior and middle managerial roles as almost 'impossible jobs' (Hargrove and Glidewell, 1990) and often only survivable in the short term. NHS management had become 'extreme work' (Buchanan *et al.*, 2013; Granter *et al.*, 2015).

Narrative management: changing what's done by changing what's said

While we were familiar with the function of language in embedding neo-liberal ideology (Massey, 2013), the ways we saw language used and controlled at various trusts was a surprise. A simple example was the shift from the term *patient* to *service user*. This change of language had an effect on the way people thought and on what they did. Patients, rather than people requiring care, became users of valuable and scarce resources; and we were regularly corrected when using seemingly out-of-date terminology. We were surprised how readily these new terms were accepted and adopted and came to think of the reorientation of narrative as a coping strategy; one used by the junior and middle managers to try to gain access to more resources. We saw how readily our managers embraced new initiatives to secure resources. There were several examples of new ideas for improving efficiency: Six Sigma, Lean Management, Total Quality Management. A prevalent example during the study was the introduction of variations of Lean management at a strategic level. At first, it was difficult to understand how managers so uncritically embraced the ideas and language of Lean management. However, as we became more consciously aware of our organizational settings and as our knowledge deepened, we discovered the expediency of this new Lean approach. By framing requests as part of Lean thinking, managers were able to gain everyday resources always in short supply – bed sheets, small maintenance tasks, new shelving. Once the supply of associated resources dried up, managers were more openly critical of the latest management fad or fashion, often through making ironic statements or jokes.

We found that the acute trust placed a heavy emphasis on communicating narratives about the hospital's strategic direction to all members of the organization. While any member of staff might see a poster encouraging them to save money by turning off lights (cost or *waste* reduction being a key narrative), it was junior and middle managers who were entrusted with actually implementing initiatives, and it was they who were the focus of senior management's efforts to instil a sense of the importance of these initiatives. The Lean Hospital Program, for instance, included in-house and professionally delivered training, visits to factories using Lean manufacturing principles, and importantly, a series of Lean Hospital Awareness events. These events allowed managers who had successfully implemented Lean practices in their units to showcase their achievements. The managers most active and engaged in the Lean Hospital implementation strategy were given the title of Lean Trailblazers.

Lean practices were framed in the trust's narrative as practices that, while necessitating some commitment of time and resources on the part of managers and junior staff alike, had the potential, ultimately, to make their work easier. This was to put it simply of course, but it is true to say that narratives of Lean management at the trust played to many managers' desires for more simplified systems (on the ward or in the office) whilst at the same time offering potential time efficiencies that would allow staff to have more contact with patients. While some nurses bought in to the vision of a more efficient and smoothly functioning hospital that the initiative created, some nurse managers were often sceptical about the Lean programme and viewed it as yet another transitory initiative '*like all the others*'. Still others viewed it more benignly but retained their sense of humour. During one Lean training session, a horse and cart passed close by the ground-floor window heading in the general direction of A&E, prompting one nurse manager to quip: '*Look – a Lean ambulance*'.

Narratives about management at the mental health trust, like those at the acute trust, included the adoption of national programmes promoting Lean management ideas such as The Productive Ward. Junior and middle managers used these programmes pragmatically – they tried to serve the stated aims of improving quality and reducing cost, but also to use the programmes to gain scarce resources as part of Productive Ward improvements. What the clinical managers noted was the shift in the language they used from a focus on patient need to attention to business goals. This had real implications for managers' roles as the development of clinical expertise, via clinical supervision, had been replaced by performance management meetings. Rapid expansion came at the expense of a specialist mental health business focus, and so the common goal became to bring in more money in the form of new contracts. In common with the acute trust, management ideas formed the basis for good-humoured banter between managers: '*The recruitment system is so un-Lean*' (Tanya, service director) so '*we'll put it on a diet*' (Ella, HR manager).

Likewise at Millford PCT, a middle manager commented that '*any training you go on, they start to talk about Toyota*'. Again, managers were not so much critical of the Lean approach *per se* as of the fact that, despite widespread training opportunities, it had not been fully '*cascaded down*'. The range of Lean applications also appeared quite wide or else, in certain instances, at variance with the original philosophies applied in the automotive industry. In a department that had been '*very good at Leaning*', one Millford PCT middle manager discussed the rather wide range of applications – from '*basic things like … organizing rooms, organizing your desks*' to the reappraisal of roles in cases where staff may take maternity leave and return on a part-time basis. The goal here appeared to be better *skill-mixing* through a process in which a department would re-examine a job and ask: '*Do we really need a Band 6 or could we use a Band 4?*' Elements of a job could be redesigned so that '*we're saving three days' worth of a Band 6*' and thus reducing departmental costs. Similar issues arose in the ambulance case study about the penetration of managerial ideology: '*We're just so keen to badge everything, instead of just getting on with the job*'.

Lean management is just one example of the kind of *narrative management* we describe. These changing language forms affected the way that care decisions were made and the care that patients received. There was increasing talk of what can be afforded in place of what might better serve the patient need. However, more troubling for us was the effect of the business discourse. Beyond the framing of patients as consumers who use up valuable resources, what seemed to be emerging was a revision of ideas about what might reasonably be expected by patients in terms of eligibility and types and length of treatment, and even what constituted an illness requiring care. At the extreme end, once an illness is declassified, no demands can be made on services. Again, we don't say this lightly. We saw managers working with doctors and nurses to distinguish clearly between health and social problems so that only the health needs might require NHS help. This happened, for example, more than once in services that dealt with the care of older people in the acute hospital and the mental health trust. This, for us, was a major threat to the principles underpinning the welfare state as social care becomes more limited and previously available healthcare excluded. The economic language of efficiencies, affordability, cost savings and controlling demand remain prevalent in the media and in everyday conversations. Yet this talk is ideological, presenting as reality the idea that '*we can't afford to care for older people*' instead of representing an economic decision made about where and how a society chooses to direct resources.

We thus found our middle managers facing highly complex situations and having to make compromises between business demands and patient care on a daily basis – striving to make their organization as effective as possible amid a fragmenting system that was creaking at the seams and lacking reasonable investment. For many, especially those with clinical backgrounds, junior and middle management might not have been a calling or vocation, but once staff found themselves in such positions, they typically expressed a desire to carry it out professionally. This meant a desire to execute their roles to the best of their abilities, to make a difference to front-line care, and to contribute to their organizations' attempts to hit their various, and at times ambitious and contradictory, targets. Such hard work and commitment at junior and middle management levels was a world away from the often caricatured public perception of NHS managers as wasteful time-servers in privileged public sector positions.

NHS managers: a rearguard against NHS deconstruction

This study has generated detailed accounts of how junior and middle managerial roles in the NHS are changing. Overall, and in common with managerial positions in other industries, the roles and behaviour of junior and middle management in health organizations appeared to be increasingly complex with the interactions between different levels of management and across different functions of the organization becoming increasingly fragmented. Managers' interpretation of, and reaction to, change measures were increasingly *businesslike*. Roles were changing because the New Public Management was shifting the job of the NHS manager away from that of a public servant and towards that of a commercially oriented business person. External hiring of professional generalist managers also appeared to be growing, with new middle managers brought in from retail, engineering, financial or other commercial organizations or else from other public sector organizations such as police or local government. Organizations were tackling financial pressures through headcount reduction and delayered hierarchies. In addition, there were some accounts of upskilling as managerial tasks were forced down the hierarchy. Middle managers in particular faced pressure as they formed the target for cuts at the same time as being responsible for implementing change. This had consequential effects of increased workload, spans of control and performance demands. Junior managers were able to draw, to some extent, upon their specialist clinical or functional area for identity and job security. However, we found consequent negative effects on careers, job tasks and responsibilities, and quality of working life. We argue that the nature of managerial behaviour has changed qualitatively and radically in ethos, from public service to business management, and that this is in keeping with international reform initiatives often labelled as New Public Management.

NHS junior and middle managers play a vital and overlooked role in their organizations. They have a wider understanding of the entire *business* of their trust and beyond, and their engagement is essential in the everyday running of trusts as well as in terms of plugging gaps, where possible, in service provision regardless of whether it is formally part of their role. NHS managerial staff constantly filled the holes in a rapidly changing system; and the present policy direction of increasingly privatized provision, aimed at stripping out layers of middle management cost, could pose threats to the everyday functioning of NHS services and potentially endanger staff and patients as resources stretch beyond working capacity.

So in our view, the NHS is hanging on precariously to its public service principles of being free at the point of need and accountable primarily to government and the people. Healthcare in England is heading back to something closer to its pre-1948 state: fragmented, offering limited services, making certain treatments accessible only to paying customers, unclear where it sits in the ministerial chain of command, and free from any bonds to 'the highest law' of public service. We take no pleasure from our critical assessment of the erosion of the welfare state. We saw the NHS beset on all sides by pressures for marketization, policy reforms and system-wide restructuring, resource shortages and increasing demand for services. Recent legislation, opening service contracts to 'any qualified provider', suits the neo-liberal agenda perfectly and reflects arrangements for rail and mail services, for example. Services can be contracted for *en bloc* and the payment process is simple; the taxpayer pays via the government. This arrangement goes beyond that in the US where health companies at least have to go to the trouble of charging individual patients. Taken together, these pressures constitute the gravest ever danger to the NHS's continued existence as they underpin the shrinkage of public service provision and the effacement of democracy by a neo-liberal 'stealth revolution' (Brown, 2015).

At the time of writing, we are still some way from the logical end point of these marketizing reforms. But our work has demonstrated that the NHS *is* being privatized, its scope of availability *is* being narrowed, and its future as a publicly provided health service *is* being questioned. As a result, we see how the NHS becomes available as a brand or *Kitemark* under which healthcare can increasingly be delivered by private providers according to the logic of market delivery.

Reconstructing the welfare state

We wonder, however, whether these processes can be reversed, or at least slowed? On one level, it is difficult to see how. We use Wendy Brown's term 'stealth revolution' because it describes the opacity of the staging posts along the way. We have shown how the penetration of neo-liberal rhetoric into public debate and the legislative changes enabling private provision of welfare have coincided to enable deconstruction to gain momentum. Governments claim, on the one hand, that the NHS will be protected yet, on the other, that a free at the point of need health service is simply too expensive. In an early examination of how the US managed care model might be applied to the NHS, Robert Royce suggests: 'Any system which subsidizes (or even makes free at the point of consumption) something as highly valued as life itself can expect a surfeit of demand over supply. Whatever its moral value, it makes for poor economics' (1997: 154).

This 'poor economics' diverts attention from social and public values, ethics and care. Talk turns to the extent to which spending on healthcare is uneconomic, wasteful or non-profitable, and spending on the sick, the injured or the depressed is simply throwing good money after bad. When such *waste* is determined economically, sick people will not fare well unless they can be transformed into income streams. The ascendency of neo-liberal ideology and governance has drastically narrowed the vision of what is considered possible or, in current parlance, *what works*. The establishment of the NHS itself shows how agendas could be structured in ways which permit a broad and expansive commitment to public healthcare, and where poor economics did not block all avenues. At a time when the country was almost bankrupt, following the Second World War, an agenda was possible in which human needs could be envisaged as superior to capital market needs.

But neo-liberal ideology is currently effective in blocking this conceptualization (Brown, 2015). Well-practised public statements about value for money, austerity, balanced budgets, wastage or bureaucracy progressively close down the space for imagining a universal, tax-funded healthcare system as a public entitlement.

Boltanski and Chiapello's writing on the 'new spirit of capitalism' (2005) nicely captures the rhetorical mechanisms in use: government is portrayed as part of the problem – bureaucratic, slow, cumbersome, remote, unresponsive. The fight against *socialized medicine* in the US is perhaps the most obvious manifestation of this process. The expansion of government-run healthcare entitlements in the US has been under constant attack by pro-market politicians and like-minded lobbies such as the pharmaceutical and insurance industries. Former Senator Bob Dole, for example, asserted that Bill Clinton's healthcare bill in the early 1990s would 'put a mountain of bureaucrats between you and your doctor' (Pious, 2008: 198).

The debates are somewhat less rhetorically charged in the UK, but discussions of the NHS and its future are still very much dominated by the notion that a universal public sector system is unaffordable and unrealistic. To make any kind of progress, we need a much fuller understanding of what might be considered in the public interest without simply confining the debate to narrow definitions of the economic interest. As legislation opening the door to commercial provision of services has already passed into law, to some extent, the debate about affordability becomes redundant. If the government pays commercial interests to provide services, larger corporate interests will be able to set the terms of the relationship and governments, as much as the public, will find corporations' interests difficult to contain. The government will probably soon rediscover the problem of increasing demand and an inability to contain costs, but now they will have powerful lobby groups to satisfy.

The NHS is a popular institution and debates that go beyond economics could be called upon in its defence. We argue that a public system of free at the point of need healthcare could and should be defended much more robustly among advanced economies. It is the US that is the outlier, and its corporate healthcare system need not be the model, or the *best practice*, to emulate. Defending public healthcare more stridently could even breathe life back into the desperately flagging ideals of citizenship and of democracy. Citizens in a democratic society, in theory at least, elect representatives to serve the public interest, not the interest of corporations and their lobbyists (Lessig, 2012). But instead, we seem to have the opposite – policy changes guided into legislation and without proper debate. A 'stealth revolution' (Brown, 2015) accurately describes the situation as the rhetoric of protecting the NHS conflicts with the reality of behind-the-scenes transfer of services into the hands of commercial enterprises (Leys and Player, 2011; Tallis, 2013).

The complex and confusing systems of NHS governance could be radically simplified in a more unified national structure. Doing so would also close the space for the intrusion of market interests, such as the purchaser–provider split, inter-service charging, consulting fees, and expensive subcontractors and personnel agencies. NHS organizations, in their survival state, need to find a way to regain their influence on contracting and providing in-house services. Somehow capacity has to be rebuilt within NHS trusts so that they can draw upon clinical judgement in allocating scarce resources of care and treatment and for them not to be subject to the *best practice* of business expediency. Poorly designed targets also go hand in hand with the market framework. They work on the basis of zero trust and represent a degraded understanding of the public service ethos. Targets are predicated on the expectation that most staff are complacent and self-serving and need to be continually pushed. This is not what we found at all. NHS middle managers were motivated by the impetus of professional judgement and the needs of patients. Some targets are practically impossible to meet, which creates tragicomic situations that encourage gaming and goal displacement. They also require an administrative control system all of their own, generating more extraneous work for everyone. The never-ending cycle of hitting and missing targets provides critics with a set of weapons to attack NHS trusts for their failings.

At the micro level, something also needs to be done about the workload that middle managers face, especially when working in the NHS can involve life or death decisions and is increasingly encircled by a culture of fear and litigation. Workload, pressure, stress and a time famine (Perlow, 1999) now add up to a basically unbearable situation for many in the NHS, a situation considerably worse than we found in Hassard et al. (2009) on private sector middle managers. NHS staff at many levels require better forms of support at work, including protection from extreme workloads and the risk of litigation that is always present. The wider the span of control and the more stressed and overloaded staff are, the greater the potential for care failures and possibilities for complaints, litigation and media criticism. None of this will be easy to achieve. Political vision and courage will be required in restarting broad-ranging debate and a radical policy agenda taking inspiration from the founding principles of the NHS.

In sum, our study of junior and middle managers in four types of NHS organization took us beyond considerations of managerial work alone. We were better able to understand the daily experiences and working lives of NHS managers by examining three levels of analysis: macro, meso and micro. Our Critical-Action perspective allowed us to examine how organizational structures and processes were influenced by overt and covert ideological factors and forces. This resulted in a series of analyses that document changes to managerial practices, but with an appreciation of how these changes serve to justify dominant political ideologies; specifically, neo-liberal market philosophies – the 'stealth revolution'. By examining how macro-level changes play out at meso and micro levels, we come to understand not only the effects of economic imperatives applied to human and ethical matters – such as what care a society should provide – but also how, in the UK, the welfare state is being progressively deconstructed.

AFTERWORD

It was almost inevitable that we would find it difficult to put down this study, not least because we continue to come into contact with NHS organizations on a regular basis in our daily lives as well as through continuing research in healthcare organizations. Since completing the manuscript for this book, we have seen the influx of commercial providers to the NHS accelerate rapidly. At the end of the study, the acute hospital already encompassed many services provided by private companies under an NHS banner, and this has continued apace. The ambulance service continued to lose contracts for patient transport to private providers, and indeed far more private ambulances are on the roads. The mental health trust still struggles with the effects of its rapid expansion, and its primary purpose is no longer to provide mental health services. And the primary care service was legislated out of existence to be replaced by local and regional commissioning and by practices operating under the logics of 'patient choice' and 'any qualified provider'. Moreover, as we continue to come into contact with NHS services, we notice the rapid increase in the names of commercial providers appearing in small type to the top right of increasingly large blue NHS signage. This 'stealth' introduction of private provision – under the *Kitemark* of the NHS – appears to be progressing with alarming rapidity.

As for the NHS managers we interviewed and observed in the course of the study, through our ongoing research into healthcare management, we continue to meet many of them at conferences, training days and their places of work. Many of these managers occupy roles similar to those they held during the course of the research, and so they are able to update us on policy issues and inform us, first-hand, of everyday changes to systems, structures and practices. On the whole, however, these managers have yet to report to us any significant improvement in their working lives or any refocusing on traditional public service values. Of course, other managers in our sample were more dramatically affected by the changes to healthcare provision that we document in this book. Of these, some found a way out of their organizations (e.g. to a new job or to early retirement); others found their roles downgraded in the various rounds of reorganization; and yet others were made redundant, by voluntary or compulsory means.

Finally, we note that the NHS – the cornerstone of the welfare state – is no longer politically untouchable. Indeed, we see private providers awarded large contracts to provide NHS services without any need to bill patients – the state pays. Nevertheless, we have also recently experienced an incipient counter-narrative to the hegemonic neo-liberalism of recent decades. In September 2015, the newly elected leader of the UK Labour Party, for example, announced his party's potential to be a 'force for humanity' and one against 'grotesque global inequity'. Perhaps resonating with Cicero's 'highest law' and Aneurin Bevan's principles for welfare and social justice, the new leader's acceptance speech declared a desire for a political movement: 'United in our quest for a decent and better society for all … we don't have to be unequal … it doesn't have to be unfair … things can and they will change.' We had wondered whether this book would merely capture a moment in time towards the end of universal health and welfare provision in Britain. Now we're not quite so sure.

REFERENCES

AACE (2014) *Annual Report 2013–2014*, London: Association of Ambulance Chief Executives.

Adams, A., Lugsden, E., Chase, J., Arber, S. and Bond, S. (2000) Skill mix changes and work intensification in nursing, *Work, Employment and Society*, 14(3), 541–55.

Aldrich, H. (2008) *Organizations and Environments*, Stanford, CA: Stanford Business Books.

Allcorn, S., Baum, H. S., Diamond, M. A. and Stein, H. W. (1996) *The Human Cost of a Management Failure: Organizational Downsizing at General Hospital*, Westport, CT: Quorum Books.

Alvesson, M. and Deetz, M. (2000) *Doing Critical Management Research*, London: Sage.

Alvesson, M. and Willmott, H. (Eds) (1992) *Critical Management Studies*, London: Sage.

Alvesson, M. and Willmott, H. (Eds) (2003) *Studying Management Critically*, London: Sage.

Anderson, P. (2000) Renewals, *New Left Review*, 1(January–February), 5–24.

Anthony, P. (1977) *The Ideology of Work*, London: Tavistock.

Anthony, P. and Reed, M. (1990) Managerial roles and relationships: The impact of the Griffiths Report, *International Journal of Health Care Quality Assurance*, 3(3), 21–30.

Appleby, J., Crawford, R. and Emmerson, C. (2009) *How Cold Will it Be? Prospects for NHS Funding 2011–2017*, London: The King's Fund.

Assinder, N. (1999) Blair risks row over public sector [online], *BBC News*, 7 July. Available at: http://news.bbc.co.uk/1/hi/uk_politics/388528.stm

Baggott, R. (2004) *Health and Health Care in Britain*, London: Palgrave.

Barley, S. and Kunda, G. (2004) *Gurus, Hired Guns, and Warm Bodies: Itinerant Experts in a Knowledge Economy*, Princeton, NJ: Princeton University Press.

Barnes, B., Ernst, S. and Hyde, K. (1999) *An Introduction to Groupwork*, Basingstoke: Macmillan.

BBC News (1998) The NHS: 'One of the greatest achievements in history' [online], *BBC News*, 1 July. Available at: http://news.bbc.co.uk/1/hi/events/nhs_at_50/special_report/123511.stm

Bechara, J. and Van de Ven, A. (2011) Triangulating philosophies of science to understand complex organizational and managerial problems. In H. Tsoukas and R. Chia (Eds) *Philosophy and Organization Theory* (Research in the Sociology of Organizations, Volume 32), Bingley, UK: Emerald Books, pp. 343–64.

Bevan, A. (1952) *In Place of Fear*, London: William Heinemann Ltd.

Bevan, G. and Hood, C. (2006) What's measured is what matters: Targets and gaming in the English public health care system, *Public Administration*, 84(3), 517–38.

Beynon, H. (1973) *Working for Ford*, London: Penguin.

BIS (2011) *Higher Education: Students at the Heart of the System*, London: Department of Business, Innovation, and Skills.

BNF (2002) *British National Formulary, No. 43*, London: British Medical Association and Royal Pharmaceutical Society of Great Britain.

Boffey, D. and Helm, T. (2011) David Cameron's adviser says health reform is a chance to make big profits, *The Guardian*, 14 May.

Boltanksi, L. and Chiapello, E. (2005) *The New Spirit of Capitalism*, London: Verso.

Bolton, S. C. (2000) Who cares? Offering emotion as a 'gift' in the nursing labour process, *Journal of Advanced Nursing*, 32(3), 580–6.

Bolton, S. C. (2003) Multiple roles? Nurses as managers in the NHS, *The International Journal of Public Sector Management*, 16(2), 122–30.

Bott, E. (1976) Hospital and society, *British Journal of Medical Psychology*, 49(2), 97–140.

Bottomore, T. (1975) Competing paradigms in macro sociology, *Annual Review of Sociology* 1, 191–202.

Boyle, M. V. (2002) 'Sailing twixt Scylla and Charybdis', negotiating multiple organisational masculinities, *Women in Management Review* 17(3/4), 131–41.

Boyle, M. V. and Healy, J. (2003) Balancing Mysterium and Onus: Doing spiritual work within an emotion-laden organizational context, *Organization* 10(2), 351–73.

Braverman, H. (1974) *Labor and Monopoly Capital*, New York: Monthly Review Press.

Brent, S. (2010) *Nee Naw: Real Life Dispatches from Ambulance Control*, London: Penguin.

Bresnen, M., Hyde, P., Hodgson, D., Bailey, S. and Hassard, J. (2015) Leadership talk: From managerialism to leaderism in healthcare after the crash, *Leadership*, 11(4), 451–70.

Brown, W. (2015) *Undoing the Demos: Neoliberalism's Stealth Revolution*, New York: Zone Books.

Buchanan, D. A., Parry, E., Gascoigne, C. and Moore, C. (2013) Are healthcare middle management jobs becoming *extreme* jobs? *Journal of Health Organization and Management*, 27(5), 646–64.

Burrell, G. (1994) Modernism, postmodernism and organizational analysis 4: The contribution of Jürgen Habermas, *Organization Studies*, 15(1), 1–19.

Burrell, G. and Morgan, G. (1979) *Sociological Paradigms and Organizational Analysis*, London: Heinemann.

Cameron, K. S., Freeman, S. J. and Mishra, A. K. (1991) Best practices in white-collar downsizing: Managing contradictions, *Academy of Management Executive*, 5(3), 57–73.

Campbell, D. and Watt, N. (2014) NHS comes top in healthcare survey, *The Guardian*, 17 June. Available at: www.theguardian.com/society/2014/jun/17/nhs-health

Caroline, N. (2008) *Emergency Care in the Streets*, London: Jones and Bartlett.

Carter, B., Danford, A., Howcroft, D., Richardson, H., Smith, A. and Taylor, P. (2013) Taxing times: Lean working and the creation of (in)efficiencies in HM Revenue and Customs, *Public Administration*, 91(1), 83–97.

Carter, M., Thompson, N., Crampton, P., Morrow, G., Burford, B., Gray, C. and Illing, J. (2013) Workplace bullying in the UK NHS: A questionnaire and interview study on prevalence, impact and barriers to reporting, *BMJ Open*, 3(6), e002628.

Cascio, W. F. (1993) Downsizing: What do we know? What have we learnt? *Academy of Management Executive*, 7(1), 95–104.

Chandler, A. D. (1977) *The Visible Hand: The Managerial Revolution in American Business*, Cambridge, MA: Harvard University Business.

CIPFA (2015) *CIPFA Briefing: The Health of Health Finances*, August [online], London: CIPFA. Available at: www.cipfa.org/~/media/files/cipfa%20thinks/briefings/briefing-paper-health-of-health-approved.pdf

Clarke, J., Gewirtz, S. and McLaughlin, E. (2000) Reinventing the Welfare State. In J. Clarke, S. Gewirtz and E. McLaughlin (Eds) *New Managerialism, New Welfare?* London: Sage, pp. 1–26.

Clegg, S. (1975) *Power, Rule and Domination*, London: Routledge and Kegan Paul.

Cooke, H. (2006) Seagull management and the control of nursing work, *Work Employment and Society*, 20(2), 223–43.

Corbett, A., Cornelissen, J. and Spicer, A. (2011) The evolution and future of management. Call for papers for *Journal of Management Studies Conference 2012*, St. Anne's College, Oxford University.

Coser, R. L. (1962) *Life on the Ward*, East Lansing, MI: Michigan State University Press.

Cousins, C. (1988) The restructuring of welfare work: The introduction of general management and the contracting out of ancillary services in the NHS, *Work, Employment and Society*, 2(2), 210–28.

CQC (2015) *Right Here, Right Now: People's Experience of Health, Care and Support during a Mental Health Crisis*, Newcastle: Care Quality Commission.

Currie, G. (1997) Contested terrain: The incomplete closure of management in the health service, *Health Manpower Management*, 23(4), 123–32.

Currie, G. and Brown, A. D. (2003) A narratological approach to understanding processes of organizing in a UK hospital, *Human Relations*, 56(5), 563–86.

Currie, G. and Procter, S. (2005) The antecedents of middle managers' strategic contribution: The case of a professional bureaucracy, *Journal of Management Studies*, 42(7), 1325–56.

Currie, G., Finn, R. and Martin, G. (2007) Spanning boundaries in pursuit of effective knowledge sharing within networks in the NHS, *Journal of Health Organization and Management*, 21(4/5), 406–17.

Davies, P. and Gubb, J. (2009) *Putting Patients Last: How the NHS Keeps the Ten Commandments of Business Failure*, London: Civitas.

Davis, J. and Tallis, R. (2013) *NHS SOS: How the NHS was Betrayed – and How We Can Save It*, London: One World Books.

de Bruijn, H. (2011) *Managing Professionals*, Abingdon: Routledge.

Deetz, S. (1996) Crossroads – describing differences in approaches to organizational science: Rethinking Burrell and Morgan and their legacy, *Organization Science*, 7(2), 191–207.

Delamothe, T. and Godlee, F. (2011) 'Dr Lansley's monster: Too soon to let it out of the lab, *British Medical Journal*, 342(7791), 237–8.

Dent, M. (2008) Medicine, nursing, and changing professional jurisdictions in the UK. In D. Muzio, S. Ackroyd and J.-F. Chanlat (Eds) *Redirections in the Study of Expert Labour*, Basingstoke: Palgrave, pp. 101–17.

Department of Health (1983) *NHS Management Inquiry: Report to the Secretary of State for Social Services* (The Griffiths Report), London: Department of Health and Social Security.

Department of Health (1991) *The Patient's Charter*, London: HMSO.

Department of Health (1992) The *Health of the Nation: A Strategy for Health in England*, London: HMSO.

Department of Health (1997) *The New NHS: Modern Dependable*, London: HMSO.

Department of Health (1998) *Modernising Mental Health Services*, London: HMSO.

Department of Health (1999) *National Service Framework: Modern Standards and Service Models*, London: HMSO.

Department of Health (2000a) *The NHS Plan*, London: HMSO.

Department of Health (2000b) *Our Healthier Nation*, London: HMSO.

Department of Health (2001) *Shifting the Balance of Power within the NHS*, London: HMSO.

Department of Health (2002) *Shifting the Balance of Power: The Next Steps*, London: HMSO.

Department of Health (2008) *High Quality Care for All: NHS Next Stage Review Final Report* (The Darzi Review), London: The Stationery Office, Cm 7432.

Department of Health (2009) Background to NHS foundation trusts [online]. Available at: http://webarchive.nationalarchives.gov.uk/+/www.dh.gov.uk/en/Healthcare/Secondarycare/NHSfoundationtrust/DH_4062852 (accessed 16 October, 2014).

Department of Health (2010) *Equity and Excellence: Liberating the NHS*, London: The Stationery Office.

Department of Health (2010) *Liberating the NHS: Legislative Framework and Next Steps*, London: The Stationery Office.

Department of Health (2013) The regulation and oversight of NHS trusts and NHS foundation trusts: Joint policy statement to accompany care bill quality of services clauses [online]. Available at: https://www.gov.uk/government/uploads/system/uploads/attachment_data/file/200446/regulation-oversight-NHS-trusts.pdf (accessed 16 October, 2014).

Diefenbach, T. (2009) New Public Management in public sector organizations: The dark sides of managerialistic enlightenment, *Public Administration*, 87(4), 892–909.

Donaldson, L. (2001) *The Contingency Theory of Organizations*, London: Sage.

Dopson, S. (1994) Management: The one disease consultants did not think existed, *Journal of Management in Medicine*, 8(5), 25–36.

Dopson, S. and Fitzgerald, L. (2006) The role of the middle manager in the implementation of evidence-based healthcare, *Journal of Nursing Management*, 14(4), 43–51.

Dopson, S. and Stewart, R. (1990) What is happening to middle management? *British Journal of Management*, 1(1), 3–16.

Du Gay, P. (2006) Machinery of government and standards in public service: Teaching new dogs old tricks, *Economy and Society*, 35(1), 148–67.

Duffield C. (1991) First-line nurse managers: Issues in the literature, *Journal of Advanced Nursing*, 16(10), 1247–53.

Eaton, G. (2013) The pre-election pledges that the Tories are trying to wipe from the internet, *New Statesman*, 13 November.

Edgell, S., Granter, E. and Gottfried, H. (2016) *The Sage Handbook of the Sociology of Work and Employment*, London: Sage.

Eisenhardt, K. (1989) Building theory from case study research, *Academy of Management Review*, 14(4), 532–50.

Enthoven, A.C., (1993) 'The History and Principles of Managed Competition', *Health Affairs*, 12, suppl 1: 24-48.

Exworthy, M. (2001) Primary care in the UK: Understanding the dynamics of devolution, *Health and Social Care in the Community*, 9(5), 266–78.

Exworthy, M. and Halford, S. (1999) Assessment and Conclusions. In M. Exworthy and S. Halford (Eds) *Professionals and the New Managerialism in the Public Sector*, Buckingham: Open University Press, pp. 121–39.

Fairclough, N. (2003) *Analysing Discourse: Textual Analysis for Social Research*, London: Routledge.

Fairfield, G., Hunter, D. J., Mechanic, D. and Rosleff, F. (1997) Managed care: Origins, principles, and evolution, *British Medical Journal*, 314(7097), 1823–6.

Fitzgerald, L. (1994) Moving clinicians into management: A professional challenge or threat? *Journal of Management in Medicine*, 8(6), 32–44.

Fournier, V. and Grey, C. (2000) At the critical moment, *Human Relations*, 53(1), 7–32.

Francis, R. QC (Chair) (2013) *Report of the Mid-Staffordshire NHS Foundation Trust Public Inquiry* (HC 947), London: The Stationery Office.

Fraser, J. A. (2001) *White-collar Sweatshop: The Deterioration of Work and its Rewards in Corporate America*, New York: W. W. Norton.

Freeman, H. (1998) Mental health policy and practice in the NHS: 1948–79, *Journal of Mental Health*, 7(3), 225–39.

Freidson, E. (1986) *Professional Powers: A Study on the Institutionalization of Formal Knowledge*, Chicago: University of Chicago Press.

Geertz, C. (1983) *Local Knowledge: Further Essays in Interpretive Anthropology*, New York: Basic Books.

Godfrey, R., Brewis, J., Grady, J. and Grocott, C. (2013) The private military industry and neoliberal imperialism: Mapping the terrain, *Organization*, 21(1), 106–25.

Goffman, E. (1961) *Asylums*, London: Penguin.

Gournay, K., Birley, J. and Bennett, D. (1998) Therapeutic interventions and milieu in psychiatry in the NHS between 1948 and 1998, *Journal of Mental Health*, 7(3), 261–72.

Graeber, D. (2015) *The Utopia of Rules: On Technology, Stupidity, and the Secret Joys of Bureaucracy*, New York: Melville House.

Granter, E., McCann, L. and Boyle, M. V. (2015) Extreme work/normal work: Intensification, storytelling, and hypermediation in the (re)construction of 'the new normal', *Organization*, 22(4), 443–56.

Greenwood, R., Oliver, C., Sahlin, K. and Suddaby, R. (Eds) (2008) *The Sage Handbook of Organizational Institutionalism*, Beverly Hills, CA: Sage.

Grey, C. and Willmott, H. C. (2005) *Critical Management Studies: A Reader*, Oxford: Oxford University Press.

Guardian, The (2002) Blair: We're at our best when at our boldest, *The Guardian*, 1 October. Available at: www.theguardian.com/uk/2002/oct/01/labourconference.labour

Habermas, J. (1964) The public sphere, *New German Critique*, 3(Autumn), 49–55.

Habermas, J. (1986) The *Philosophical Discourse of Modernity: Twelve Lectures*, Cambridge, MA: MIT Press.

Hales, C. (1986) What do managers do? A critical review of the evidence, *Journal of Management Studies*, 23(1), 88–115.

Hall, S. (1997) *Representation: Cultural Representations and Signifying Practices*, London and Thousand Oaks, CA: Sage.

Ham, C. (2009) *Health Policy in Britain*, London: Palgrave.

Ham, C. (2010) *GP Budget-holding: Lessons from Across the Pond and from the NHS*, Birmingham: Health Services Management Centre.

Hardy, C., Phillips, N. and Clegg, S. (2001) Reflexivity in organization and management theory: A study of the production of the research 'subject', *Human Relations*, 54(5), 531–60.

Hargrove, E. and Glidewell, J. (Eds) (1990) *Impossible Jobs in Public Administration*, Lawrence, KS: University of Kansas Press.

Harney, S. (2007) Socialization and the business school, *Management Learning*, 38(2), 139–53.

Harrison, S. (1982) Consensus decision-making in the NHS: A review, *Journal of Management Studies*, 19(4), 377–94.

Harrison, S. (1999) Clinical autonomy and health policy: Pasts and futures. In M. Exworthy and S. Halford (Eds) *Professionals and the New Managerialism in the Public Sector*, Buckingham: Open University Press, pp. 50–64.

Harrison, S. and McDonald, R. (2008) *The Politics of Healthcare in Britain*, London: Sage.

Hassard, J. (1993) *Sociology and Organization Theory: Positivism, Paradigms and Postmodernity*, Cambridge: Cambridge University Press.

Hassard, J. and Wolfram Cox, J. (2013) Can sociological paradigms still inform organizational analysis? A paradigm model for post-paradigm times, *Organization Studies*, 34(11), 1701–28.

Hassard, J., McCann, L. and Morris, J. (2009) *Managing in the Modern Corporation: The Intensification of Managerial Work in the USA, UK and Japan*, Cambridge: Cambridge University Press.

HCC (2009) *Investigation into Mid Staffordshire NHS Foundation Trust*, London: Healthcare Commission.

Hearn, J. and Parkin, W. (1983) *Sex at Work*, New York: St Martin's Press.

Heckscher, C. (1996) *White Collar Blues*, New York: Basic Books.

Heller, R. F., Edwards, R., Patterson, L. and Elhassan, M. (2003) Public health in primary care trusts: A resource needs assessment, *Public Health*, 117(2), 157–64.

Hewison, A. (2004) *Management for Nurses and Health Professionals: Theory into Practice*, Oxford: Blackwell Science Ltd.

Hewlett, S. A. and Luce, C. B. (2006) Extreme jobs: The dangerous allure of the 70-hour workweek, *Harvard Business Review*, 84(12), 49–59.

Hinshelwood, R. D. and Skogstad, W. (Eds) (2000) *Observing Organisations*, London: Routledge.

Hodgson, D. (2000) *Discourse, Discipline and the Subject*, London: Ashgate.

Holt, R. and Sandberg, J. (2011) Phenomenology and organization theory. In H. Tsoukas and R. Chia (Eds) *Philosophy and Organization Theory* (Research in the Sociology of Organizations, Volume 32), Bingley, UK: Emerald Group Publishing Limited, pp. 215–49.

Hood, C. (1991) A public management for all seasons, *Public Administration*, 69(1), 3–19.

Hood, C. (2006) Gaming in Targetworld: The targets approach to managing British public services, *Public Administration Review*, 66(4), 515–20.

Hoque, K., Davis, K. and Humphreys, M. (2004) Freedom to do what you are told: Senior management team autonomy in an NHS acute trust, *Public Administration* 82(2), 355–75.

Hosking, D. M., and McNamee, S. (Eds) (2006) *The Social Construction of Organization*, Oslo: Liber.

HSJ (2014) Open letter in full: Respect for NHS managers [online], *Health Services Journal*, 4 December. Available at: www.hsj.co.uk/topics/workforce/open-letter-in-full-respect-for-nhs-managers/5077419.fullarticle

Hunter, D. (1984) NHS management: Is Griffiths the last quick fix? *Public Administration*, 62(1), 91–4.

Hunter, D. (1996) The changing roles of personnel in health and health care management, *Social Science and Medicine*, 53(5), 799–808.

Hutchinson, S. and Purcell, J. (2010) Managing ward managers for roles in HRM in the NHS: Overworked and under-resourced, *Human Resource Management Journal*, 20(4), 357–74.

Huy, Q. N. (2001) In praise of middle managers, *Harvard Business Review*, 79(8), 72–9.

Hyde, P. and Thomas, A. B. (2002) Organisational defences revisited: Systems and contexts, *Journal of Managerial Psychology*, 17(5), 408–21.

Hyde, P. and Thomas, A. B. (2003) When a leader dies, *Human Relations*, 56(8), 1003–22.

Hyde, P., Granter, E., McCann, L. and Hassard, J. (2012) The lost health service tribe: In search of middle managers. In H. Dickenson and R. Mannion (Eds) *The Reform of Health Care: Shaping, Adapting and Resisting Policy Developments*, Basingstoke: Palgrave, pp. 7–20.

Jackall, R. (1988) *Moral Mazes: Inside the World of Corporate Managers*, Oxford: Oxford University Press.

Jacobs, M. D. and Hanrahan, N. W. (2005) Re-envisioning civic life: Normative and critical lessons from the Blackwell Companion. Paper presented at the *Annual Meeting of the American Sociological Association*, Philadelphia, 12 August.

Jennings, P., Perren, L. and Carter, S. (2005) Guest editors' introduction: Alternative perspectives on entrepreneurship research, *Entrepreneurship Theory and Practice*, 29(2), 145–52.

JESIP (Joint Emergency Services Interoperability Programme) (2013) *Joint Doctrine: The Interoperability Framework*, London: Home Office.

Jones, C. (2005) Practical deconstructionist feminist Marxist organization theory: Gayatri Chakravorty Spivak, *Sociological Review*, 53(S1): 228–44.

Jordan, K. (2010) The human factor: Obstacles to change, *Design Management Journal*, 8(4), 40–6.

Kanter, R. M. (1977) *Men and Women of the Corporation*, New York: Basic Books.

Kerr, A. and Sachdev, S. (1991) Third among equals: An analysis of the 1989 ambulance dispute, *British Journal of Industrial Relations*, 30(1), 127–43.

Kilner, T. (2004) Educating the ambulance technician, paramedic, and clinical supervisor: Using factor analysis to inform the curriculum, *Emergency Medicine Journal*, 21(3), 379–85.

King's Fund, The (2015) Satisfaction with NHS overall, 2014, 29 January [online]. Available at: www.kingsfund.org.uk/projects/bsa-survey-2014/satisfaction-nhs-overall?gclid=C NOKi8nSpcYCFcPMtAodPbYCzA

Klein, N. (2007) *The Shock Doctrine: The Rise of Disaster Capitalism*, London: Penguin.

Klein, R. (2010) *The New Politics of the NHS: From Creation to Reinvention*, 6th Edition, Oxford: Radcliffe Publishing.

Klikauer, T. (2013) *Managerialism: A Critique of an Ideology*, Basingstoke: Palgrave.

Korczynski, M. (2003) Communities of Coping: Collective Emotional Labour in Service Work, *Organization*, 10(1): 55–79.

Kunda, G. (1992) *Engineering Culture: Control and Commitment in a High-tech Corporation*, Philadelphia, PA: Temple University Press.

Lawson, N. (1992) *The View from No. 11: Memoirs of a Tory Radical*, London: Bantam Press.

Le Grand, J. (2003) *Motivation, Agency, and Public Policy: Of Knights and Knaves, Pawns and Queens*, Oxford: Oxford University Press.

Lessig, L. (2012) *Republic Lost: How Money Corrupts Congress – and a Plan to Stop It*, New York: Twelve.

Lewis, M. and Grimes, A. (1999) Metatriangulation: Building theory from multiple paradigms, *Academy of Management Review*, 24(4), 672–90.

Leys, C. and Player, S. (2011) *The Plot Against the NHS*, London: Merlin Press.

Lindorff, M. (2009) We're not all happy yet: Attitudes to work, leadership, and high performance work practices among managers in the public sector, *Australian Journal of Public Administration*, 68(4), 429–45.

Linstead, S. (2002) Organizational kitsch, *Organization*, 9(4), 657–82.

Lipsky, M. (1980) *Street-level Bureaucracy: Dilemmas of the Individual in Public Services*, New York: Russell Sage Foundation.

Lister, J. (2008) *The NHS After 60: For Patients or Profits*, London: Middlesex University Press.

Llewellyn, N. and Hindmarsh, J. (Eds) (2010) *Organisation, Interaction and Practice: Studies in Ethnomethodology and Conversation Analysis*, Cambridge: Cambridge University Press.

Luhrmann, T. M. (2000) *Of Two Minds: An Anthropologist Looks at American Psychiatry*, New York: Vintage Books.

Lyng, S. (Ed.) (2004) *Edgework: The Sociology of Risk-Taking*, Abingdon: Routledge.

McCann, L. (2014) *International and Comparative Business: Foundations of Political Economies*, London: Sage.

McCann, L. (2016) From management to leadership. In S. Edgell, E. Granter and H. Gottfried (Eds) *The Sage Handbook of the Sociology of Work and Employment*, London: Sage, pp. 167–84.

McCann, L., Morris, J. and Hassard, J. (2008) Normalized intensity: The new labour process of middle management, *Journal of Management Studies*, 45(2), 343–71.

McCann, L., Granter, E., Hyde, P. and Hassard, J. (2013) Still blue-collar after all these years? An ethnography of the professionalization of emergency ambulance work, *Journal of Management Studies*, 50(5), 750–76.

McCann, L., Granter, E., Hassard, J. and Hyde, P. (2015a) 'You can't do both – something will give': Limitations of the targets culture in managing UK healthcare workforces, *Human Resource Management*, 54(5), 773–91.

McCann, L., Hassard, J., Granter, E. and Hyde, P. (2015b) Casting the lean spell: The promotion, dilution and erosion of lean management in the NHS, *Human Relations*, 68(10), 1557–77.

McKay, P. (2012) Why is Dave risking such ill feeling over health reform? *Daily Mail*, 12 February.

McLellan, A. (2012) Does the government really have a Plan B for NHS reform? [online], *Health Service Journal*, 9 February. Available at: www.hsj.co.uk/comment/leader/does-the-government-really-have-a-plan-b-for-nhs-reform/5041372.fullarticle

McMurray, R. and Cheater, F. (2003) Partnerships for health: Expanding the public health nursing role within PCTs, *Primary Health Care Research and Development*, 4(1), 57–68.

Martin, G. and Learmonth, M. (2012) 'A critical account of the rise and spread of leadership': The case of healthcare, *Social Science and Medicine*, 74(3), 281–8.

Massey, D. (2013) Neoliberalism has hijacked our vocabulary, *The Guardian*, 11 June. Available at: www.theguardian.com/commentisfree/2013/jun/11/neoliberalism-hijacked-vocabulary

Merali, F. (2003) NHS managers' views of their culture and their public image: The implications for NHS reforms, *International Journal of Public Sector Management*, 16(7), 549–63.

Metz, D. L. (1981) *Running Hot, Structure and Stress in Ambulance Work*, Cambridge, MA: Abt Books.

Mills, C. W. (1959) *The Sociological Imagination*, Oxford: Oxford University Press.

Mintzberg, H. (1971) Managerial work: Analysis from observation, *Management Science*, 18(2), B97–B110.

Mintzberg, H. (1973) *The Nature of Managerial Work*, London: Harper and Row.

Mintzberg, H. (1998) Covert leadership: Notes on managing professionals, *Harvard Business Review*, 76(6), 140–7.

Morgan, G. (1980) Metaphors, and puzzle solving in organization theory, *Administrative Science Quarterly*, 25(4), 605–22.

Morgan, G. (1986) *Images of Organization*, London: Sage.

Mouzelis, N. (1975) *Organization and Bureaucracy*, London: Routledge and Kegan Paul.

Newdick, C. (2014) From Hippocrates to commodities: Three models of NHS governance, *Medical Law Review*, 22(2), 162–79.

NHS Choices (n.d.) The NHS in England [online]. Available at: www.nhs.uk/NHSEngland/thenhs/about/Pages/overview.aspx

NHS Confederation (2015) Key statistics on the NHS, *NHS Confederation* [online], 9 June. Available at: www.nhsconfed.org/resources/key-statistics-on-the-nhs (accessed 8 July, 2015).

NHS Future Forum (2011) *Summary Report on the Proposed Changes to the NHS* [online], London: Department of Health. Available at: https://www.gov.uk/government/uploads/system/uploads/attachment_data/file/213748/dh_127540.pdf (accessed 23 December, 2015).

NHS Leadership Academy (2014) About the Academy [online]. Available at: www.leadershipacademy.nhs.uk/about/ (accessed 16 October, 2014).

Noordegraaf, M. (2007) From 'pure' to 'hybrid' professionalism: Present-day professionalism in ambiguous public domains, *Administration & Society*, 39(6), 761–85.

Nuffield Trust (n.d.) UK spending on public and private health care [online]. Available at: www.nuffieldtrust.org.uk/data-and-charts/uk-spending-public-and-private-health-care

O'Dowd, A. (2011) GP consortiums will need first class management support, says Nuffield Trust, *British Medical Journal*, 342: d337.

O'Hara, R., Johnson, M., Siriwardena, A. N., Weyman, A., Turner, J., Shaw, D., Mortimer, P., Newman, C., Hirst, E., Storey, M., Mason, S., Quinn, T. and Shewan, J. (2015) A qualitative study of systemic influences on paramedic decision making: Care transitions and patient safety, *Journal of Health Services Research and Policy*, 20(S1), 45–53.

Okhuysen, G. and Bonardi, J.-P. (2011) Editors' comments: The challenge of building theory by combining lenses, *Academy of Management Review*, 36(1), 6–11.

Oroviogoicoechea, C. (1996) The clinical nurse manager: A literature review, *Journal of Advanced Nursing*, 24(6), 1273–80.

Orr, J. (1996) *Talking about Machines: An Ethnography of a Modern Job*, Ithaca, NY: Cornell University Press.

Osterman, P. (2009) *The Truth about Middle Managers: Who They Are, How They Work, Why They Matter*, Cambridge, MA: Harvard Business School Press.

Oxman, A. Sackett, D., Chalmers, I. and Prescott, T. (2005) A surrealistic mega-analysis of redisorganization theories, *Journal of the Royal Society of Medicine*, 98(12): 563–8.

Parker, M. (2002a) *Against Management*, Cambridge: Polity Press.

Parker, M. (2002b) Utopia and organizational imagination: Outopia. In M. Parker (Ed.) *Utopia and Organization*, Oxford: Blackwell, pp. 1–8.

Parry, L. (2010) PCT to be abolished in radical NHS shake-up, *Ipswich Star*, 13 July.

Peck, J. (2010) *Constructions of Neoliberal Reason*, Oxford: Oxford University Press.

Peck, E. and Parker, E. (1998) Mental health in the NHS: Policy and practice 1979–98, *Journal of Mental Health*, 7(3), 241–59.

Perlow, L. A. (1999) The time famine: Toward a sociology of work time, *Administrative Science Quarterly*, 44(1), 57–81.

Peters, G. (2005) *Institutional Theory in Political Science: The 'New Institutionalism'*. New York: Continuum.

Phillips, N., Sewell, G. and Jaynes, S. (2008) Applying critical discourse analysis in strategic management research, *Organizational Research Methods*, 11(4), 770–89.

Pierson, P. (1994) *Dismantling the Welfare State? Reagan, Thatcher, and the Politics of Retrenchment*, Cambridge: Cambridge University Press.

Pious, R. M. (2008) *Why Presidents Fail: White House Decision Making from Eisenhower to Bush II*, New York: Rowman and Littlefield.

Pollitt, C. (1996) Business approaches to quality improvement: Why they are hard for the NHS to swallow, *Quality in Health Care*, 5(2), 104–10.

Pollock, A. (2003) Foundation hospitals will kill the NHS, *The Guardian*, 7 May. Available at: www.theguardian.com/politics/2003/may/07/publicservices.comment (accessed 16 October, 2014).

Pollock, A. (2005) *NHS Plc: The Privatization of our Health Care*, London: Verso.

Porter, A. (2010) Biggest revolution in the NHS for 60 years, *The Daily Telegraph*, 9 July.

Porter, A., Snooks, H., Youren, A., Gaze, S., Whitfield, R., Rapport, F. and Woollard, M. (2008) Covering your backs: Ambulance crews' attitudes towards clinical documentation when emergency (999) patients are not conveyed to hospital, *Emergency Medicine Journal*, 25(5), 292–5.

Power, M. (2000) *Audit Society: Rituals of Verification*, Oxford: Oxford University Press.

Preston, D. and Loan-Clarke, J. (2000) The NHS manager: A view from the bridge, *Journal of Management in Medicine*, 14(2), 100–8.

Primary Care Trust Network NHS Confederation (2010) *The Legacy of Primary Care Trusts*, London: NHS Confederation.

Private Eye (2011) Is anybody listening, *Private Eye*, 13 May, p. 30.

Reedy, P. (2009) *The Manager's Tale: Stories of Managerial Identity*, Farnham: Ashgate.

Reynolds, T. (2006, 2009, 2010) *Blood, Sweat, and Tea: Real-Life Adventures in an Inner-city Ambulance*, London: The Friday Project.

Rhodes, L. (1991) *Emptying Beds: The Work of an Emergency Psychiatric Unit*, Los Angeles, CA: University of California Press.

Rose, M. (1985) *Industrial Behaviour*, Hardmondsworth: Penguin.

Royce, R. (1997) *Managed Care: Practice and Progress*, Abingdon: Radcliffe Medical Press.

Sandel, M. (2013) *What Money Can't Buy: The Moral Limits of Markets*, London: Penguin.

Savage, J. and Scott, C. (2004) The modern matron: A hybrid management role with implications for continuous quality improvement, *Journal of Nursing Management*, 12(6), 419–26.

Scheid, T. L. (2004) *Tie a Knot and Hang On: Providing Mental Health Care in a Turbulent Environment*, New York: Aldine De Gruyter.

Schultz, M. and Hatch, M.-J. (1996) Living with multiple paradigms: The case of paradigm interplay in organizational culture studies, *Academy of Management Review*, 21(2), 529–57.

Scott, W. R., Ruef, M., Mendel, P. J. and Caronna, C. A. (2000) *Institutional Change and Healthcare Organizations: From Professional Dominance to Managed Care*, Chicago: University of Chicago Press.

Sergeant, H. (2003) *Managing Not to Manage: Management in the NHS*, London: Centre for Policy Studies.

Silverman, D. (1970) *The Theory of Organizations*, London: Heinemann.

Smith, J., Walshe, K. and Hunter, D. J. (2001) The 'redisorganization' of the NHS, *British Medical Journal*, 323(7324): 1262–3.

Smith, R. (2011) Cancer cash wasted on NHS salaries, *Daily Telegraph*, 23 November. Available at: www.telegraph.co.uk/news/health/news/8911379/Cancer-cash-wasted-on-NHS-salaries.html

Smith, V. (1990) *Managing in the Corporate Interest: Control and Resistance in an American Bank*, Berkeley: University of California Press.

South West Thames Regional Health Authority (1993) *Report of the Inquiry into the London Ambulance Service*, London: SWTRHA.

Sparrow, A. and Womack, S. (2002) Union fury as Blair blames 'the wreckers', *The Telegraph*, 4 February. Available at: www.telegraph.co.uk/news/uknews/1383653/Union-fury-after-Blair-blames-the-wreckers.html

Steger, M. and Roy, R. K. (2010) *Neoliberalism: A Very Short Introduction*, Oxford: Oxford University Press.

Stewart, R. (1989) *Leading in the NHS: A Practical Guide*, Basingstoke: Macmillan.

Stewart, R. (Ed.) (2003) *Evidence-based Management: A Guide for Health Professionals*, Oxford: Radcliffe Medical Press.

Styhre, A. (2014) The influence of neo-liberalism and its absence from management research, *International Journal of Organizational Analysis*, 22(3), 278–300.

Tallis, R. (2013) Introduction. In J. Davis and R. Tallis (Eds) (2013) *NHS SOS: How the NHS was Betrayed – and How We Can Save It*, London: Oneworld.

Tangherlini, T. L. (1998) *Talking Trauma: A Candid Look at Paramedics through Their Tradition of Tale-Telling*, Jackson, MS: University Press of Mississippi.

Tangherlini, T. L. (2000) Heroes and lies: Storytelling among paramedics, *Folklore*, 111(1), 43–66.

Taylor, F. (1911) *Principals of Scientific Management*, New York: Harper.

Taylor, J. D. (2013) *Negative Capitalism: Cynicism in the Neoliberal Era*, Alresford, UK: Zero Books.

Tengblad, S. (2006) Is there a 'New Managerial Work'? A comparison with Henry Mintzberg's classic study 30 years later, *Journal of Management Studies*, 43(7), 1437–61.

Tengblad, S. (2012) Overcoming the rationalistic fallacy in management research. In S. Tengblad (Ed.) *The Work of Managers: Towards a Practice Theory of Management*, Oxford: Oxford University Press, pp. 3–17.

Theodosius, C. (2008) *Emotional Labour in Health Care: The Unmanaged Heart of Nursing*, Abingdon: Routledge.

Thomas, R. and Davies, A. (2005) Theorizing the micro-politics of resistance: New Public Management and managerial identities in the UK public services, *Organization Studies*, 26(5): 683–706.

Thomas, W. I. and Thomas, D. S. (1928) *The Child in America: Behavior Problems and Programs*, New York: Knopf.

Tope, D., Chamberlain, L. J., Crowley, M. and Hodson, R. (2005) The benefits of being there: Evidence from the literature on work, *Journal of Contemporary Ethnography*, 34(4), 470–93.

Tsoukas, H. and Chia, R. (2002) On organizational becoming: Rethinking organizational change, *Organization Science*, 13(5), 567–82.

Turner, B. (1972) *Exploring the Industrial Subculture*, London: Heinemann.

US Department of Transportation (1995) Star of Life [online]. Available at: www.ems.gov/vgn-ext-templating/ems/sol/HS808721.pdf

Van Maanen, J. (2011) *Tales of the Field: On Writing Ethnography*, 2nd Edition, Chicago: University of Chicago Press.

Vincent, A. (2012) *NHS on the Brink of Financial Collapse: Response to Mike Farrar's Stark but Honest Warning* [online], Derby: Medicademy. Available at: www.nhsinsights.co.uk/articles/NHS-on-the-brink-of-financial-collapse.pdf

Vuic, K. D. (2009) *Officer, Nurse, Woman: The Army Nurse Corps in the Vietnam War*, Baltimore, MD: Johns Hopkins University Press.

Walby, S. (1986) *Patriarchy at Work*, London: Polity.

Walshe, K. and Ham, C. (2011) Can the government's proposals for NHS reform be made to work? *British Medical Journal*, 342: d2038.

Walshe, K. and Smith, J. (2015) Tackling the NHS's unprecedented deficit and securing reform, *British Medical Journal*, 351: h4670.

Walton, P. (2000) Psychiatric care: A case of the more things change, the more they stay the same, *Journal of Mental Health*, 9(1), 77–88.

Wankhade, P. (2012) Different cultures of management and their relationships with organisational performance: Evidence from the UK ambulance service, *Public Money and Management*, 32(5), 381–8.

Wanless, D. (2002) *Securing our Future Health: Taking a Long-term View. Final Report*, London: HM Treasury.

Waring, J. and Bishop, S. (2010) Lean healthcare: Rhetoric, ritual, resistance, *Social Science and Medicine*, 71(7), 1332–40.

Watson, T. J. (1977) *The Personnel Managers: A Study in the Sociology of Work and Employment*, London: Routledge and Kegan Paul.

Watson, T. J. (1994) *In Search of Management*, London: Routledge.

Watson, T. J. (1996) *In Search of Management: Culture, Chaos and Control in Managerial Work*, London: Thomson Business.

Watson, T. J. (2011) Ethnography, reality and truth: The vital need for studies of 'how things work' in organisations and management, *Journal of Management Studies*, 48(1), 202–17.

Weber, M. (1930) *The Protestant Ethic and the Spirit of Capitalism*, trans. Talcott Parsons, London: Allen and Unwin.

Whitehead, M., Hanratty, B. and Popay, J. (2010) NHS reform: Untried remedies for misdiagnosed problems? *The Lancet*, 376(9750), 1373–5.

Willis, E. (2006) Taking Stock of Medical Dominance, *Health Sociology Review*, 15(5), 421–31.

Willis, P. (1977) *Learning to Labour*, Farnborough: Saxon House.

Willmott, M. (1998) The new ward manager: An evaluation of the changing role of the charge nurse, *Journal of Advanced Nursing*, 28(2), 419–27.

Willshire, L. (1999) Psychiatric service: Organising impossibility, *Human Relations*, 52(6), 775–803.

Womack, J., Jones, D. and Roos, D. (1990, 2007) *The Machine that Changed the World*, London: Simon and Schuster.

World Health Organization (2000) *The World Health Report 2000: Health Systems: Improving Performance*, Geneva: World Health Organization.

INDEX

Page numbers in *italics* denotes a table/figure